DATE DUE

Serving Country and Community

Serving Country
and
Community

Who Benefits from National Service?

Peter Frumkin and JoAnn Jastrzab

DISCARDED

Harvard University Press
Cambridge, Massachusetts
London, England
2010

Library of Congress Cataloging-in-Publication Data

Frumkin, Peter.
Serving country and community : who benefits from national service? /
Peter Frumkin and JoAnn Jastrzab.
p.   cm.
Includes bibliographical references and index.
ISBN 978-0-674-04678-8 (alk. paper)
1. National service—United States.   2. Voluntarism—United States.   3. Volunteers in
Service to America.   4. AmeriCorps (U.S.)   I. Jastrzab, JoAnn.   II. Title.
HD4870.U6F78   2010
361.6—dc22   2009046634

Contents

Acknowledgments

We benefited a great deal from the help of others while writing this book and it is our pleasure to acknowledge them here. At both Abt Associates and the University of Texas, we tapped the collective wisdom of our colleagues who generously shared their ideas and suggestions with us. The Research and Policy Development staff at the Corporation for National and Community Service—headed over time by Lance Potter, David Reingold, and Robert Grimm—wrote the original requests for proposals for the AmeriCorps and Volunteers in Service to America (VISTA) studies and then supported the lengthy and painstaking process of collecting the data. In addition, Christopher Winship, Doug McAdam, and the other members of the projects' technical working groups played a vital role in framing and developing the core data collection and analysis strategies from their inceptions. We want to thank Ryoko Yamaguchi, Carrie Markovitz, Leanne Giordono, Larry Orr, Fatih Unlu, and the other current and former analysts at Abt Associates who relentlessly pursued contact information, carried out interviews, assembled data, and generally helped keep two large and complex projects on track for eight years. Katherine Chen and Sarah Dryden-Peterson traveled extensively across the country for this project and we are grateful for their efforts. In addition, we thank graduate students Margaret Vaaler, Brendan Miller, Paul Sutherland, and Adam Greeney, who served as research fellows on this project and provided critical support as the book moved from concept to completion.

Few projects make it to completion without funders who believe in the value of the work and invest in it. We are very grateful for the financial support of the Smith Richardson Foundation, the Bradley Foundation, the Surdna Foundation, Abt Associates, and the RGK Center for Philanthropy and Community Service at the University of Texas at Austin, along with the Center for Public Leadership and the Hauser Center for Nonprofit Organizations, both located in Harvard's Kennedy School of Government. A special thank you to Greg Kozmetsky for providing a quiet and comfortable off-campus office, where the final push to complete the manuscript was made.

Finally, we are grateful to the leadership of the Corporation for National and Community Service, in particular Chief Executive Officer David Eisner and Board Chair Steve Goldsmith, who shared their insights on national service, took a long-term perspective on program evaluation, and invested in both the longitudinal study of AmeriCorps and the retrospective study of VISTA, the two main data sources on which we build here.

Serving Country and Community

— 1 —

Visions of National Service

The United States has a long and rich history of citizens banding together, volunteering, and rendering service to their communities. When Alexis de Tocqueville toured America in the early nineteenth century, he commented on the American penchant for voluntary effort aimed at advancing the common good.[1] As early as 1910, Americans began envisioning citizen service on a national scale. With roots in Franklin D. Roosevelt's Civilian Conservation Corps of the 1930s and 1940s, an institutionalized service movement has developed and grown over time. In the early 1960s, President Kennedy established the Peace Corps, expanding national service to the international community. Later in that decade, the Economic Opportunity Act expanded domestic national service with the creation of Volunteers in Service to America (VISTA), the National Teacher Corps, and the Neighborhood Youth Corps. More recently, the National and Community Service Trust Act of 1993 furthered the national service movement by creating the Corporation for National and Community Service, a public agency that provides Americans of all ages and backgrounds with opportunities to serve their communities. The act also established AmeriCorps, a large-scale national service program that places young people in community service positions across the country.

The national service movement received a substantial boost in 2009 with the passage of the Edward M. Kennedy Serve America Act. By eventually increasing the size of AmeriCorps from 75,000 positions to 250,000, this legislation will make national service not just an experience that a few select people have, but rather a formative year for a very large number of young adults. The expansion represents a fulfillment of President Obama's pledge to build upon one of the most visible programmatic legacies of the

1

Clinton presidency. In addition to providing a huge number of new positions in AmeriCorps, the legislation also creates a part-time service option for sixth to twelfth graders, which will expose them early on to the idea of civic service. President Obama and his family have been active community volunteers, and have made a point of encouraging everyone to serve their community.

With many decades of experience in hand and with billions of dollars expended on service programs to date, one might think that the slated expansion of national service is grounded in a deep and penetrating understanding of how service works and how it shapes the lives of young people. This, however, is not the case. Even with hundreds of thousands of volunteers since creation of the first national service programs,[2] it is still unclear who benefits from service, under what conditions these programs work best, and how exactly they contribute to the strengthening of communities. Now, at a time when the call to service is again being sounded loudly and these programs are scheduled for expansion, there is a clear need to understand what has worked, what has not, and how most effectively to direct resources into the programs that lie at the center of the idea of national service.

Progress on understanding national service has been hindered by recurring squabbles over the idea itself. Over the past two decades, political disagreements about the wisdom of subsidizing volunteer activity for any purpose have largely displaced reasoned analysis that is based on data. The politics surrounding this issue are strident and complex, often driven more by assumptions than facts, and differentiated mostly by underlying political ideology. In the eyes of their supporters, programs like AmeriCorps hold out the potential to breed a new kind of idealism and public spiritedness that can only empower individuals and strengthen democracy.[3] By injecting volunteers into community organizations and giving them the ability to engage in community projects, some see national service as leading to open-mindedness and compassion. Moreover, the opportunity to serve one's country and community might also be a potentially important way to insure that youth are given employment and educational opportunities that can lead to more productive lives. Efforts such as VISTA were a central component of the War on Poverty and they still revive memories of a time when we had a more activist government and when the public sector had a desire to be an agent of social change. Today, with the shifting of political tides favoring progressives, these activist desires have come back to the fore. National service has a distinct additional attraction above and beyond its link to social change: It can be used to build trust, create greater levels of solidarity within communities, and combat trends of civic disengagement. To communitarians, programs like AmeriCorps represent tools for the construction or reconstruction of social capital in communities that have suffered too long from isolation and anomie. By bringing people together to carry out service projects as varied as planting public gardens or tutoring children, service programs may well build new networks of collaboration and understanding that will have value and use long after the service work is completed. Not just communities but civil society itself, some have argued, can be revived through service.[4]

Critics of national service see things very differently. They counter that national service may be a dangerous threat to individual freedoms because it involves the incursion of government into the world of volunteerism.[5] Some fear that the autonomy of the nonprofit organizations that host government-subsidized workers will be undermined in the long run by these efforts, that volunteer activity will be reduced to low-grade employment, and that a new and costly government bureaucracy will be created. Detractors have often ridiculed the idea of paying people to volunteer, seeing this as a gross perversion of Tocqueville's early observation that voluntary action among citizens was a critical training ground for democratic politics.[6] They believe that the only true service is voluntary service.[7] Service for pay, even if the pay is modest, has been described as "coercive utopianism," only slightly disguised. The higher education establishment has always objected to a requirement of service in exchange for federal student aid eligibility, arguing that the system encourages only the poor to serve in order to attend college.

To date, the claims on both sides of the issue have not been challenged, explored, or tested fully. In this book, we start with the premise that many of the concerns about service can and should be treated as testable hypotheses to be eventually supported or refuted by a thorough exploration of data related to the performance of the largest and most significant national service programs.

Visions of National Service

Above and beyond partisan projections onto the concept of national service, it is important to ask why we have national service. Programs like

AmeriCorps and VISTA promise to do everything from revitalizing our democracy to transforming local communities. Although the base of support for the idea of service has grown noticeably over the past several decades as citizens across the country have had a chance to experience service in their communities firsthand, there is still considerable debate and confusion[8]—not just about national service's political implications but also about its actual effects. This is not surprising because the stakes are high and the subject touches on the nature of citizenship. Programs like AmeriCorps have come to symbolize many of our aspirations for what our country represents. As a large and flat screen, national service today has many visions and images of America projected upon it.

Part of the confusion stems from national service's diffuse and multifaceted nature. There are more than 900 AmeriCorps programs alone, and two-thirds of all funds allocated to AmeriCorps are given directly to states as block grants. Evaluating and understanding what is happening and which programs are effective is no small task. There are many possible targets of analysis and many different program models to choose from when determining the impact of national service. To date, aside from a number of narrow and short-term efforts, little substantive progress has been made in reaching a well-grounded conclusion about the effectiveness of national service.

Many of the basic disagreements over national service arise because observers bring to the task widely divergent normative frames. Whether national service is considered a good or bad idea, or even just whether it is effective, will depend on what measures and standards are applied to the assessment and which outcomes are defined as worth tracking and measuring. In 1990, Williamson Evers wrote, "American usage of the term [national service] is now in a muddle . . . Do not expect those debating national service to share a precise meaning for the term."[9] More recently, E. J. Dionne and Kayla Meltzer noted that the results of service are also contested: "Americans differ widely over which kinds of national service are genuinely valuable."[10] To set the stage for a detailed analysis of national service programs, we begin by attempting to bring some conceptual order to this field and we sketch the competing underlying assumptions and visions that are behind the debate over national service.

To help us begin to understand the many ways in which national service has been conceptualized, we conducted fifty interviews with policy and practice leaders in the field all across the country. We asked people to explain what they thought the fundamental purpose and rationale for national service might be. Our interviewees varied greatly in what they found most unique, essential, or precious in national service. Reasonable people, coming from widely different backgrounds and holding divergent political views, ended up conceptualizing national service very differently, based on their personal experiences and worldviews. Strange and outlying visions aside, the conversations we had slowly began to fall into a recognizable pattern in which four fundamental visions or conceptions of the purpose and impact of national service emerged: citizenship and civic engagement, personal growth, social capital, and public work. These conceptions were distilled from interviews with program staff at large AmeriCorps-supported programs and small community-based programs in both urban and rural locations around the country, as well as with leading thinkers and researchers, notable national service critics, and those involved in crafting the 1993 legislation and implementing it at the Corporation for National and Community Service.

Our goal was to capture a broad landscape of informed perspectives on national service and include what people believed these programs could achieve, as well as what they had actually seen these programs accomplish. All interviews were taped and summarized, and the interviewees' conceptions of national service were coded and organized into categories. The many initial categories overlapped one another in a number of ways and called for refinement. After some reframing and analysis, a smaller number of distinct categories of thought and perspective started to emerge. The four conceptions presented here represent the framing that demonstrates the greatest consistency in relation to the analysis we did of our interviews, while at the same time constituting an economical and practical framework for the empirical examination of claims about national service.

Citizenship and Civic Engagement

The concepts of national service, citizenship, and civic engagement are often closely linked. Those who believe national service is a way of cultivating citizenship tend to also hold that service will render participants more informed and civically engaged. However, in the same way that there are many ways to conceptualize the goal of national service, there are a variety of ways to understand what makes an engaged and active citizen. We can think of citizenship as consisting in a number of interconnected dimensions.[11] Citizenship is a complex concept in itself, and it involves the recognition and appreciation of a set of legal rights and obligations, the fulfillment of democratic responsibilities through civic engagement, and commitment to country and fellow citizens.

Several of our interview subjects acknowledged, however, that national service may not directly contribute to a greater understanding of, and appreciation for, constitutional rights and responsibilities. AmeriCorps, for example, does not require its programs to educate their members about these rights and responsibilities. There is no curriculum on what it means to be a citizen who is part of a national service program. Furthermore, AmeriCorps explicitly prohibits members from engaging in political activities (e.g., working with a political party).[12] All these constraints aside, national service still can be a potent laboratory for learning what it means to be a citizen. Volunteers may get a sense of responsibility as citizens simply by virtue of acting to help others, observing the capacity of politics to transform a community, or learning about an issue and growing committed to addressing it through grassroots action.

National service may also cultivate a sense of generalized reciprocity, making members more inclined to seek to exercise their rights and uphold their responsibilities after their year of service has been completed. Through the giving and receiving that occurs in service and through interacting with local community-based institutions, members learn civic habits that translate to different levels of public life. National service also promotes critical active citizenship by exposing members to injustice and suffering that they would not otherwise experience firsthand, which can lead to future citizen action. As a researcher noted, "Privileged kids come face to face with individuals whose needs aren't being met. And realizing that causes them to question, well what kind of society is this? They were actually moved by the belief that the system ought to work and it wasn't working for some people."

AmeriCorps was forced from the start to set limits on the kind of political work that young people could undertake. This was a function of a widespread concern that the program could easily be politicized. A leading practitioner explained that while the "experience of otherness" is a powerful moment for young people that takes them outside their comfort zones, the strict prohibitions on advocacy work, which were needed to win initial approval of AmeriCorps in Congress, have limited the ability of the program to really teach active citizenship: "The compromises that were made getting AmeriCorps out of the business of advocacy were terrible, terrible compromises, because the history of our country speaks to the importance of people understanding political institutions and the role of a citizen and advocating for change. It cost them the soul of the program." She went on to explain that, aside from these problems and limitations, "I still think doing direct service work is a way to expose people to issues and challenges and if we complement the direct service with some sort of historical analysis we can make up for some of the things we've lost in not having a direct action component to AmeriCorps."

Citizenship can also be cultivated when individuals are empowered and made to believe that their engagement and participation matters.[13] National service increases the appetite of participants for change and tends to attract young people interested in finding a way to become more active and engaged citizens.[14] An AmeriCorps program manager commented about the energizing nature of national service: "You don't come to our organization because you want to maintain the status quo and keep people oppressed regardless of your political background. You come here because you think something is wrong and there might be something you can do about it. People come here to address an issue."

A number of our interviewees described ways that national service can cultivate a deep commitment to one's fellow citizens and to the country as a whole. Serving together under a shared purpose can create new ties and connections to Americans from whom one might otherwise feel disconnected. By creating a broader understanding of "us," patriotism is also built. An alternative approach to developing a sense of patriotism is through an appreciative inquiry into what makes America great, which would come in the form of American history and civics lessons. It would be possible to incorporate this kind of education into national service, but it is not a central part of national service programs today.

Citizenship may be constructed simply through the act of working for others. Connecting citizenship with community work has not yet gained widespread acceptance, but by reframing democracy, politics, and what it means to be a citizen, some of the existing debates and disagreements have the potential to be transcended and reconciled. A leading proponent of this conception explains: "I think of politics in an older, richer sense to be everywhere, not just elections, which is an entirely modern concept. Politics is not ideological but is instead Aristotelian, the negotiation of difference. And then the work angle of vision also highlights the productive/

creative side of politics which the more distributive understandings don't, which see it as a matter of who gets what." After noting that most people have a narrower conception of what citizenship is and where it comes from, he concluded: "Democracy is something created by the whole society, including all sorts of institutions as well as citizens. The key question to ask about policies is in what ways do they enhance civic capacities, power and responsibility and capacities for collaborative work and build a democratic way of life? This is different from a distributive perspective in which citizens are just seen as rights bearing voting individuals and customers."

In this framework, good citizens work together to create material goods and services of lasting civic and public value. This work can take place in any sector or across sectors, may be paid and/or voluntary, and includes everything from discussion and debate to direct service and problem solving, but it also may involve direct action and protest, depending on the situation. People engage this work out of an enlightened sense of self-interest and commitment to a common good approach. Another person with experience running a large youth service program explains how national service may develop this kind of citizenship: "By actually participating in a year or more of service to the nation, a person gets to experience what a citizen needs to experience to understand the common good. As you move citizens through the institutions that govern our lives, you create a cadre of people who bring fresh ideas, energy, and change to the institutions as they go through them." This is significant because these young people "go on for the rest of their lives with that perspective and see themselves as citizens of the nation, of their community. These citizens cannot have the wool pulled over their eyes."

Among national service's more ardent supporters, there is a tendency to view civic engagement—built through national service—as the gateway to a life full of political participation and community involvement. Some caution is needed, however, before claiming that service stimulates civic participation. A leading expert on civic engagement warned that the link between national service and broader forms of lasting civic engagement has not been conclusively demonstrated to date: "Providing direct service has been argued to be one of the first steps through a succession of stages toward which civic engagement and political and social action would be among some of the other steps. However, there is little evidence that suggests that it leads to later civic engagement."

Because it is framed as nonpolitical, service does not provide people with social action skills. It is possible that AmeriCorps could even dissuade people from civic and political engagement by engaging them in simple and nondescript community improvement projects or the delivery of traditional forms of direct human services. Of course, some believe that national service programs should be granted permission to participate in the political process and be allowed to advocate and lobby Congress and other lawmaking and rule-making bodies, which would greatly contribute to their ability to develop a more activist dimension of citizenship. This would need to be done carefully because there is a fine line between encouraging democratic participation and using government resources to fund narrow ideological agendas.[15] To date, national service has steered toward less-contentious aspects of promoting active citizenship.

Our research looks at a number of different dimensions of citizenship, though we focus heavily on civic and political engagement. The idea that national service increases young people's enthusiasm for participation in civic life was one of the most common starting points in all our discussions of the impact of service. Regardless of how one conceives of citizenship, most of our interviewees expressed confidence that national service could indeed contribute to some aspect of its development. National service may not promote all dimensions of citizenship equally and it may ultimately favor some aspects of citizenship over others. In some cases, this is due simply to the nature of national service and the design of programs. In other cases, it is a function of particular policies and implementation decisions that could be changed or adapted to refocus service on different objectives.

Personal Growth

In their most basic form, AmeriCorps and other national service programs start with the input of discounted labor when young people commit to work in community service positions for modest stipends.[16] In reality, the real starting point of service is the impulse to help that young people have. One reason why people volunteer is an earnest desire to do something socially useful and to help others. There is a second reason for volunteering, which is connected neither to the urgency of community needs nor to the nature of the volunteers' social commitments: Many people are drawn to volunteering and helping work because it is a way for them to enact their values and live out their convictions.

It is not hard to think about national service in terms of the personal growth it generates for those it touches, particularly the volunteers but also the nonprofit staff who works alongside the volunteers and community members who come in contact with these young people. Service creates an opportunity to work on problems of public concern and participate in the lives of others. In a structured and supportive environment, service also allows people to cross paths with individuals they would otherwise never meet. As they experience making a difference for others, corps members grow and mature, and also develop new skills and talents. National service imbues members with benefits that far exceed its usually meager financial stipends. Those who participate in service benefit from a broadened perspective on work and life, the development of workplace skills, and greater awareness of public issues.

One reason personal growth can be achieved through service is that many AmeriCorps programs are animated by a can-do culture of optimism. Young people often apply to and then join national service programs because they believe, or at least are open to the possibility, that they can make a difference in the world. Through a self-selection bias that favors these idealistic individuals against hardened cynics, a culture of idealism often permeates the programs. It is also worth noting that most AmeriCorps members are young adults, who are on average more idealistic upon entry into service than older adults. Still, this culture of idealism contributes to creativity and innovation because there is a greater openness to trying new things, or sometimes simply trying old things a second time. A program manager who had experience working with AmeriCorps commented: "What I've seen with having younger folks involved is a high degree of energy—an ability and a desire to work hard. You'll see young people really tackle work that others don't want to do, and bring enthusiasm to that." She also pointed out that as part of the process of recruiting and motivating people, it is essential to stress the larger vision. In her organization's case, this larger vision was the goal of eliminating substandard housing. When this is done, volunteers work hard and are generally more focused because they enjoy chasing a vision or goal. They see themselves as part of something larger than themselves and enjoy the potential to deepen their understanding of the world and their role in it.

Those who hold this developmental view of national service tend to believe that the way to unlock our nation's potential is through the development of our human capital. The impact of a program like AmeriCorps is the sum of the transformation of the many individual lives it touches. As these individuals go about their lives, they carry with them all that they learned during their time of service. The experience informs and influences their choices, providing an understanding of, and appreciation for, the public interest. All of this results in increased prosocial behavior. Service builds within them the character traits, skills, and motivation they need to make a difference in their workplaces and communities.

Within this broader frame of individual growth and development, our interviewees described a number of different impacts of service and underlying mechanisms through which AmeriCorps changes those who serve. Some focused on the increased understanding and broader perspective that comes from exposure to new situations and people, which helps young people understand their place in society and the way they can make a contribution to the community. Service takes individuals out of the constraints or "boxes" within which they are locked and opens up new opportunities and perspectives. As one practitioner explained, "We have so many forces in society that are driving us into certain boxes. For example, if you're in business school you're on a business track and you should go to work for a business. The same is true for education. It is very easy to get into a box fairly young in life and not have the full picture of the world. I believe the community benefits tremendously by people learning about those other worlds." One important benefit of national service is thus thought to reside in its ability to open up the minds of young people to the full range of life choices that are available to them. While corps members are working for others during service, they can and do end up learning about themselves.

The idea that service can lead to personal growth is significant on a broader level. Not only are individual horizons broadened but, collectively, there is also a chance to create consensus and understanding of critical public problems. A thought leader in the field elaborated on this effect: "If every eighteen-year-old spent a year or even less in a homeless shelter, I would guarantee that in a generation homelessness would disappear, not necessarily because of the work they did in those shelters, but because there would be a shared generational conversation about homelessness, a shared outrage and creativity about it." While it is possible that some of this growth and learning could be channeled into a movement, it is more likely to simply raise awareness and increase sensitivity to certain persistent social problems. It is also likely that many young people do not enter service with this goal in mind. In some poor rural areas, for example, the modest AmeriCorps stipend is actually financially attractive, particularly to young people with limited options. Some young people thus join to earn money when others are not offering them jobs. As a result, not all members come with a strong service ethic. Some may sign up because of uncertainty about what to do next in their lives, while others might be attracted by the prospect of having something to do, and for yet others it may just be a first line on their résumés. The director of a program that serves the frail elderly explains: "Many of our members come in with a 'it's all about me' mentality, not having had an opportunity to do service before. My experience is that over the course of the year most of them develop a service ethic, which they carry forward in their lives. The community appreciates the transformation of the members and they see it too."

Other policy and practice experts have focused less on identity and perspective changes and more on the development of practical skills. They see the potential of AmeriCorps in terms of workforce development, providing participants with training in both hard, technical skills and soft, interpersonal "workplace" skills. Service not only exposes young people to a skill set but also provides supervised opportunities to practice those skills. This kind of broad skill development results in more informed career choices, makes members more attractive to employers, and creates a stronger workforce: "If you look at what employers are looking for, and the debate about the qualifications of entry level workers, you'll find people wanting workplace skills and certainly wondering how to get them. AmeriCorps provides one example." Thus, above and beyond the maturity and awareness that service may impart, there are more practical considerations at play. Service may also help young people train and acquire work skills.

Finally, some of those we spoke with pointed out ways that AmeriCorps develops the leadership skills of volunteers and the staff in nonprofits that host AmeriCorps programs. Because these programs provide opportunities for members to demonstrate responsibility and to take action in a supportive and structured context, they experience firsthand that they can make a difference for themselves and others. This builds a sense of efficacy, reinforces their idealism, and inspires them to assume greater responsibility in the future. The communities in which national service operates can be classrooms in which important lessons about leadership and responsibility are learned.[17] Some of these lessons may be immediately clear, while others may take years to fully come into focus. The head of a large nonprofit began by reflecting on the most pressing need in her organization:

"Our organization's greatest need is not money or other resources, it is leadership. Because if you have good leadership, the rest will follow along." In stressing the importance of finding and developing the leaders of tomorrow, this expert also noted: "I think that [leadership development] is one of the most important aspects of what AmeriCorps does, and why I'd like to see it broadened in terms of the job descriptions. Anytime you can take a young person and give them an experience where they have to exhibit leadership, we're building a stronger country and a stronger world." This sort of leadership development is an explicit goal of many Ameri-Corps programs, both for faith-based programs that emphasize "the blessings you receive are to be shared," and for secular programs that may talk about moving people up the "ladder of service." Some programs even choose to invest in alumni networks so they can encourage and monitor service after members complete their AmeriCorps year: "In the same way we've always looked at growing the capacity of our volunteers, we want to provide the same challenge to our members. We call it 'cultivating persons of service.'" This head of a state commission also suggested that national service not only develops the leadership of members but also the leadership of everyone touched by a well-designed AmeriCorps program.

The idea that service enlarges vision and develops skills is held deeply by most of its proponents. It is part of the rationale that they have constructed for the often difficult and challenging work of engaging young people in public problem solving over the course of an entire year. AmeriCorps can bring out the best in individuals and in a community, often allowing people to serve for perhaps the first time in their lives. Individuals who in the past may have been consumers of service are invited to step from the sidelines and be a full contributor, even if they never thought they could meaningfully serve their communities. This can create a feeling of self-worth and build self-esteem. The promise of individual growth is also important to participants; it provides some of the attraction of national service. One program director who originally served as a member had this to say: "People are willing to sacrifice a year of their lives and live on a pittance if they can say, 'Wow! I really grew from that in a way that I would not have been able to if I just worked for that organization. And I think it's worth it.' That's certainly why I'm still here."

To become a reality, the conceptualization of national service as a driver of individual growth ultimately depends on a number of factors related to program design and implementation. Achieving these benefits is not simple or straightforward and requires meaningful preservice training, a clever initial program design, and strong site management and oversight. Without each of these elements, service experiences designed to encourage personal growth can just as likely result in greater alienation, frustration, a decreased sense of personal efficacy, and a kind of civic stunting that would be hard to reverse. Beyond these issues related to execution, this second conception of national service was critiqued by some on the grounds that the urgency of the problems we face as a nation are too significant to spend any time trying to promote personal growth. Some of those we spoke with even suggested that the focus on individuals is misguided, pointing to the importance of institutions and communities. These observers placed greater emphasis on community capacity building and the building of social capital. Finally, more than a few people felt strongly that government should have no role in the moral and personal development of young people, which has long been the responsibility of family and church.

Social Capital

Different from either human or financial capital, social capital refers to the networks, norms, and trust that make community coordination and cooperation possible.[18] The existence of social capital has important consequences for the quality of civic engagement and politics. Although the idea of trust is an old one,[19] it has in recent years become a powerful organizing concept for researchers studying markets, politics, and trust.[20] Putnam has argued that in the United States there has been a precipitous drop-off in social capital in recent decades. Measured in terms of involvement with clubs, Parent-Teacher Associations (PTAs), unions, and other forms of socializing, Americans over the past half century have slowly receded into increasingly isolated private lives. Putnam's most memorable image is that of the bowler who has forgone the camaraderie of a league and instead simply bowls alone. While the decline of bowling leagues has significant economic consequences for bowling lane proprietors, Putnam notes that the real significance of this trend "lies in the social interaction and even civic conversations over beer and pizza that solo bowlers forgo."[21]

Service has a unique role to play in forging the ties that link people together in ways that allow them to accomplish collective tasks.[22] In the process of meeting to form a neighborhood crime patrol or in volunteering at the local shelter, individuals make new acquaintances that can be useful for some time. The relationships and ties created by the pursuit of common purposes may seem rather pedestrian at the time they are being constructed, but over time they can prove to be a critical stock of resources on which neighborhoods can draw. While working together with residents to put together a youth sports program for a poor community may seem like an unremarkable activity for AmeriCorps members to undertake, this kind of work forges linkages, and individuals soon see one another in public space and begin to match names and faces. Relationships are created and friendships emerge. Thus, when it comes to enticing people outside their narrow networks of family and friends, service at the community level can be a powerful instrument for the forging of ties that bring people into contact with one another and create trust where once there was none.

It seems clear that service at the local level does connect people to one another and to the public sphere in many different ways. These connections can be somewhat limited in their character and depth, however. Many community groups struggle with the task of building extensive networks of ties that actually span the boundaries of income, race, and ideology. From churches that minister to narrow demographic groups to PTAs that draw only nearby suburban parents, individuals tend to associate with others who look, act, and think like they do. At one level, the fact that social capital is often built among people that have much in common seems only natural. The impulse to associate and "bond" is often driven by a desire to find others that share an interest or concern. This can be a significant shortcoming, however, because "bonding social capital" is more naturally abundant than "bridging social capital," which connects across long-standing divides. To make connections across groups and interests is a fundamental challenge for national service. Coalition building, which is a critical part of programs like VISTA, often entails reaching across traditional boundaries to find partners who are not the usual suspects, but who can advance a common agenda that spans long-standing differences of nationality, race, class, and economic position. If national service builds social capital, it will inevitably build our capacity within our communities and across the nation.[23] And to the extent that national service establishes ties that cross traditional divides of class, race, and ethnicity, it also may reunite an increasingly diverse America in our shared commitment to one another.

People who conceive of national service as social capital building see its strength not in the work that gets done, in the transformation of individuals, or even in the development of particular institutions and organizations, but instead in the relationships and connections that form between these individuals as they associate with one another.[24] These relationships become a critical source of creativity, energy, and coordination, and ensure that the associational life of the nation remains strong, which many, including Alexis de Tocqueville, believe has made our country both successful and democratic.[25] How then does national service foster these relationships and connections? What sorts of connections does it promote, specifically? The most common way mentioned was through what might be called the building of a broader "we." According to this understanding of national service, when programs bring together diverse people under a shared purpose of their own choosing, this shared purpose, in combination with an intensive year-long experience together as equals, creates a strong environment in which the members can develop new understanding and appreciation for each other. As one program director noted, "Individuals and groups that may have entered with a frame of 'us' and 'them,' leave as just 'us.' "

Social networks are valuable to the individual (e.g., consider the importance of one's own Rolodex) and they are even more valuable to the broader community. Communities where people know and trust each other have better schools, better local government, better public health, and better economic performance. "Bridging" social capital is particularly important because these ties are less likely to form on their own, and because it breaks down stereotypes. Only with a broader vision of social equality or justice and a store of social capital can some of the most complex and enduring community problems ever be addressed and ultimately solved. Personal friendships that bridge from one side of the tracks to the other are a way of importing clout into disadvantaged communities.

Social capital is important because it may also increase understanding and tolerance. With more connections to persons different from themselves, AmeriCorps members may gain in their appreciation of cultural diversity. A number of practitioners and leaders in the national service movement commented on the role national service can play in reducing stereotypes, whether it be of the elderly, immigrants, young people, or the disabled. The lines between servers and beneficiaries become blurred as those who have traditionally given become receivers, and those who have received now give. This helps strengthen and spread a norm of reciprocity. One program director who works with older volunteers explained: "We have lots of life extension technology now, which means longer lives for individuals we care about, which is great. But as a nation we see this as a bad thing because we see it as one giant cost center. This creates a negative attitude towards older people. ExperienceCorps [an AmeriCorps program for those older than fifty-five] changes the ideas about what it means to be old in America, what's expected of you, how you're valued." The manager of an AmeriCorps program that serves developmentally delayed persons and isolated seniors by working on their skills and giving them service opportunities, elaborated on this point: "The integration that occurs because of the support of AmeriCorps members is very difficult to measure, but has a double effect on the person and the community. It gives the person with disability (or the seniors) the chance not only to participate in society but also give back to society." These comments also point out the importance of "showcasing" these service efforts, which can extend their impact beyond the individuals involved to the broader community. When service is done in one's own community, these programs shift stereotypes and present an alternative to the self-interested individualism,[26] and plant the seeds for future cooperation upon which other work can be accomplished.

A norm of reciprocity may also be reinforced between institutions and individuals through national service. For example, members are rewarded for their service with an education award and all AmeriCorps programs are required to have significant member development that accompanies their service. Investments like these emphasize the social contract between the members, their community, their country, and the hosting nonprofits. Finally, through service, members develop a deeper appreciation for their interdependence and they are exposed to the intrinsic rewards of service, perhaps for the first time. This has the effect of merging their own self-interests with an appreciation for the needs of others, creating an "enlightened" sense of self-interest. In this way, national service as social capital building can be thought of as the projection of individual transformation to a community level.

Some former volunteers thought the experience was important for how it affected their horizons and their sense of connection to something bigger than themselves: "I found an incredibly rewarding reciprocity through service. Everything from exploring a neighborhood I'd never otherwise know, to meeting new people, to challenging myself to understand what's going on outside my own world. That discovery of that reciprocity lit me on fire and became insatiable." The construction of networks of reciprocity and social capital can fuel a long-term commitment to public service. In the case of one former volunteer, it led to years of community service: "As I found more of that [feeling of reciprocity], I wanted to bring others to that too, taking on leadership. And that's what I've done. I participated in AmeriCorps for two years. My original plan was to go to law school, but I determined that wasn't the right move for me, and I've been working with service organizations ever since."

While social capital and trust may seem like things that adhere only to individuals, they can and do connect organizations and communities together.[27] Social capital can be built through collaborations between organizations and joint service delivery efforts that rally entire communities toward a common goal. This sort of community-wide social capital was mentioned by many of the people we spoke with, a number of whom noted that these collaborations and connections were not always planned intentionally but emerged organically through running a national service program. One program director and part-time academic talked about the impact his program had within his university: "Our AmeriCorps program brought together people from different parts of the university who would not have come together otherwise, to work on common projects. This creates cross-fertilization." One concern about social capital is that it may be ephemeral and require lots of regular maintenance. In the case of this university-centered project, the connections and relationship outlasted even the formal presence of the national service project: "Each part of the university that participated was represented on a campus coordinating committee, which was unprecedented at my university. It brought together different service efforts and became a vehicle for future collaborative projects, even though our AmeriCorps program is no longer funded." National service can thus be seen as a tool for building social capital within large clusters of institutions and across entire communities. By engaging people in public problem solving, national service may also be able to address some of the dangerous trends toward isolation and disengagement that Putnam and others have signaled.

Social capital may also appear in the space among national service programs that operate nearby one another. One program director found this effect among the organizations where her members worked: "In cities where we have several AmeriCorps members placed, they also seem to be able to form networks and cross-pollinate. They identify service gaps and make contact so that their organizations can partner to get something done." These interorganizational linkages proved very important when it came time to lobby for AmeriCorps' continued funding during a recent fiscal crisis. One person suggested that the ability of the Save AmeriCorps Coalition to form and recruit a large amount of support so quickly was a testament to the social capital that has been created. A mobilization of that scale would not have been possible without it: "The activity of the Save AmeriCorps Coalition validated what we had been saying on faith, that it was out there and it was making a difference. It is insinuating itself, in the best sense of the word, into American life." The main problem, however, with seeing national service primarily as a builder of social capital, tolerance, and trust is that these are very hard concepts to measure. This proved to be particularly problematic given the early criticism leveled at national service by its detractors that its goals were too ambiguous.

Social capital and norms of reciprocity are not inevitable by-products of AmeriCorps programs. It is also possible for stereotypes to be reinforced, animosity to grow, and connections to be weakened because of the close working conditions and intensity of feeling surrounding many of the projects undertaken by national service programs. Furthermore, AmeriCorps programs are not mandated to engage diverse constituents, which means that these programs may not create bridging ties at all. A number of interviewees emphasized the importance of skilled facilitation to ensure that when people are brought together they have positive experiences and to demonstrate possibilities they might not be aware of otherwise. They also emphasized the need to intentionally design programs with reciprocity in mind. The director of a faith-based program used the Greek concepts of *kononia* and *diaconia* to structure their program, or as she put it: "Building community, but in service to the broader community and world." Investments are made in members, beneficiaries, and their congregation, but with the explicit intention that they will in turn use their new capacity to serve and invest in others, creating a virtuous cycle of community building.

The vision of national service that focuses on social capital formation tends to be embraced by those who felt uncomfortable with the prospect of imposing narrow boundaries around the potential impact of these programs. In fact, when national service is stripped down to its essential elements, one observer noted, "I am not convinced that there is something unique about the work that gets done [through national service] that is significantly different than typical volunteer work." This expert went on to note that the real contribution of AmeriCorps lies "in the more unique opportunity to build bridging social capital and to change the norms regarding what is expected of citizens." This broader conception of the purpose of AmeriCorps represents the core of the vision of national service as social capital builder. Later in this book, our analysis translates this vision into constructs that are measurable: trust, tolerance, and community connections.

Public Work

Far less complex and contingent than the concept of social capital is the idea of public work. In its most basic terms, national service has long been about meeting critical public needs and filling gaps created by government and market failures. Volunteers are part of a system designed to deliver at low cost important public services that otherwise would not be available to communities.[28] National service is believed by many to be an alternative means of addressing public needs without reliance on traditional forms of contracting or direct public service employment. In all these functions, service is a form of production and a way of meeting critical needs, particularly in the focal areas of education, human services, environment, and public safety.

Most people think about national service in terms of the simple instrumental ends it accomplishes. The slogan adopted by the corporation for conveying this vision was "getting things done," a phrase that was emphasized during the early years of AmeriCorps. This emphasis was partly a matter of political expediency. Under pressure to show that the expense of national service was producing something of value for taxpayers, the corporation spent a great deal of time and expense documenting for Congress what was in fact getting done. Counting the number of shrubs planted by a service project or documenting the number of tutoring hours delivered is much easier to track and communicate than a change in the level of civic engagement, a significant contribution to participants' personal growth, or increased social capital formation.[29] But the attraction of defining national service in terms of what it gets done reflects the broader debate in which we found ourselves immersed. There has long been a tension in American society between those who see citizenship from the lens of civic education, identity development, and patriotism and those who conceive of it in terms of the results that are achieved. The latter perspective has grown in popularity in recent years, as the former has slipped in credibility due to a lack of good evidence and empirical data to support its plausibility.

To understand national service in terms of what it concretely accomplishes for communities and the nation is simple and straightforward enough. The immediate, direct results of the service undertaken are the most visible and easily comprehensible artifacts within and outside the service movement. It can be documented whether intended outputs are being produced and the costs of producing these outputs are also identifiable. Outputs or units of service—for example, the number of empty lots cleared of garbage or the number of elderly persons served meals at home—can be measured, tracked, and even aggregated across communities. Given the obvious challenges and uncertainties in measuring the other impacts of national service, and the inherent importance of building support for the work being undertaken, a number of the observers and experts we spoke with felt it was entirely appropriate to conceive of national service in large measure along these instrumental terms. Still, some we spoke with hesitated to focus on these instrumental achievements, drawing a distinction between *outputs,* which track short-term units of service delivered, and *outcomes,* which are broader and more complex units of analysis that imply changes in client or community conditions. At the end of this debate about what can be measured and what is worth measuring, the basic question remains: What does national service actually accomplish for communities or the nation?

Even if one sets aside the question of measurement and accepts that judging service in terms of what it accomplishes for communities is reasonable, there is a more interesting question about whether all the local outputs that AmeriCorps generates together constitute a coherent vision of "national" service. Questions abound: What really is the relationship between community-level service and our national needs? Can this link be plausibly made? Do all the small victories and narrow accomplishments add up to a coherent vision for national service? How are these achievements related to one another? Do they need to be related? These are some of the questions that arose as we explored this more tangible vision of service with those who know these programs best. Some interviewees saw and fixated on a definite distinction between community work and national needs, pointing to things like military service and public infrastructure projects as constituting national needs, but positing that most of what AmeriCorps does remains strictly at the community level.

Other interviewees were willing to consider some areas where Ameri-Corps and VISTA are active and focused as constituting a national need, such as the education of disadvantaged children, but not areas such as neighborhood beautification. Still others considered anything of community value to be nationally valuable.

Interestingly, those with concerns about the coherence and value of what national service produces tended to favor greater central control and oversight over these programs, aimed at bringing greater coherence to the work that is done: "I think AmeriCorps in some ways has suffered from a thousand flowers blooming, funding so many things, and having a hard time really saying this is what's fundamentally different in this country as a result of the service." With a personal commitment to helping kids, one program director wished for more convergence around her substantive area: "We strongly believe that out of school time should be a much more central and strategic focus of AmeriCorps. If there were central funding and baselines around achievement of children in programs that were AmeriCorps funded, I think that would be part of how we could strengthen the whole field."

Not everyone agreed that bringing uniformity or even alignment to the public work of national service would be wise or desirable. Those who thought that diverse public work in communities aggregated to a clear national contribution actually argued for greater autonomy and local control over the direction of service. As a service leader put it: "I think Ameri-Corps would be weaker if every member did tutoring, for example. It would tend to draw people who thought they wanted to spend a year being tutors. It wouldn't necessarily attract people who wanted to do other things. Part of the strength of AmeriCorps is to have local communities say what their needs are."

Even some of those who are concerned more with individual growth, citizenship development, and social capital building sometimes put the instrumental goals of AmeriCorps first. One interviewee drew an analogy with the military: it does an excellent job developing individuals and citizens, but these goals are entirely secondary to the main instrumental goal of the military, which is national defense. He pointed out that if the military were conceived more in terms of the development of human capital, it likely would not only fail to achieve that ambiguous end but also fail to provide effective defense. Moreover, there is something about putting one's own needs second to the good of the community and nation for a

period of time that may inherently promote personal development. Therefore, although these developmental goals may be most important, some of
their promoters still choose to conceive of national service as "getting
things done" for the nation—seeing it as an essential means to the other
ends of service.

Beyond perhaps serving as the stepping-stone to achievement of the
other intended impacts of national service, the public work conception has
an additional dimension. Getting things done may involve actually delivering a certain amount of service to a community, but it can also mean
building the capacity of the organizations in the community so that they
can "get things done." In this sense, the instrumental vision of national service has both direct and indirect components. The direct component involves using volunteers to actually do the work, while the indirect component depends on nonprofit capacity building to get things done on a larger
and lasting scale, even after specific service initiatives have ended and national service slots are moved to other communities. Evidence is growing
that AmeriCorps does indeed impact the hosting nonprofits and an increasing number of people believe these effects to be significant. Capacity
building was also an explicit priority under President George W. Bush.

Those who advocate this perspective see a variety of different ways that
AmeriCorps builds capacity. AmeriCorps can help expand the reach of
existing programs or stimulate the creation of innovative new programs.
It can institutionalize systems, processes, and best practices that leave
behind a lasting infrastructure. It can develop management capacity and
promote a more intensive focus on mission. It can increase the awareness
of additional resources and help leverage strategic partnerships. The underlying logic of capacity building as the anchor of public work is that by
developing the capacity of the nonprofit sector, one can increase the ability
of the sector to respond effectively to important national needs once local
programs have ended and are moved to other needy communities. Capacity building thus promises to turn one dollar of program investment into
many dollars of long-term social value.[30]

The most basic kind of capacity building is through expansion of existing programs. A program can use AmeriCorps resources to be able to offer
the same services to more clients. Examples of this model would be many
tutoring programs, which add members as full-time tutors and thus can
serve more children. This sort of capacity exists only as long as AmeriCorps
funding is sustained. However, if the community sees that the organization

is successfully getting things done, even the short-term presence of national service resources can increase long-term capacity by attracting new funding and other volunteer commitments from the community.

Based on what we heard in interviews with those delivering programs, there are at least three reasons why the capacity to get things done that is developed through AmeriCorps may persist after funding has ended. In some cases, the systems, processes, and practices established with the creation of their programs proved more broadly beneficial and were retained. An example of this would be the continued use of previously unused performance measures and regular evaluations. The second reason might be called the "Possibility Effect," in which a community becomes aware of possible achievements through AmeriCorps, and seeks out new and creative ways to enable these activities to continue. The third reason is connected to using the capacity provided by national service programs to move beneficiaries from dependence to self-sufficiency. Having the capacity to cross this threshold can free the organization to take on new challenges, expand its scope, or otherwise advance its mission. In this way, the beneficiaries and nonprofits go from "survive" to "thrive" together.

The temporary nature of funding is a powerful reason why organizations tend to plan early for sustainability.[31] The very structure of one-year service positions may inherently help to build the capacity to get things done in the future. Because members must get up to speed quickly, the organization must develop its training, policies, procedures, and systems. Oftentimes, the members themselves develop these resources before they leave at the end of their year. This planning for sustainability is emphasized particularly with VISTA members. However, a few interviewees noted that in some cases the one-year appointments are too short, suggesting that some of the ways an organization may invest in members are never fully "repaid." This is particularly the case where heavy training and regular oversight by nonprofit managers are needed for the program to succeed. Similarly, the funding structure of AmeriCorps grants themselves may help organizations focus more directly on their mission, although there were conflicting opinions on this point. Some interviewees complained that the funding they receive through AmeriCorps is insufficient to cover essential aspects of their program, particularly evaluation, training, and technical assistance. As a result, they feel they underinvest in these areas, which undermines their ability both to get the most out of AmeriCorps members and to advance their mission.

Another way that public work builds the capacity of communities is by allowing nonprofits to leverage additional volunteers. A program director with years of experience explained, "We have a surplus of unskilled, short-term volunteers. AmeriCorps really helps us by allowing us to use those legions of volunteers in an effective and productive manner. We consider it ideal when you have about one skilled person for every four to five unskilled volunteers. On a staff level, we never hit that. We just can't afford it. But AmeriCorps makes that possible." Other interviewees mentioned similar effects with regard to funding. Not only can participating in a national service network increase their awareness of funding opportunities, but it can make their organizations more attractive to funders: "What we have discovered in meeting the requirements of the AmeriCorps grant is that it has opened the door for corporations and business to feel comfortable that we in the faith-based community are doing what we need to do to be good caretakers of the funding." The accomplishment of goals through national service thus encourages additional funders to support other organizational means to get things done.

National service may not just add to the capacity of existing organizations but may also fuel the formation of new capacities for addressing public problems. National service may actually stimulate creative problem solving focused on our most pressing public problems. A number of the people interviewed suggested that one of the most important effects of national service is to promote civic innovation and social entrepreneurship.[32] Underlying this perspective is an assumption, sometimes stated and sometimes implied, that the key to addressing our problems as a nation is not working harder in the same ways, but working instead in smarter and more creative ways. By reinventing the way we conceive of and address problems, we can develop the potential to transcend the limitations of past approaches and respond to the many significant and ongoing changes in American society.

One observer drew an analogy to the business sector where companies like Dell Computer, Wal-Mart, and Southwest Airlines have reinvented and disrupted established conventions, creating more value in the process. They point to the growing trend in social entrepreneurship, in which the entrepreneurial mind-set has been brought to bear on problems in the social sector, leading to new strategies, growth, and higher levels of effectiveness. In fact, some of the nonprofits best known for their entrepreneurship have affiliations with AmeriCorps, including City Year,[33] Jumpstart, and

Teach for America. Organizations like these and the people who lead them are innovative, resourceful, and tend to see opportunities when pursuing practical solutions to problems and the creation of public value. Unfortunately, there are limits to this kind of innovation through experimentation because of the way programs are administered and funded. As one veteran of the service movement allowed, "Failing is important for learning and there is no tolerance [within AmeriCorps] because there are federal taxpayer dollars involved and because AmeriCorps has always been under intense political scrutiny. There's also no space for failure or honest evaluation, so you can't learn by trial and error. It's never been an option to have an evaluation of a program and find it's not so good . . . If it were a venture capital thing, you hit one out of twenty and you're rich. With AmeriCorps, you screw up one out of 250 placements and you're dead broke."

What at first glance appeared to be obvious—counting what gets accomplished through service—turns out thus to be more complex. Part of complexity relates to the fact that the process of getting things done involves not just the production of community benefits but also the construction of capacity and the leveraging of additional resources outside national service. In this sense, the public work conception is linked to other intervening conceptions of service that are broader than the simple question of how many midnight basketball games were organized in a given community to help keep young people from getting into trouble. It is about everything that happens around the game and what this means for the community over the long haul.

Why National Service?

Given all the confusion and contestation around the purpose of national service,[34] the question still lingers: "Why national service?" One reason is that Americans are optimistic and idealistic, and the idea of service fits nicely with this national outlook. Still, because it aims at big things like citizenship, self-actualization, and community cohesiveness, it is hardly surprising that there are many competing views about how to channel and maximize the impact of programs like AmeriCorps and VISTA. With hundreds of thousands of people moving through these programs, the national service movement has created its own base of support among alumni, even though policy makers of all political stripes continue to ask tough questions.

The four visions of national service elaborated here transcend the ungrounded and ideological arguments about national service as either an enactment of American idealism or a corruption of the Tocquevillian vision of grassroots volunteer action. These four conceptions are clearly not hermetically sealed and independent, however; there are clear overlaps and intersections between them. It may be that the instrumental logic behind seeing national service as public work may be critical to achieving some of the broader and more expressive ends of service that relate to the development of human potential. Similarly, it may be that supporting citizenship development and personal growth, and even constructing social capital, depend at bottom on national service being about something far more concrete and real. Only when public work actually gets done can it be possible to achieve some of the deeper and more ambitious visions of national service.

The four main visions of national service that we defined from our interviews may not exhaust all the possibilities, but they do reflect the full diversity of the perspectives articulated in our interviews. They represent our interpretation and our effort to fashion a coherent framework that will form the basis of the empirical analysis that follows. They are idealized conceptions. Our core challenge in this book is to use data to test the effectiveness of national service programs in realizing these competing visions. While there is an attempt to test claims about national service and cut through some of the fog that envelopes the field, it is our hope that this project will stimulate dialogue between those holding these four different visions and that this will in turn slowly move us toward greater agreement regarding the role of national service in American society. In carrying out this work, we made some difficult decisions to focus on a limited range of issues and questions. We do not attempt to say which vision of service is "correct" or which should guide the future of national service. What we do attempt is to provide evidence about whether and under what conditions national service programs may be able to achieve the complex and ambitious ends implied in each of the competing visions of service.

Within the debate over what national service actually accomplishes, we intervene in the following chapters with data—a lot of data. In the middle chapters, we present not one but two major new data sets related to the efficacy of national service programs, along with a large amount of qualitative data culled from in-depth interviews with thousands of corps members and hundreds of volunteer program managers.[35] Armed with this data and guided by the question of who benefits and in what ways from national service, we proceed by laying out some historical background on national service, sketching the broad contours of the evidence to be used in this book, and then delving into each of the visions of national service with as much evidence as we can muster. Finally, after all the data is examined and discussed, we conclude by offering some ideas about how national service might be improved, regardless of one's vision of what service should ultimately attempt to achieve. While the world of national service is filled with people animated by a passionate commitment to their work, there is still room, we believe, for new ideas and proposals that everyone should be able to embrace. With these formalities now complete, it is time to examine more closely the kaleidoscope of intentions that is national service.

— 2 —

The Evolution of National Service

The idea of national service is deeply rooted in American political values that can be traced back to the origins of this country. Over the past two centuries, a wide array of contrasting conceptions of the role of government has shaped the many forms national service has taken in the United States. Just as politics change over time, national needs and priorities have shifted and the focus of national service has changed in response. The content and form of service has been a function of incremental changes in program emphasis and what the political climate has dictated. Popular attitudes toward national service have also evolved over time as citizens have seen and experienced the reality of service in their own communities.

What does it mean to serve the nation? This remains the central animating question behind national service. Some might immediately think of national service in terms of its current programmatic incarnations, including AmeriCorps, Volunteers in Service to America (VISTA), and a host of other programs targeted at specific populations. AmeriCorps, the largest program in the portfolio, engages primarily young citizens across the country in direct service to address pressing needs in their communities for a year. National service is, however, a much broader idea than any specific programs now in place. It is an idea that has been with us since the founding and which can even be traced back to the first democracy in ancient Athens.

National service has always been closely linked to important national needs. The original national need, and some argue the only true national need, is military defense.[1] A nation cannot continue to exist without protecting its boundaries and its people from outside threats. In ancient times, every able-bodied man was required to contribute to defense through military service. Today, many countries around the world still require some form of military service from its citizens. Beyond national defense, democracies have other needs and they often depend on their citizens to perform at least some of the functions of government. These needs include holding public office, sitting on juries and voting, and providing services such as fire protection. The structure and term of these services varies significantly, but they are all essential to the health of a nation and should be considered forms of community and public service. Throughout history, many experiments have been conducted in which these critical duties were performed either through voluntary or mandatory service.[2] By tracing some of the ideas about and aspirations for service, a historical grounding can be laid here for the study of contemporary forms of national and community service.

Volunteerism in Early America

Defense was the first need the American colonies faced after they declared their independence from Britain and became a sovereign nation. The Revolutionary War presented an extremely compelling and complex challenge for the fledgling United States: how to defend its independence once it was declared. Americans responded with a structure that was familiar to them from their time in England and that also matched well with their political values and convictions. They formed a series of local militias. Valuing their freedom and angry with what they perceived to be the unreasonable demands of the British monarchy, Americans resisted investing too much power in central government. The militia system, which would become the origin of the modern National Guard, involved universal compulsory short-term military training and service under local officers. States held the power to draft men to serve in the Continental army, but they notably denied George Washington's desire to draft at the national level. All of this was designed to avoid a central authority making demands on localities. The ranks of short-term citizen soldiers were augmented with a smaller group of professional long-term volunteers who enlisted into what later became known as the U.S. Army.[3] These volunteers—drawn primarily from the young and the disadvantaged—signed up for a combination of religious, patriotic, and economic reasons, because of social pressure, or out of a desire for adventure. George Washington once remarked, "It may be laid down as a primary position, and the basis of our system, that every

Citizen who enjoys the protection of a Free Government, owes not only a proportion of his property, but even of his personal services to the defense of it."[4] Service in the early Republic was not organized and directed by a central body, but it was still a potent source of community problem solving.

The forms of national service have reflected the political debates of the day. Federalists like Madison and Hamilton argued with Republicans like Jefferson over the appropriate amount of power to vest in the central government versus the amount to retain at the state and local levels.[5] The balance of compulsory versus voluntary service was a response to disagreements over the nature of freedom and the appropriate balance of rights and responsibilities in the face of a clear threat and a need for immediate action. There were at least two different perspectives: moralists, who believed that people should serve out of a sense of responsibility, and capitalists, who argued that a system of incentives to serve would yield the best outcome. A professional force can be trained extensively and can achieve high levels of competence through experience, but average citizens stepping forward to serve may possess a deeper sense of purpose and be animated by strongly held beliefs. Their service may have more lasting effects in terms of training the citizenry, developing a valuable sense of patriotism, and contributing to a lifetime of public service. The need for citizens to organize for the purpose of service is seen in the Federalist Papers. Federalist Paper No. 57 states that citizens "will enter into the public service under circumstances which cannot fail to produce a temporary affection at least to their constituents."[6]

Nonmilitary forms of public service were also common in early American life, even before independence, although primarily at a local rather than national level. By 1835, Alexis de Tocqueville was famously struck by the intensive and extensive use of civil associations at the community level to accomplish what the government would provide in other countries: "Americans of all ages, all stations of life, and all types of disposition are forever forming associations. In democratic countries knowledge of how to combine is the mother of all other forms of knowledge; on its progress depends that of all the others . . . In every case, at the head of any new undertaking, where in France you would find the government or in England some territorial magnate, in the United States you are sure to find an association." Tocqueville noticed in these associations both a way of getting collective tasks accomplished and an ingenious way to curb the expansion of state power. By relying on civil associations and by allowing these groups to support the formation of political associations, Americans were finding a way both to meet community needs and to build active civic engagement.[7] While these early associations were local and informal, and while they did not resemble modern structured volunteer "programs," America's early associational tradition still sets the stage for later efforts to channel this community spirit toward larger purposes.

What did these early volunteer associations actually accomplish? Associations were used to provide collective goods, such as caring for the elderly and infirm, dealing with bad crops and hard winters, constructing public buildings, and clearing blocked intersections. Most of these community services were performed voluntarily out of a sense of fellowship, often among members of a religious congregation,[8] but it is important to note that some essential nonmilitary civic duties were considered mandatory, including holding public office.[9] Volunteer firefighting groups may be perhaps the best known of the nonmilitary forms of public service. The first "Mutual Fire Society" was created in Boston in 1711, and many more followed soon thereafter. The members of these fire societies came to each other's aid when one of their houses caught fire. Benjamin Franklin borrowed this idea for implementation in Philadelphia in 1733, but made an important revision: fire societies there would be for the general benefit of all citizens rather than only the participating members. Members purchased their own equipment and even voluntarily assessed fines within the group when a member failed to attend a meeting or arrive for firefighting duty.[10] In a *Pennsylvania Gazette* article of 1733, Franklin noted how fires were being fought in Philadelphia: "Soon after it [a fire] is seen and cry'd out, the place is crowded by active men of different ages, professions and titles who, as of one mind and rank, apply themselves with all vigilance and resolution, according to their abilities, to the hard work of conquering the increasing fire."[11]

By and large, from the founding up until modern times, American political culture has been partial to, and had faith in, decentralized, bottom-up, voluntary solutions to social problems. These early associations are the origins of what is now called the nonprofit and voluntary sector, which today contributes hundreds of billions of dollars to the U.S. economy and employs an important part of the workforce. Over the past two centuries, much of the activity within this sector has been informal in nature and delivered by volunteers rather than professionals.[12] There have been significant historical differences in how these voluntary associations and early public-serving organizations were organized by different states. Some states channeled resources into public organizations, including universities and hospitals. A more informal approach was taken in New England, where resources were allowed to flow to private charitable organizations and new organizations created by private donors were encouraged.[13] There was a general preference for decentralized solutions and there was no single "American model" for the delivery of public services. Instead, there was a diversity of perspectives and approaches that represented local tastes and customs. This diversity is still present in modern national service in the sense that the form taken by service varies greatly and is shaped heavily by the local context. Community service is thus an old idea. Debates during America's first century about service eventually succeeded in bringing out into the open fundamental differences in opinion about the nature of American democracy and the role of active citizens in it.

Framing the Modern Idea of National Service

Throughout much of the first half of the nineteenth century, the only form of national service in the United States—public service at the national level—was military in nature. Given that the majority of conflicts during this time were limited and sporadic, a small, voluntary, full-time army was augmented in times of need by a locally raised but federally financed and controlled force of citizen soldiers.[14] The first mandatory service at the national level was introduced during the Civil War, given the need for massive numbers of troops on both sides. Despite the tremendous need, conscription was very controversial at the time because of the numerous exemptions that were offered to the privileged, many of whom were allowed to buy their way out of service. Religious pacifists were also allowed to perform alternate, nonmilitary service. The draft was used later in World War I, but without as many exceptions. Only conscientious objectors were given reprieve.[15] As a result, there was not a repeat of the draft riots that were common during the Civil War.[16]

In 1906, philosopher William James wrote an influential essay entitled "The Moral Equivalent of War," which many point to as the origins of the idea of modern civilian national service. In his article, James observed that there is a wide array of positive indirect benefits associated with external threats and war. As a pacifist, this was a troubling fact for him to accept. Foremost among these benefits were the forging of a national unity and the development and exercise of civic virtue among the citizenry:

> Militarism is the great preserver of our ideals of hardihood, and human life with no use for hardihood would be contemptible . . . We should get toughness without callousness, authority with as little criminal cruelty as possible, and painful work done cheerily because the duty is temporary, and threats not, as now, to degrade the whole remainder of one's life . . . All the qualities of a man acquire dignity when he knows that the service of the collectivity that owns him needs him . . . So far, war has been the only force that can discipline a whole community, and until an equivalent discipline is organized [civilian national service], I believe that war must have its way.[17]

These indirect benefits are clearly quite important in and of themselves: social cohesion, patriotism, individual character development, investment in national infrastructure, and strengthened civic habits among the citizenry. Given the diverse purposes that national service is actually trying to achieve, some people today continue to consider these indirect benefits of primary importance. To adherents of this view, the direct instrumental goals of the service are almost irrelevant. James's essay raised several important questions for national service that remain unanswered to this day: What is the ultimate purpose of national service? Is universal service a requirement of a healthy and strong nation?[18] Does service need to be military? What would a civilian form of national service aim to achieve? These questions remained a part of the public conversation about service and citizenship until times got tough enough that answers were needed.

The staggering unemployment of the Great Depression in the 1930s presented an extremely compelling national challenge, which demanded a direct response on a large scale. How should the crisis be addressed? As might be expected, key debates in American political culture surfaced as the country grappled with developing a recovery plan. For example, there was much debate over the issue of how much responsibility affected individuals bore for righting their own situations compared to the duty of government to help. Many wanted a decentralized, market-based approach, but others wanted more direct government intervention. A major initiative aimed at tackling the challenges of the times was the National Recovery Administration (NRA). The NRA sought to provide incentives for employers to treat employees well, primarily by permitting participating businesses to put a blue eagle in their window and on their products. This eagle was a way to put social pressure on employers, but it was later ruled unconstitutional. It was not until this decentralized, voluntary solution was tried and failed that the federal government took more direct action.

One important action was the creation of the Civilian Conservation Corps (CCC) 1933. The CCC marked the first time that a nonmilitary service program was implemented at the national level in the United States. It represented an innovative response to a new need that was based on experience with previous local forms of service and informed by James's ideas. President Roosevelt presented the bill, and Congress passed it quickly and easily, given the urgency and depth of the employment problems facing the country. Roosevelt believed that there was plenty of work to be done across the nation: "We face a future of soil erosion and timber famine. It is clear that economic foresight and immediate employment march hand in hand, in the call for the reforestation of these areas. In so doing, employment can be given to a million men. That is the kind of public work that is self-sustaining."[19] He also argued that "More important than material gains, will be the moral and spiritual value of such work. We can take a vast army of the unemployed out into healthful surroundings. We can eliminate to some extent at least the threat that enforced idleness brings to spiritual and moral stability."[20]

The CCC was first and foremost a jobs program, but it was also explicitly a conservation program. Roosevelt touted it as a multilayered investment in the country's future. It engaged 250,000 young men ages eighteen to twenty-eight and enrolled them on a temporary basis to work on federal lands, doing much of the work to create our national park system. The work varied from camp to camp and from month to month, but most of the work was done in teams and all of the projects were concrete and tangible: planting trees, tending trails, and building lookout towers, small dams, and bridges, among other things. As Charles Moskos noted in his historical summary of service: "In the original design, enrollees were unemployed, single males aged eighteen to twenty-five years with no criminal record. Enrollment was for a six-month period, renewable up to two years. Participants received food, shelter, uniforms, and a monthly payment of $30, two-thirds of which was sent directly to the enrollee's family. It was not much, but given the harshness of times, the corps had few problems attracting applicants."[21] There was no explicit citizenship or educational component built into the program, but it is generally agreed that overall the camps had an energizing effect on the young men who participated.[22] Unlike subsequent national service programs, it had a clear focus on getting public work done in the arena of environmental conservation and public land development.

Developing and Shaping National Service Programs

The attack on Pearl Harbor and the entry of the United States into World War II represented a major shift in the nation's foremost needs. Jobs were no longer a problem, but instead national defense was a primary concern. The CCC ended and conscription was reinstated. Over time, 10 million men were drafted and 6 million eventually enlisted. The war effort was felt at home in other ways. Women entered the workforce for the first time in large numbers to meet the demand. During World War II, millions of women worked in manufacturing plants that produced munitions, taking the place of male employees who were away fighting in the war. Rosie the Riveter became a cultural icon, appearing in films and posters that were used by the U.S. government to encourage women to go to work in support of the war effort.

The major innovations in national service during this period were the GI Bill and Reserve Officers' Training Corps (ROTC) scholarships, both of which provided education assistance to those who served in the military as an incentive and reward for service. In this way, a national norm of civic reciprocity was fostered. In total, more than 7 million people were reached by these scholarships, representing more than half of all veterans and well in excess of anyone's expectations. These awards turned out to be far more than handouts; they were a huge and valuable investment in the nation's human capital. The acknowledged architect of the bill, Harry Colmery, a veteran and former national commander of the American Legion, wanted to avoid the painful experiences that returning veterans faced after World War I: "The burden of war falls on the citizen soldier who has gone forth, overnight, to become the armored hope of humanity. Never again, do we want to see the honor and glory of our nation fade to the extent that her men of arms, with despondent heart and palsied limb, totter from door to door, bowing their souls to the frozen bosom of reluctant charity."[23]

Many in higher education were originally fearful of the idea. James Conant, then president of Harvard, initially opposed the bill, expecting that it would undermine academic standards. He later changed his mind, going as far as to concede that "World War II veterans were the best students Harvard ever had." Most historians tend to agree, considering the GI Bill to be one of the single most successful investments ever in the health and strength of the nation. The link between education scholarships and national service continued during the Korean and Vietnam Wars, but was financed at lower levels. Scholarships for civilian service also were instituted later, in the form of the National Defense Student Loan Program in 1958 and the National Teacher Corps, both of which supported people who agreed to serve as teachers in areas of national need. These were followed by other programs like the National Health Service Corps for health professionals.

The 1950s were a time of relative peace and prosperity, certainly in contrast with the previous two decades. With the end of World War II, the beginnings of the reconstruction of Europe assisted by the Marshall Plan, and the creation of the United Nations, Americans came to see themselves as a major force for development around the globe.[24] Some even began to talk about the idea of voluntary international service by individual citizens.[25] But what really brought this proposal to the fore was the growing perception of communism as an increasing threat to developing nations, to the power of the United States abroad, and to the future of democracy. Thus, preserving democracy and the American way of life became an important national need at that time. President Kennedy remarked on the unique position of the country: "The United States and a few other fortunate nations are part of an island of prosperity in a worldwide sea of poverty. Our affluence has at times severed us from the great poverty stricken majority of the world's people. It is essential that we demonstrate that we continue to be aware of the responsibility we fortunate few have to assist the efforts of others at development and progress."[26]

Some believe it was the communist threat that led President Kennedy to create the Peace Corps in 1961 as a way to win the hearts and minds of citizens in the developing world, particularly those in countries at greatest risk of falling under the spell of communism. The real reasons are more complex and multidimensional. The Peace Corps was to be a youth corps, in many ways similar to the CCC, but different in that volunteers were to be college-educated professionals trained to assist with economic development projects, and would serve as individuals or in small groups dispersed through partner countries. Some of the inspiration for the Peace Corps came as much from the tradition of missionary work—familiar to many from their religious traditions—as from the CCC.

Public figures of the 1970s had a range of things to say about the Peace Corps. On 1 March 1968, President Lyndon Baines Johnson wrote to Congress, "If you would confirm your faith in the American future—take a look at the Peace Corps." Johnson asserted that the lives of Peace Corps volunteers "have been changed by their service in the Corps. They have become aware—in a unique and profound way—of the bond of suffering and hope that unites men and women on every continent . . . no more valuable experience can be gained by any man."[27] Robert Shaffer, dean of students at Indiana University, hoped that the Peace Corps would provide "a period of personal challenge by shattering the actual and mentally imposed limitations of provincialism, tradition, and custom and would also combat conformity and anonymity."[28] John Kenneth Galbraith revealed a common attitude among progressives at the time: "If you design programs to promote social change in Latin America, word will drift back to Congress; some won't like what you do, but the Peace Corps must be on the side of economic democracy . . . there is no alternative for the Peace Corps to political sophistication."[29]

The Peace Corps was ultimately much smaller than the CCC, owing to the fact that the case for international service was not as politically compelling as joblessness at home during the Depression. The Peace Corps has continued to this day, but it has remained a modest program, servicing less than 5,000 volunteers annually around the world.[30] Some observers even suggest that its permanence as an American institution is due largely to its symbolic power as a memorial to President Kennedy. The real impact of the Peace Corps is still debated.[31] Does it actually improve the lives of people in the developing world, or is it more of a benefit to volunteers in terms of expanding their horizons? Or is it a citizenship development program? A large number of returned Peace Corps volunteers do continue in one form of public service or another, and there are concrete project outcomes related to Peace Corps work overseas. There are convincing anecdotes on each side of this debate, but there is little definitive research on the topic. Just like the contemporary debates about what AmeriCorps is truly seeking to accomplish, there was and remains plenty of room for interpretation about the ultimate purpose and impact of the Peace Corps.

Poverty and the Call to Action

The next major challenge facing the nation was a domestic issue: poverty. Urban poverty in particular was painful and visible. The expenditure of $13.2 billion for public welfare in 1971 was a dramatic reminder of the persistence of poverty in the United States. Even as employment became more available, the unemployment rate for minorities remained high. In 1970, unemployment averaged 7 percent among blacks compared to 3.8 percent among whites.[32] In general, there was great optimism about the future in the 1960s, but there was also a growing awareness of fundamental inequality in the United States. This tension between a sense of what was possible and the limitations of reality led to widespread activism on a number of fronts—most important, including poverty. President Johnson, seizing this popular spirit and believing in the efficacy of an active, hands-on federal government in addressing national problems, set in motion an ambitious multipoint agenda that he called the Great Society. One of the many programs created by President Johnson was VISTA, described as a "domestic Peace Corps," both to help the general public understand it and to leverage the existing political support for the Peace Corps. VISTA volunteers served in placement structures similar to those of the Peace Corps, focusing on capacity-building projects, and working through existing nonprofit and community agencies in disadvantaged areas. A central goal of these efforts was to foster greater self-sufficiency. VISTA intended to cultivate the participation of recipients in their communities by working together to address common needs.

Like the Peace Corps, VISTA was not a jobs program; its focus was on the communities being served, not the volunteers. But one major difference was that people from the communities being served worked as VISTA volunteers themselves. VISTA was premised on the notion that developing "indigenous" leadership within communities was a powerful way to build permanent capacity and to develop the skills and knowledge to get things going. For VISTA, this resulted in a much more diverse corps than in the Peace Corps or the CCC in terms of class, formal educational attainment, age, and race. Bringing together a diverse group of participants who would work together toward a shared purpose had the potential benefit of developing new social capital, creating ties across boundaries that were usually difficult to bridge.

VISTA persists to this day, having become part of AmeriCorps. In terms of scope, VISTA has had approximately half the number of members as the Peace Corps, but the annual enrollment has varied significantly with its political fortunes. Under Presidents Nixon and Reagan, vigorous efforts were made to kill the program, or at least reduce it and direct it away from activism, community organizing, and other activities that challenged power structures, and toward a focus on working within existing structures and supporting social service delivery. C. R. Lane, acting director of VISTA under President Nixon, stated his intentions bluntly: "VISTA is no longer going to be this place where you can do your own thing . . . especially if that means confronting the establishment. We hope, predict, and are striving for a new type of volunteer who will work within the system and lower the noise level."[33]

Under Presidents Johnson and Carter the corps was larger and more activist in its orientation, taking on more controversial projects such as community organizing and empowering citizens to influence local politics,[34] which provoked the ire of conservatives. VISTA programs were involved in community organizing and a whole range of activities that bled into local politics, and many of these efforts were aimed at helping the poor and disenfranchised to find their voice. The extent of national service's political involvement was—and remains—an ongoing point of contention stemming primarily from fundamental differences in what people consider to be the program's priorities. Whose interests matter? What problems are tractable? Who are the key actors and where is the leverage? What is the relationship between service and politics? These are just a few of the questions that were swirling around VISTA and service programs during this period of transition and change.[35]

In addition to VISTA, there were several federal experiments during the 1970s aimed at exposing young people to service and based on the model of the CCC. The Youth Conservation Corps (YCC) was created in 1970 as a summer employment program for teenagers, riding the wave of concern at that time over the state of the environment. The first Earth Day was organized the same year. The YCC eventually grew to 34,000 participants. The Young Adult Conservation Corps (YACC) followed on its heels in 1978, focusing in particular on unemployed sixteen- to twenty-three-year-olds. The unique feature of this federal program lay in that it was implemented in a decentralized way, organized under small state-level offices. The success of these state programs varied widely, with the California Conservation Corps as the most notable model. The YCC came to be seen primarily as an alternative model of poverty alleviation that focused on workforce development. The idea was to build the skills of the poor and improve their employability through a variety of service learning opportunities and apprenticeships. By providing a supportive learning environment and a structured, disciplined experience, corps members learned a wide range of job skills that included technical skills like carpentry. More important, general workplace skills like teamwork, problem solving, and personal responsibility were cultivated.

More Recent Programmatic Formulations

The federal youth corps was eliminated through the new Job Training Partnership Act in 1982 under President Reagan, who believed in a different model of workforce development that worked more closely with the business community and did not require the federal government to run the programs. But the youth corps continued in various shapes and forms at the state level in pockets around the country where they still had political support, eventually banding together into the National Association of Service and Conservation Corps. This association organized replication projects across the United States with the support of private foundations. At the same time, high school and collegiate service and service learning began to grow with the support of national nonprofits like the Campus Outreach Opportunity League (COOL) and the Campus Compact.[36]

Those involved in youth service began to notice the wide range of programs as well as the growth of interest in service. In 1985–1986, Youth Service America (YSA) was founded to begin to unify these efforts into a coherent framework. The YSA was instrumental in persuading President George H. W. Bush to establish the Office of National Service at the White House. President Bush believed in the importance of volunteering—particularly after a decade known for its self-serving materialism—and he sought ways to promote it, eventually creating the Points of Light Foundation in 1990. Individuals who did significant things in their communities on a volunteer basis began to be recognized.[37]

During this period of recasting and rethinking, several national service bills were introduced into Congress. With the championing of Senator Edward Kennedy, who evoked President Kennedy's association with service and who had experience with service corps like City Year in Boston, the National and Community Service Act of 1990 was passed. This bill was informed by all of the learning and experimentation of previous national service programs, but particularly the experience of the 1980s. One of the key lessons learned was that national service need not exist as an operating program at the federal level. The U.S. government could act more as a grant maker to fund programs and bring existing initiatives to scale, something few private foundations could do alone. Innovative pilot projects and promising local programs could be funded and those that demonstrated their ability to produce results could be expanded. This "new paradigm" of national service bridged a key ideological divide between Democrats, who favored federal intervention, and Republicans, who preferred to promote local action, all of which allowed national service to gain new support. There was also bipartisan support for linking financial aid with service, emphasizing the reciprocity of service. President Bush's administration was still skeptical of "paid volunteerism," as civilian national service was framed, but was willing to support a pilot program, partially due to the support of Republican senator Orrin Hatch, a Mormon familiar with the benefits of youth service from the Mormons' Mission Program.[38]

During the 1992 campaign, service figured in both the platforms of President Bush and then governor Clinton, but their visions diverged considerably. President Bush advocated letting local heroes define and solve local problems with the support of the Points of Light Foundation, while also promoting increased episodic volunteering in communities around the country. With bigger plans in mind, Clinton wanted to create a link between financial aid for college and a year or two of national service that would involve many more young people in full-time, stipended service. Soon after President Clinton's inauguration, he signed into law the National and Community Service Trust Act of 1993, creating AmeriCorps and funding the education awards and stipends for its members. This did not happen without a great deal of public debate and wrangling in Congress, however.[39] Newt Gingrich and libertarian-leaning conservatives sought to kill the legislation. Social conservatives found some resonance with the idea in that it focused on civic responsibilities, but they did not like that it was associated with Clinton and they certainly did not want to fund liberal activism. Most liberals argued for a national identity and a more activist orientation, although some expressed concerns that linking it to education would undermine equal opportunity. Some wanted service to be mandatory, making the responsibilities of citizenship explicit. The final bill reflected all of these influences and perspectives.

Unlike previous incarnations like the CCC or the Peace Corps, Ameri-Corps was unique in the history of national service in the United States because there was no clear and compelling national need driving it forward. At the time of AmeriCorps' founding, several rationales for service were offered. One was the general decline in community and civic engagement in the United States. The "new paradigm" of a federally funded but decentralized national service program made it possible to fund services and community capacity building that addressed the huge and diverse range of social challenges in the United States. In the past, diffuse national needs had not been seen as sufficient justification. The loose model and the multiple rationales for service created a big tent under which many interpretations, local adaptations, and experiments were possible. This breadth of purpose was at once a strength and a weakness. Even some original supporters of the bill that created AmeriCorps viewed the generalized vagueness that resulted from compromises as an unfortunate and perhaps even fatal flaw. AmeriCorps would be seen and understood as being at once about everything and nothing.

Despite its politics at the national level, AmeriCorps has steadily grown over the years so that by 2008 it was supporting 75,000 members, and this was under a Republican president during a time when the nation's attention was focused outside the United States on terrorism and the war in Iraq. AmeriCorps has also continued to gain the support and admiration of governors and local citizens across the country, both Democrats and Republicans, as they have experienced the program firsthand. When Ameri-Corps faced a huge funding cut in 2001 to reconcile accounting irregularities within the agency administering the program, it received a large and swift wave of support in the form of the Save AmeriCorps Coalition, which was rapidly generated to defend the program and service the movement.[40]

Given the flexibility of the AmeriCorps legislation, debates over the direction of the program continue to rage. But most of the debates are familiar, reflecting long-standing tensions in American political culture: Should service be voluntary or compulsory? How much federal coordination and oversight is needed? How can we harness the natural associational tendencies of the American people? Should social service work be done by permanent professionals or by temporary citizen volunteers? Should service be compensated in order to provide incentives for disadvantaged populations to participate, or should it come from purely altruistic motivations?

Are there any obligations that come with the rights of citizenship? Is it important to intentionally foster a sense of national unity? Is it wise to place AmeriCorps volunteers in federal, state, or local government agencies, or only in independent nonprofit organizations?[41] Are the tangible results of the service most important, or are the indirect character- and citizenship-building effects that come with the service paramount? Is service primarily for the server or for the served? Is activism an inherent part of service?

National service today is a modern and regimented extension of the tradition of using associations as tools for civic problem solving, an approach that can be traced back to the founding of our country. The problems may be more complex and interdependent nowadays, requiring more sophisticated forms of organization, but the essence of national service remains unchanged: citizens coming together voluntarily to address the problems we face collectively.

Unifying and Institutionalizing National Service

Amid the changing political tides around it, the mission statement of the Corporation for National and Community Service (CNCS) has changed little since 1995, when it first reported to Congress: "The Corporation will engage great numbers of Americans in a wide range of service activities designed to address America's most fundamental societal issues, and create results that can be seen. In so doing, the Corporation seeks to inspire good citizenship, strengthen community, and provide educational opportunity in exchange for substantial work." While the main elements of this mission remained stable, there were subtle changes and modifications to the corporation over time that reflected both enduring ambitions and changing circumstances. Specifically, the 1995 mission statement pledged that the corporation would engage Americans of all ages and backgrounds in community-based service, and that this service would address the nation's education, human, public safety, and environmental needs to achieve direct and demonstrable results. By contrast, the 2005 mission statement says that "the Corporation will provide opportunities for Americans of all ages and backgrounds to engage in service that addresses the nation's educational, public safety, environmental and other human needs to achieve direct and demonstrable results and to encourage all Americans to engage in such service. In doing so, the Corporation will foster civic responsibility, strengthen the ties that bind us together as a people, and provide educational opportunity for those who make a substantial commitment to service."

The revised mission statement no longer promises to engage Americans of all ages and backgrounds in service. Instead, it promises to provide them with opportunities to engage. Similarly, the revised mission to statement contains no promise that community service will address the nation's human needs, as well as needs in education, public safety, and the environment. It more realistically states that some human needs other than education, public safety, and the environment will be addressed. Finally, the 2005 mission statement articulates an original principle not previously specified: to encourage all Americans to engage in service.

Significantly, the slogan of the corporation from its start was "Getting things done." This phrase was designed to render service concrete and to speak to the political environment and the general public. In claiming to be about "getting things done," the corporation sought to reinforce the fact that national service was not just about youth development, self-actualization, and idealism but also that it could lead to concrete results in communities. The precise nature of the "things" that would be done has always been very broad, including planting trees, painting houses, tutoring children, and assisting the elderly. More important politically than the precise nature of the work carried out by volunteers was the fact that "things" would indeed be "done" and that the program would be practical.

The corporation has always had three primary programs to translate mission principles into product: Learn and Serve, AmeriCorps, and the National Senior Service Corps.[42]

LEARN AND SERVE.   The National and Community Service Trust Act of 1993 defines service learning as an educational method having the following main characteristics: "students or participants learn and develop through active participation in thoughtfully organized service that is conducted in and meets the needs of a community. Activities are coordinated within an elementary school, secondary school, institution of higher education, or community service program, and with the community; programs help foster civic responsibility; the work is integrated into and enhances the academic curriculum of the students, or the educational components of the community service program in which the participant is enrolled; and the effort provides structured time for students or participants to reflect on the service experience." The goal of service learning is thus to make service an integral part of the education and life experiences of all young people, building a lifelong ethic of responsibility and service. The corporation's service learning programs are administered by its Department of Service Learning, primarily through schools, community-based organizations, and colleges and universities.[43] Grant awards are made by the department to state education agencies for local competitive distribution and to school-based programs operated by or in conjunction with Indian tribes, U.S. territories, and community-based organizations.

AMERICORPS.   While the corporation has many commitments, AmeriCorps remains the core program of the CNCS. It engages Americans age seventeen and older in community service and provides educational awards in exchange for service. AmeriCorps programs are run through local, state, and national organizations with which AmeriCorps forms partnerships. Examples are Habitat for Humanity, Boys and Girls Clubs, Big Brothers/Big Sisters, YMCAs, and faith-based organizations. "AmeriCorps members recruit, train, and supervise community volunteers, tutor and mentor youth, build affordable housing, teach computer skills, clean parks and streams, run after-school programs, help communities respond to disasters, and build the capacity of nonprofit groups to become self-sustaining, among many other activities. In 2008, AmeriCorps supported a record 75,000 opportunities for Americans to provide intensive service to their communities and country through their programs. In exchange for a year of full-time service, AmeriCorps members earn an education award of $4,725 that can be used to pay for college or graduate school, or to pay back qualified student loans. Since 1994 more than 500,000 Americans have served in AmeriCorps."[44] AmeriCorps articulates five goals that parallel the mission goals of the corporation: (1) *Getting Things Done:* AmeriCorps helps communities meet critical needs in the areas of education, public safety, the environment, and other human needs through direct and demonstrable results; (2) *Strengthening Communities:* AmeriCorps helps unite a diverse group of individuals and institutions in a common effort to improve communities through service. It acts as a catalyst to build community capacity by leveraging resources and linking volunteers to existing service efforts; (3) *Expanding Opportunity:* AmeriCorps members broaden their own individual perspectives and receive scholarships to help pay for college, vocational training, or student loans; (4) *Encouraging*

Responsibility: Through service experiences and civic education, corps members learn to take responsibility for helping to solve community problems; and (5) *Supporting Service Infrastructure:* Through its competitive processes and involvement, AmeriCorps strives to help existing programs and organizations become more efficient and effective. Within AmeriCorps, there are three principal programs: AmeriCorps National Civilian Community Corps (NCCC), AmeriCorps State and National, and AmeriCorps VISTA.[45]

AmeriCorps National Civilian Community Corps (NCCC) is a tenmonth, full-time, residential service program for men and women between the ages of eighteen and twenty-four. Inspired by the Depression-era Civilian Conservation Corps, the program combines the best practices of civilian and military service. AmeriCorps NCCC members live and train in teams at five regional campuses, and serve nonprofit organizations and government entities in communities across the country. Three of the five campuses occupy closed military bases in South Carolina, Colorado, and California, and the other two are located in a medical facility for veterans in Maryland and a municipal building in Washington, D.C. During their ten-month full-time service period, NCCC members spend considerable time off-campus providing services throughout the region, living temporarily in schools or other facilities provided by the community. Some NCCC members also participate in disaster relief efforts such as flood relief or fighting wildfires. In 1999–2000, NCCC members spent approximately half their time away from campus, providing services throughout the states in their regions.[46] Members work in teams, and receive a $4,000 annual living allowance plus room and board. They are eligible to receive an education award upon successful completion of service. Teams generally consist of ten to fifteen members. They work on projects in the four areas identified in the corporation mission statement: education, public safety, the environment, and other human needs. AmeriCorps NCCC emphasizes disaster relief and leadership for large numbers of community volunteers. NCCC develops partnership relationships with existing organizations such as FEMA (Federal Emergency Management Administration), the American Red Cross, and the U.S. Forest Service. At NCCC's fifth anniversary, 5,000 corps members and team leaders graduated from the program.[47]

AmeriCorps State and National is the largest and most visible of the AmeriCorps programs, supporting participants through a network of local community-based organizations, educational institutions, and other agencies. One-third of AmeriCorps State and National grant funds are distributed by a population-based formula to governor-appointed state service commissions, which in turn make grants to local nonprofits and public agencies. Roughly 20 percent of grant funds are awarded to national nonprofits that operate national service projects in two or more states. The remaining grant funds are awarded to state service commissions on a competitive basis to fund local nonprofit and public entities that operate community service programs. AmeriCorps State and National members are recruited by nonprofits, schools, and other agencies to help address local community needs. About three-quarters of the members serve full-time in any given program year, with the remaining members engaging in sustained part-time service. AmeriCorps State and National programs address community needs in the areas of education, public safety, human needs, homeland security, and the environment. The organizations receiving grants, referred to as *sponsoring organizations,* are responsible for recruiting, selecting, and supervising AmeriCorps members. In most programs, AmeriCorps members provide services at their sponsoring organizations, some of which include schools and neighborhood health clinics. Members of AmeriCorps State and National must be at least seventeen years old. Full-time AmeriCorps State and National members must serve at least 1,700 hours over nine to twelve months in local service programs operated by one or more grantees that are nonprofit agencies, local and state government entities, Indian tribes, colleges or universities, local schools, or police districts. To be eligible for participation, grantee organizations must meet community needs in education, public safety, the environment, and other human needs through direct and demonstrable results. Individual members who complete the program are eligible for an education award of $4,725, and a living allowance that ranged from $10,600 to $21,200 in 2005–2006. High school diplomas, or their equivalent, are required before the education award can be utilized.[48]

AmeriCorps VISTA is the third AmeriCorps program. Volunteers in Service to America (VISTA) was originally created in 1964 by the Economic Opportunity Act, was reauthorized under the Domestic Volunteer Service Act of 1973 with the passage of the Domestic Volunteer Service Act (DVSA), and became part of a new federal agency called ACTION, the Federal Domestic Volunteer Agency. It has evolved considerably over its long history, reflecting presidential priorities. In 1994, VISTA was added to the newly formed portfolio of programs operated by the Corporation for National and Community Service. Historically, VISTA has been a highly decentralized program. Its members serve individually or in small groups and focus primarily on building capacity in local communities. In contrast, State and National and NCCC members focus on the provision of direct services. Since the VISTA experience and member profiles differ appreciably from State and National and NCCC, the effects of service participation may be different for its members. VISTA is dedicated to poverty alleviation. Its main activities involve strengthening and expanding the capacity of local organizations to help people out of poverty through programs in education, technology, health and nutrition, housing, economic development, and public safety. VISTA members are assigned to local project sponsors and serve full-time for at least one year, and receive an annual living allowance. They may also be eligible to receive health insurance, child care, liability insurance, and an education award.[49]

NATIONAL SENIOR SERVICE CORPS.   The National Senior Service Corps provides opportunities for Americans older than fifty-five to serve their communities through a network of local projects. State offices of the corporation award grants to state and local nonprofit organizations—called sponsors—that have the responsibility to recruit, place, and support participants in the Senior Corps. Examples of sponsors are United Way, the Red Cross, Catholic Charities, Lutheran Social Services, community colleges, civic organizations, and more. There are four Senior Corps programs: RSVP (Retired Senior Volunteer Program), the Foster Grandparent Program, the Senior Companion Program, and Senior Demonstration Programs.[50] Sponsoring agencies decide what program models to adopt. In 2006, there were an estimated 500,000 Senior Corps members working in fifty states, Washington, D.C., Puerto Rico, and the Virgin Islands. Senior Corps members receive a modest stipend.[51]

In our analysis of the impact of national service, we focus in the balance of this book on AmeriCorps (including both State and National and NCCC) and VISTA. While the other programs are important and do reflect a broader interpretation of the call to service, we have chosen to collect data and delve deeply into the two programs that represent the most recognized face of national service today.

An Idea in Search of Evidence

In the United States, national service programs have gained increasing support in times of compelling national need, such as the Great Depression and the period following September 11. As the country's needs have evolved, so has the nature of the service. Today, national service is a permanent fixture of American life, drawing on values embedded deep in our political culture and democracy generally. With support from the Obama administration, the scope of national service is slated for real expansion over the coming decade. While not universal, service will become ubiquitous as the size of the AmeriCorps program expands to reach increasing numbers of young people. However, given its many possible purposes and the wide-ranging rationale that may lie behind national service, the ongoing political struggle for the heart and soul of national service will likely continue.

Although support for national service has become more bipartisan of late, tensions still persist beneath the public debate. In the eyes of its liberal supporters, programs like AmeriCorps represent the fulfillment of the ideal of an active and informed citizenry. It is a way to bring social justice to poor communities and to mobilize the disenfranchised. By putting people to work in communities and by building the capacity of local nonprofit agencies, national service represents a major labor donation by the government to the people who can benefit most from it. In the process, those who serve will be awakened and energized for a lifetime of activism, political participation, and volunteering.[52]

The communitarian perspective today may be the most familiar in the context of service. According to this view, a citizenry needs a stock of social trust and shared, deeply held civic values to remain strong. Some communitarians, like Amitai Etzioni and Robert Bellah, emphasize not only values but also the shared practices and habits of cocreative citizenship.[53] National service is promoted as a way to build trust, socialize people to civic values, and train people in the practices of associational democracy. For communitarians, national service is just as important for what it symbolizes as for what it accomplishes. Service is a critical part of a community of caring and committed citizens, held together by a sense of the public good.[54]

Conservative critics of national service still see few of these benefits. Instead, they see the potential for political manipulation in the doling out of slots to community groups. They also worry about what subsidized labor does to the efficient working of labor markets. But most of all, conservatives today worry about ever-growing deficits, the expansion of the state into new realms of life, and the bureaucratization of the one aspect of American life that has long been uncoerced and free, namely volunteerism.[55]

In the end, the evolution of national service in America has seen many different interpretations of what these programs should aim to accomplish. Those who admire the CCC model tend to believe that concrete infrastructure projects should be the central focus of service. Those who see immediate human needs going unmet everywhere have become proponents of providing direct human services. And still others would like to see service focused exclusively on tutoring and education. Those who are focused on individual responsibility and developing self-sufficiency want to channel resources in ways that equalize opportunity and support people in helping themselves. Institution builders concentrate on organizational capacity-building efforts. Activists want to empower the poor and change the balance of power through grassroots mobilization and organizing. Systems thinkers want to explore why problems persist and identify and attack root causes, whatever they may be. Free market advocates feel the whole enterprise is misguided because government involvement is bound to do more harm than good to both volunteers and communities due to bureaucratic failure and political corruption. In other words, almost everyone has an opinion and an aspiration when it comes to national service.

National service manages to excite the passions across the political spectrum. It is at once a blank screen upon which all kinds of different political views can be projected and a huge collection of competing intentions, with contrasting visions butting up against one another. To begin to sort out what national service actually does accomplish, we must turn to the data and let it begin to speak to us about which visions of national service are supported by evidence and which are not.

— 3 —

The Shape of National Service Today

National service programs can be seen as having impact at two different conceptual levels. First, at an individual or micro level, national service attempts to contribute to the growth and development of the people who give their time and effort to service. The programs are about shaping lives and building human capital one young person at a time. Second, at the community or macro level, national service is concerned with building new networks of collaboration by bringing communities together to complete significant community projects. Service programs are also about meeting needs and delivering critical services. There is some tension in the prioritization of these levels that has shaped the way programs have been developed and implemented over the years.[1]

Still, it is useful to think of national service as a nested system that operates at both levels simultaneously, with abundant interaction between these levels. In setting out to assess the impact of national service programs, we confronted a significant challenge in the form of asymmetric information. In our project, we were able to collect very detailed quantitative and qualitative data about what happens to the young people who take part in service. While building on previous research, the data in this book are entirely new and never have been collected at this scale, in longitudinal form, and with the quasi-experimental design that anchored this project. We ground much of our analysis in this individual-level data. Because so many other studies had previously sought to document the community-level impact of service, most often through the counting of outputs and units of service delivered, we decided to go a different route by focusing more on the individual level of impact. Before laying out our data and analysis, it is useful to frame carefully the way these two levels of analysis differ and how they relate to the four fundamental visions of service outlined in Chapter 1.[2]

Individual- and Community-Level Impacts of National Service

A substantial body of research exists on the individual-level effects of national and community service. There are many theories and empirical studies that address the impacts of service on maturation and youth development.[3] This human development research treats service as a tool for the cultivation of the psychological and social growth of young people. The effects of service as a pedagogical tool—where it is actually integrated into educational curriculum—and, more generally, as an inspiration for better learning, have been reviewed by education theorists.[4] Some sociologists and psychologists believe that integrating service experience with a structured environment (e.g., classroom instruction) provides a balance of instructional and reflective components to a curriculum, assisting adolescent students in the critical task of establishing a "social-historically coherent identity" from which to grow.[5] The theory is based on Piaget's premise that reality is not given but constructed by individuals reflecting on their actions in order to make sense of past experience and anticipate their own future actions. In addition, attitudinal effects of national service are the subject of several studies on race, class, ethnicity, and gender in national service programs. Some researchers theorize that service learning changes lives forever, while others are more circumspect in measuring attitudinal change and personal development in the long and short term.[6] Much of the research "data" consists of compelling stories, and each individual anecdote is likely representative of countless others, pointing to the conclusion that students exposed to community service in combination with a thoughtful curriculum are profoundly and positively affected by their experiences.

A lingering question is whether, and to what degree, community service fosters positive moral development in young people.[7] Moral development involves the formation of social values—an appreciation for difference, tolerance, respect, compassion, and agency.[8] Agency is a person's perceived capacity to act and make a difference. Generally, it has been found that high school students engaged in community service, and given concurrent opportunities for structured individual and group reflection, manifest increased moral sensitivities at the life stage when moral identities are being formed. Students often claim a moral awakening and profess intentions to make service a part of their lives. However, once again, long-term program success, described in terms of deeply instilled individual values and lifetime social commitment, is still largely unknown.[9] Across many studies, the effects of service on volunteers has thus been explored and analyzed in a number of different ways.[10] This heterogeneity further demonstrates that a consensus has yet to emerge about what national service is trying to accomplish when it shapes the lives of those called to service.

Outcome data on community-level effects of national service are sparse. Theories abound about how national service builds social capital and trust, but few claims are supported by reliable data. With community-level impacts—more so than with individual-level impacts—it is difficult to establish causality between AmeriCorps program activity and improved complex community indicators.[11] Whereas an AmeriCorps member—through pretesting and posttesting—can demonstrate personal growth that is attributable to the AmeriCorps experience, it is difficult for a community to link a specific social outcome directly to AmeriCorps, given the presence of so many confounding factors. Thus, it would be very hard to establish that, for example, reduced rates of poverty in a neighborhood or higher rates of literacy in a city are in fact the result of AmeriCorps work. The scale of intervention is often modest and the problems very complex and multidimensional. Also, because there is so much "noise" around the complex social systems that determine community-level outcomes, establishing causality can appear quixotic. This may be one reason why hard data on the community-level impacts of AmeriCorps is so sparse, and that the major studies on community impacts have almost always focused on simply counting outputs or measuring the opinions of community leaders about AmeriCorps' effectiveness, rather than data showing quantified improvement in conditions.[12]

Theories of community disintegration and individual withdrawal from civic life are now familiar warnings about modern American society. Looking at many different indicators of connectedness and community, Putnam claimed that social capital—the store of trust and networks of collaboration—was diminishing. This finding was troubling because social capital is a critical resource among individuals, organizations, and communities.[13] However, not all observers of American community life have been as pessimistic as Putnam. Robert Wuthnow suggested that the case for declining social capital was not conclusive since new, less formal, and sometimes virtual forms of connectedness were emerging to replace earlier institutions such as fraternal clubs and neighborhood associations. Among the many researchers and critics who later weighed in on this debate over the state of associational life, there has emerged a general agreement on the importance of a strong civil society, either as a vehicle for collective problem solving independent of government (a proposition attractive to conservatives and libertarians) or as the starting point for building grassroots support for a government that is responsive and energetic (a priority for progressives).[14]

Regardless of one's perspective on the state of social capital in America or one's underlying politics, strong communities appear essential to a vibrant civil society. This connection is clear because civil society ultimately depends on small units of grassroots action and collaboration through communities defined by interests, geography, and identity. The role of national service in strengthening communities was affirmed at the Presidents' Summit for America's Future in 1997, and incorporated into the Corporation for National and Community Service's (CNCS's) 1997 strategic plan as a key goal: "Communities will be made stronger through service."[15] Experience has shown, however, that it is possible for untrained workers and disorganized programs to damage communities, and that building community through service is a complex task.[16] Recent studies commissioned by the CNCS have attempted to address the effects of national service on community. One study began with the question "Do AmeriCorps programs build strong communities?" and sought to measure community effects by looking at such things as more involved institutions, engaged local organizations, improved community infrastructure, improved linkages between community organizations, and improved community morale.[17] The study identified a list of fifteen measures of project performance deemed relevant to the achievement of community strength. Researchers asked community leaders to rate AmeriCorps' project accomplishment on measures such as overall project impact, impact on community, strengthening of community ties, working across organizational boundaries, community mobilization, cultivation of community leadership, and other measures of community building. But these are very subjective and difficult to measure phenomena. The study did find that community representatives overwhelmingly agreed that the effects of AmeriCorps programs are positive. The bigger question of whether communities had changed as a result of AmeriCorps work within them was not broached, however.

Faced with the challenge of overcoming impressionistic assessments of community impact, the CNCS and the research community have tended to translate the challenge of measuring community-level impact into something far simpler: whether or not the projects accomplished useful things and "got things done." Of course, this motto of national service simply claims that public work is getting completed and sidesteps the more elusive issue of whether community building and social capital construction have occurred in neighborhoods. To date, there has been no real effort to measure community-level impacts and to relate these effects to those produced at the individual level. This is an area where we also faced some obstacles because both of our large studies were focused heavily on individual-level impacts.

To explore the individual-level effects of service, we focus on measures of member development in the areas of civic engagement, personal growth, and social capital (focusing on trust and tolerance). While Chapters 4, 5, and 6 contain member-level data, this data also tells us something important about community-level change. Social capital may be measured in terms of changing individual attitudes and beliefs. However, there is a broader community-level impact associated with the construction of social capital as greater levels of trust imbue the community with the capacity to solve problems collectively in new ways. For this reason, we represent social capital in our unified model as straddling both the individual and community levels. While public work creates clear benefits for neighborhoods and communities, it does require individuals to commit to their work and see it through to a successful conclusion. Thus, it is important to see the two levels of service as overlapping and reinforcing, rather than hermetically sealed. To clarify the linkage between levels, in Chapter 7 we provide two different examinations of the public work dimension of service: a case exposition of the nature of public work carried out in AmeriCorps programs and accounts of the nature of work carried out by Volunteers in Service to America (VISTA) volunteers over the past four decades, which illustrate in concrete terms how national service penetrates the community.

Toward a Unified Model

While there is certainly room to argue about the precise meaning and scope of these two levels of intended impact, it is useful to think of national service as an integrated system that works at both individual and community levels simultaneously.[18] To clarify how these levels operate and how they differ substantially from one another, we sketch next a theory of change with two levels and four stages leading toward the fulfillment of

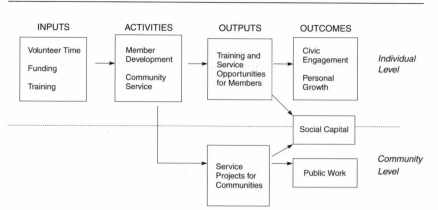

Figure 3.1. General theory of change for national service

the many goals of service.[19] The "General Theory of Change for National Service" (see Figure 3.1) illustrates how it is possible at each level of analysis to sketch out a series of causal linkages that lead from the inputs needed to the activities or processes that take place to the outputs or units of service that are produced in the short run, all the way to the outcomes that the efforts ultimately generate.

In exploring and testing our model, we focus on the AmeriCorps and VISTA programs because they represent large and enduring efforts to make full-time community service a part of the lives of tens of thousands of young people each year. They are also the most visible programmatic manifestations of the drive to transform individuals and communities through service. Our goal is to render a grounded judgment about the relative success of national service programs in achieving the ends embodied in the four visions of service outlined in Chapter 1.

Data Description and Sampling Design

The landscape of national service is broad and populated by several interconnected programs. AmeriCorps is comprised of three discrete programs: AmeriCorps State and National, AmeriCorps VISTA, and AmeriCorps National Civilian Community Corps (NCCC). Of the three, AmeriCorps State and National is by far the largest and is funded at a much higher level than the NCCC, which is a much smaller program.[20] In exchange for a year of full-time or sustained part-time service, AmeriCorps participants, referred to often as *members,* receive an education award that can be used toward higher education or vocational training, or to repay qualified student loans. Members also receive a subsistence stipend while they serve.[21]

Many of the findings we report here come from the *Longitudinal Study of AmeriCorps,* which focuses on AmeriCorps State and National and AmeriCorps NCCC.[22] In the 1999–2000 program year (the year from which the study sample was drawn), more than 38,000 members enrolled in these two AmeriCorps programs. The primary purpose of this study was to compare changes in the behaviors and attitudes of those who participated in AmeriCorps over time to other individuals not enrolled in AmeriCorps. The qualitative data we present for AmeriCorps VISTA are based on the *40th Anniversary Retrospective Study of VISTA,* which focuses on a representative sample of individuals who enrolled in the program since its inception in 1965 through 1993, the year the program was integrated into AmeriCorps. During that period, 55,838 individuals enrolled in the program. The principal purpose of the retrospective study was to assess the long-term effects of participation in VISTA, compared with those outcomes for individuals who enrolled but did not extensively participate in the program. Table 3.1 presents succinctly the key features of the three AmeriCorps programs that are discussed throughout this book.

These two national studies cover all three major components of the AmeriCorps program. In this and the following three chapters, data from these studies are used to assess the effect that participation in national service has on members by addressing two questions: (1) Who participates in national service? and (2) Does participation in national service effect participants' subsequent civic engagement, personal growth, and social capital?

We answer these questions in the central chapters of this book. Before showing our results, however, we need to provide more specific information about each of the three AmeriCorps programs and lay out the methodology underpinning the two studies, the data sources and outcome measures used, and our analytic methodology. To set the stage for the analysis that follows, we begin by reporting on the characteristics of the study members, which addresses the first question of who participates in national service. The middle chapters of this book take up the second research question, which focuses on the effects of service.

The AmeriCorps study relies on a complex quasi-experimental design to prospectively track outcomes associated with participation in full-time

Table 3.1

Characteristics of AmeriCorps State and National, NCCC, and VISTA Programs (2005 program year)

	State and National	NCCC	VISTA
Enrollment	66,830	1,152	6,707
Locations	Nationwide	3 regional campuses	1,638
Age Range of Members	17+	18–24	17+
Operated by	Local, state, national nonprofits, government agencies	CNCS	Local, state, national nonprofits, government agencies
Recruitment	Local and national	National	Local and national
Type	Primarily nonresidential	Residential	Nonresidential
Participation	Full-time and part-time	Full-time	Full-time
Fiscal Year Funding—2006	$403.42 million[a]	$26.73 million	$95.46 million
Corresponding Evaluation	Longitudinal	Longitudinal	Retrospective

[a]Amount includes grants and education awards.

service. The study captures comprehensive quantitative information collected through multiple surveys of participants and their counterparts in the comparison group. In contrast, the VISTA study is a retrospective assessment that collected information from individuals up to forty years after they joined the program. Data sources for that study are surveys and in-depth interviews with former VISTA members along with their counterparts in the comparison group—individuals who enrolled in the program but did not continue their participation. It may be useful to think of the AmeriCorps study as going very wide and the VISTA study as going very deep.

Studying AmeriCorps

The longitudinal study of AmeriCorps includes the State and National and NCCC programs.[23] From the outset, the goal of this extensive and expensive study was to describe AmeriCorps members and then to assess the impact of AmeriCorps on their attitudes and behavior, compared with similar individuals not in service programs. The ideal approach to ensuring that participant and nonparticipant groups differed only in their participation and not some other vital feature (e.g., inclination to serve) would have been to implement a perfect experiment in which study participants were randomly assigned to either participant or nonparticipant groups. However, random assignment of subjects to AmeriCorps and comparison groups was not possible due to the low enrollment rates of many programs during the study period. Given the voluntary character of the program, a quasi-experimental design was implemented to address the core questions. Separate comparison groups, composed of persons who had expressed interest in national service programs but had not enrolled, were selected for State and National and NCCC because differences exist in the nature of the two programs and in the characteristics of their participants. Each individual had two potential conditions arising from the opportunity to join AmeriCorps, either participation or nonparticipation. The objective in selecting the comparison group was that the expected values of their outcomes would be the same as the expected values for the AmeriCorps group outcomes *if the AmeriCorps members had not chosen to participate in AmeriCorps*. Since the AmeriCorps members did choose to participate, our model identifies the changes that occurred as a result of participation as distinguished from those changes that would have occurred even in the absence of service. Therefore, this research builds upon a quasi-experimental design that estimates program impacts by comparing the changes that occur in AmeriCorps members (treatment group) with changes in a comparable group of individuals (comparison group). The design overcomes many of the obstacles that have stood in the way of getting a clear picture of the net effects of national service on participants.

Data for the longitudinal study were collected primarily through four rounds of surveys of study participants, as shown in Appendix A. Baseline information was collected from members and the comparison groups at the beginning of their terms of service (1999–2000).[24] Postprogram information was collected from State and National members one to two months after completing service, from NCCC members during the final weeks of service, and from the comparison groups during a similar time period (2000–2001). A follow-up survey was conducted approximately three years after baseline to collect additional data (2002–2003). A fourth round of data collection on this study was implemented early in 2007.[25]

In addition to the participant surveys, information about programmatic characteristics was obtained through a survey of the project directors of the AmeriCorps State and National programs represented in the study. The survey was completed at the end of summer 2000, corresponding to the close of the AmeriCorps program year. The survey was conducted primarily by mail, with some telephone follow-up. All 109 project directors from programs included in the study completed the survey. A parallel survey of NCCC regional directors was not implemented due to the cross-region consistency of that program and the small sample size of regions (three of five) in the study.

The study sample comprises a nationally representative sample of more than 2,000 AmeriCorps members from more than 100 AmeriCorps State and National programs and three (of five) AmeriCorps NCCC regional campuses, as well as almost 2,000 nonmembers in comparison groups. The State and National member sample comprises members who enrolled in a nationally representative selection of 108 programs out of the approximate 700 AmeriCorps State and National programs operating during the 1999–2000 program year. The NCCC member sample comprises all first-year members enrolled at three (of five) NCCC regional campuses. Both samples include members who enrolled between September 1999 and January 2000.[26]

The comparison groups comprise individuals who demonstrated both awareness of AmeriCorps and interest in service. The State and National comparison group included individuals who inquired about AmeriCorps but did not actually enroll. The comparison group for the State and National programs is comprised of individuals who contacted the corporation's toll-free information line to request information about the program but did not enroll in AmeriCorps during the study period. The group is limited to those individuals who contacted the information line during the same period of time when future members were filling out applications and being accepted into AmeriCorps. The assumption implicit in the selection of this comparison group is that these individuals will be similar to members by virtue of expressing knowledge of, and interest in, the AmeriCorps program. (See Table 3.2.)

Table 3.2

AmeriCorps Participant and Comparison Group Samples

	State and National Members	State and National Comparison Group	NCCC Members	NCCC Comparison Group	Total
Baseline sample	1,752	1,524	476	401	4,153
Postprogram sample	1,385	1,153	461	301	3,300
Postprogram supplemental sample	1,242	1,032	419	282	2,975
Observations after top 5% of propensity score distribution eliminated	830	833	279	241	2,183
Long-term follow-up sample	917	780	337	206	2,240
Observations after top 5% of propensity score distribution eliminated	882	969	289	194	2,334

For the NCCC, the comparison group is comprised of individuals who were selected for the 1999–2000 programs but did not enroll. These individuals completed the entire application process and were determined by the corps to be eligible for the program, but declined to enroll or did not enroll because of limited space in the program. We expect that this group is similar to program participants, by virtue of taking the time to complete the application and interview process, thereby indicating a strong interest in the program and national service.

The next challenge was to settle on a small group of critical areas of individual-level effects to study. Following our conversations with key leaders in the field, the program outcomes identified were separated into three categories that are consistent with the goals of the corporation for AmeriCorps member development and with the first three visions of service outlined in Chapter 1: (1) civic engagement, (2) personal growth, and (3) social capital development. Composite measures were created to characterize a broad outcome related to these three visions of service.[27] These composite measures were taken at baseline and at follow-up to create "gain scores."[28] Most program outcomes were analyzed in terms of *gains*—the changes between baseline and postprogram values of the same measures. These gains (which could be negative as well as positive) were then compared between program members and comparison group members. Across the core chapters of this book, we focus on fifteen outcomes, organized into the three main categories of civic engagement, personal growth, and social capital development.

The gain scores produced several measures of civic engagement. Our discussion is focused on six of them—three attitudinal and three behavioral. The first outcome, *volunteer participation,* assesses whether the respondents served as volunteers at any point. The next three outcomes represent the respondents' *attitudes* toward civic engagement. *Neighborhood obligations* represent respondents' opinions about the importance of being active in their neighborhoods. *Community problem identification* tracks how much respondents feel they know about health, education, and environmental problems in the community. *Grassroots efficacy* is a measure that focuses on how confident respondents feel about carrying out community projects on their own. The last two outcomes, *active in community affairs* and *national voting participation,* are behavioral and ask whether respondents have become active in their community and whether they voted in the 2000 and 2004 national elections.

Five outcomes are used to measure the effect of AmeriCorps participation on the personal growth of members. *Personal growth through community service* represents how respondents assess the impacts of their volunteer activities during the previous year with respect to personal growth, including exposure to new ideas, changing beliefs, and learning about the real world. *Personal effectiveness of community service* represents the respondents' opinion about the impacts they made through their service and reflects the respondents' judgment about their own competence and relative achievements. Educational behavior measured as *educational progress* indicates the level of education attained three years after baseline (during fall 2002 and winter 2003; not a gain score).[29] *Basic work skills* identify the amount of experience respondents have with fundamental work skills, including gathering and analyzing information, motivating coworkers, and managing time. Additionally, *public service employment* indicates whether respondents were employed in the public sector three years after the baseline survey.[30] Public sector employment was defined as holding a job in the fields of education, social work, public safety, arts, religion, or full-time military service.

Social capital outcomes measure the members' connection to community, their level of trust and tolerance, and the quality and frequency of their group interactions. Four social capital outcomes are discussed here. The respondents' *connection to community* represents their opinion about the strength of their connection to the community, as represented by the strength of feelings toward the community, including attachment, awareness, and commitment. To measure the members' tolerance, *appreciation of cultural and ethnic diversity* tracks the respondents' opinions about the importance and desirability of relationships between people who do not share the same cultural and/or ethnic background. Two measures of respondents' behavior in groups are evaluated. *Constructive group interactions* provide an assessment of the frequency with which respondents participated in group situations during which constructive interactions occurred, such as working out conflicts and sharing ideas. Lastly, *constructive personal behavior in groups* provides respondents' reports of the frequency with which they personally use techniques for fostering constructive group interactions, such as encouraging participation by other team members and supporting the rights of others to be heard. A complete list of survey questions used to construct the composite gain scores is included in Appendix B.

Our impact analysis estimated the effects of participation by comparing changes in the outcomes for AmeriCorps members over time with changes in the outcomes for similar individuals who did not enroll in AmeriCorps, using Propensity Score Analysis (PSA) to address possible selection bias.[31] The use of a comparison group enables the description of the *average effects of treatment on the treated*.[32] The effects of participation were estimated separately for State and National and NCCC programs.[33]

To do a thorough job in matching respondents across the treatment and comparison groups, a considerable amount of data was collected about background and motivational factors.[34] Armed with this data, we were able to use PSA to estimate the effects of program participation on member outcomes. In its simplest terms, PSA estimates treatment effects by comparing treatment cases with comparison group cases that have a similar probability of selection into treatment. In other words, the use of PSA allows a comparison of treatment individuals to control individuals with similar probabilities of service in order to focus on the impact of the AmeriCorps service program rather than simply reflecting the underlying differences between the individuals in the treatment and comparison groups.[35] Stated again even more succinctly, a propensity score is the estimated probability of participation conditioned on pretreatment characteristics. While some of the underlying math is complex, the basic approach is simple. We matched up people one to one in the group that did national service and in the group that did not who were equally likely, ex post facto, to participate in national service. We looked to see if there were differences in the key outcomes of interest over time.

PSA begins with an equation to predict the probability of selection into treatment.[36] In our model, we included baseline demographic measures, preprogram background measures, and measures of alternative opportunities that could potentially affect both participation and postprogram outcomes.[37] After careful consideration, we decided to use *stratification* as our method of adjustment.[38] The combined groups of control and treatment individuals were divided into seven (State and National) or six (NCCC) strata based on their propensity scores. Research has indicated that at least five strata are generally sufficient for removing 90 percent or more of the bias due to the covariates.[39] We estimated the propensity score in two steps. First, we calibrated a logistic model using the variables and respondents from the baseline survey.[40] In the second step, we added selected variables from the postprogram supplemental survey (PPSS) to the first model.[41] Propensity scores were calculated separately for State and National and NCCC samples.[42]

We excluded from the impact analysis those individuals who were almost certain to have joined AmeriCorps (people with estimated probabilities of 95 percent or more). We found only a few members of the comparison group who matched the characteristics of these near-certain participants. Because we did not know with any precision what would have happened to these hyperengaged participants had they not joined, our estimates for their treatment effect had very large standard errors—so large that they sometimes doubled the standard error of the total estimate of treatment effect. In other words, we removed outliers from our treatment group when it was impossible to match them accurately with individuals in the comparison group. Substantial numbers of participants in both the NCCC and State and National programs have patterns of characteristics that are associated with very high probabilities of participation. For example, more than a third of the participants in both the State and National programs and the NCCC had estimated participation probabilities between 90 and 100 percent. Very few people with these characteristics inquired about AmeriCorps but then decided not to serve. We observed twenty such cases for the State and National programs, and only five for the NCCC.[43]

While the cornerstone of our work is this matching technique aimed at ferreting out the net impact of service on young people, we do include some other forms of data analysis. In the analyses reported in Chapters 4–6, we provide additional analyses that focus exclusively on the treatment groups (State and National and NCCC programs). We analyze the influence of sociodemographic characteristics, experiences in AmeriCorps, and (for those in State and National programs) program characteristics (as reported by program directors, from the program director survey).[44] This allows us to come to conclusions about who benefits most from national service and under what circumstances those in national service get the most out of the experience.

In sum, we have collected data on what happens to AmeriCorps members compared to similar people who expressed interest in AmeriCorps but did not enroll in the program. The analysis is technical, but the basic approach is simple—we want to find out and explain what difference Ameri-Corps makes in the lives of young people. We do this by tracking them over time and comparing them to others with similar characteristics who did not serve in order to isolate and quantify the net effect of service on the individual.

Studying VISTA

The retrospective study of VISTA was commissioned in part to assess the legacy of the program in its more than forty years in operation. Previously there had been limited rigorous research about the program. The central purpose of the study was to explore the life decisions of VISTA participants in comparison with similar individuals who may have enrolled in VISTA, but who dropped out early in the preservice training component or who only participated in VISTA for a few days.[45]

Part of the challenge of developing a study design had to do with the amount of time that had passed since service. The retrospective study was intended to focus on individuals as much as forty years after their experience in the program. There was no pre-VISTA or baseline information and there were no systematic records available on participant characteristics. The program began before automated record-keeping systems were routinely used. VISTA has historically been administered in a highly decentralized manner and transferred across federal agencies, along with its records. The only records available for selecting the study sample and identifying and contacting potential sample members were through a recent CNCS effort to create an electronic database, pieced together from various aging hard copy files and computer printouts. The database contained only name and mailing addresses for individuals at the time they were VISTA enrollees, along with their Social Security numbers. There was some indication of period of service (start and end dates), but no systematic or reliable information on member demographics.

The most rigorous evaluation design, employing random assignment, was not feasible due to the retrospective nature of the study. Instead, a quasi-experimental design was adopted, intended to compare individuals enrolled in VISTA (the treatment group) with like counterparts who did not enroll in the program (a comparison group). The design of our study was patterned on Doug McAdam's groundbreaking study, *Freedom Summer,* which integrated quantitative survey data with data from in-depth interviews to assess the long-term impact of participation in that civil rights initiative.[46] (VISTA began around the same time as the civil rights movement, and the two initiatives often attracted the same individuals.) However, unlike in the case of the Freedom Summer study, records were not available for individuals who were accepted into VISTA but never enrolled in the program. Therefore, we encountered the challenge of identifying an appropriate comparison group. Ideally, individuals would have known about VISTA and expressed interest in the program, but would not have actually enrolled. Since no records existed for such individuals, our solution was to identify a group of people who had very limited exposure to the program. During many of the periods covered by our study, VISTA required the completion of an intensive up-front training (up to six weeks) prior to actual placement in the program. We determined that for purposes of the project, the best match for VISTA participants would be individuals who dropped out of the program during training or during the periods of the program where preservice training was more limited, in the first week or two of service. Thus, our treatment group was comprised of individuals who were enrolled in VISTA for nine months or longer, and our comparison group was formed of individuals who expressed interest in serving in VISTA but who dropped out, or were asked to leave, very early in their VISTA experience.

A second design challenge was presented by the fact that all the evidence suggested three distinct versions of the VISTA program, shaped by programmatic and social changes over time. Programmatic changes influenced the recruitment strategies (national versus local), the length of preservice training, and placement strategies (stay in current community or deploy to another geographic area). These versions closely mapped on corresponding presidential administrations and the social events that influenced them.

Taking these factors into account, we settled on three versions of VISTA, defined by the following years of operation and programmatic emphasis:

- *Early VISTA:* 1965–1972, with emphasis on community organizing, and national recruitment for placement of VISTA participants in different geographic areas from where they were living at time of enrollment. This version had the most intensive training program leading into service.
- *Second Phase of VISTA:* 1973–1980, which saw some decrease in community organizing and more recruitment of professionals such as teachers, lawyers, and medical practitioners. This version relied on a mix of local and national recruitment and a more limited preservice training period.
- *Third Phase of VISTA:* 1981–1993, characterized by primary reliance on individuals living in the communities where they served, and some use of the program to develop the job skills of welfare recipients. Preservice training was limited to three days, and accompanied by periodic in-service training.

Not surprisingly, since there were three versions of the program spanning our study period, the types of individuals who were attracted to and enrolled in VISTA varied across the three programmatic variations. Because VISTA members differed across the three program versions, it was necessary to select individuals for the comparison group of near members from each of the three different time periods (see Table 3.3).

Our research design called for a two-stage sampling, in which individuals would first be contacted to complete a telephone interview, then a sample of those respondents would be asked to complete a longer, more

Table 3.3
VISTA Study Sample

	Treatment	Comparison	Total
Early Phase	352	252	604
Second Phase	367	169	536
Third Phase	266	133	399
Total	985	554	1,539

in-depth, in-person interview. Our final study challenge involved locating and interviewing sample members. Much of the contact data available for use in tracking sample members was out-of-date and not usable. Although we relied on other electronic locating services, we were only able to achieve an overall response rate of 38 percent, much lower than had been desired. Somewhat surprisingly, we achieved the highest response rate with individuals who had enrolled in the early years of the program. Those respondents had tended to have stable lifestyles with permanent homes and credit accounts. In contrast, individuals who enrolled in VISTA more recently were more transient and difficult to locate. We attempted a limited study of nonresponse, but without available demographic information, we were unable to draw any conclusions about the extent of response bias. Given the low response rate, we do not believe it is appropriate to assess statistical significance. Therefore, we report only descriptive data. The final sample sizes by programmatic version of VISTA are presented in Table 3.3. The demographic differences between the three VISTA cohorts are detailed in Appendix C.

We selected the sample of respondents for the in-depth interviews from the pool of telephone survey respondents, clustered by six geographic areas where a sizable number of telephone respondents resided: Boston, Massachusetts; Madison, Wisconsin; Chicago, Illinois; San Diego, California; Seattle, Washington; and Birmingham, Alabama. Across those locations, we completed sixty-four in-depth, in-person interviews with respondents to the telephone survey. The in-depth interviews lasted two to four hours and provided valuable insight and an explanation of the telephone survey findings.

Profiling AmeriCorps and VISTA Members

What do we know about the people who enter AmeriCorps?[47] As shown in Table 3.4, the sample of AmeriCorps members in the State and National programs was predominantly female, more than half white, and most had some college experience or were college graduates. The average age of participants in the State and National programs was twenty-eight years. The majority of participants and nonparticipants assigned to either the State and National or the NCCC programs had performed some form of volunteer work in the past.[48] These patterns are consistent across programs: The samples of members and nonparticipants assigned to the NCCC and VISTA programs were also predominantly female, at least 80 percent in both the treatment and comparison groups were white, and the majority of all respondents either had some college experience or were college graduates. The average age of participants in the NCCC programs was twenty-one years, noticeably younger than the average age of participants in the State and National programs (twenty-eight years). Additionally, we know that 94 percent of NCCC participants and nonparticipants had volunteered in the past.[49] At first blush, this demographic dispels at least one myth about national service, namely that the program "looks like America." In fact, AmeriCorps is at once more white, more female, and more educated than the general population.

The descriptive statistics and baseline data on participants' civic engagement, personal growth, and social capital outcomes in the State and National and NCCC groups were scrutinized carefully. Individuals in the State and National programs were fairly similar to the NCCC participants. There were two notable divergences: Treatment group members from both the State and National and NCCC programs show a lower rate of voting in national elections and a lower sense of civic responsibility than their counterparts in the comparison groups. These and other small variations aside, the comparisons we make between the young people who complete national service and those who do not are based on groups that look remarkably similar at baseline.

Sixty-one percent of members assigned to State and National programs completed the AmeriCorps program at follow-up. This means that a sizable number of national service participants simply drop out. One other surprising fact was that 3 percent of the programs were housed within faith-based organizations.[50] While we tend to think of national service as

Table 3.4

Demographic Comparison of State and National, NCCC, and VISTA at Baseline

	State and National (1999–2000)					NCCC (1999–2000)					VISTA (1964–2004)			
	Treatment Group		Comparison Group		Mean Diff.	Treatment Group		Comparison Group		Mean Diff.	Treatment Group		Comparison Group	
Characteristic	Mean	S.D.	Mean	S.D.		Mean	S.D.	Mean	S.D.		Mean	S.D.	Mean	S.D.
Demographic Characteristics														
Female	.72	.45	.79	.41	**	.68	.46	.74	.42	*	.64	.48	.66	.47
Age (in years)	28.00	10.20	27.70	9.50		21.50	1.70	21.30	2.00		27.60	9.20	26.70	9.80
White	.52	.50	.61	.49	**	.88	.34	.86	.35		.84	.35	.81	.39
African American	.33	.47	.29	.45	**	.05	.21	.05	.22		.08	.28	.09	.29
Hispanic	.16	.37	.08	.28	***	.04	.18	.08	.28	*	.04	.21	.05	.22
Other Races	.10	.30	.11	.31		.05	.16	.08	.27		.03	.17	.04	.18
High School Diploma or Less	.31	.46	.16	.37	***	.23	.42	.27	.44		.14	.35	.23	.42
Some College (or two-year associate's degree)	.40	.49	.44	.49		.27	.42	.40	.49		.34	.47	.32	.46
College Graduate	.28	.44	.40	.48	***	.48	.09	.32	.46		.50	.50	.44	.49
Have Volunteered in the Past:														
Ever	.81	.42	.89	.28	**	.94	.21	.94	.31		—	—	—	—
Past 5 Years	.77	.49	.81	.33	*	.90	.25	.92	.37		—	—	—	—
Past 12 Months	.57	.61	.58	.42		.69	.39	.70	.58		—	—	—	—

*p < .05 **p < .01 ***p < .001
Note: For AmeriCorps sample, volunteered at age seventeen or younger.

a secular experience, there is a faith component that is at least part of the experience for some members. When it comes to the actual size of the programs, we found that the average AmeriCorps enrollment for the 1999–2000 program year was eighty-nine members. Finally, just under half of the AmeriCorps State and National programs have AmeriCorps members working in teams.

For the most part, we are able to report that there is a relatively good match between the individuals in the VISTA treatment group and their counterparts in the "near VISTA" comparison group. Along a large number of dimensions that include political participation, employment, and education, there is a pretty good match between the two groups. Among the items we noted was the fact that 89 percent of the former VISTA members completed the program. During their service with VISTA, only 2 percent of respondents lived with a host family, while 34 percent lived with other VISTA participants, and 36 percent lived with others not enrolled in VISTA. We also scrutinized the data by VISTA cohort to see if there was much variation across time between those who served and those who did not. In terms of those who enrolled and stayed in VISTA, the overall trend reflects increased participation over time by women, older (but still relatively young) individuals, and persons of color. The percentage of college graduates peaked during the middle programmatic version, reflecting that era's emphasis on recruiting individuals from the professions.

Study participants were asked the relevance of different factors in their decision to apply to VISTA.[51] Among VISTA members (from the treatment group), 70 percent reported they had a desire to participate in service as a means to reduce social or economic inequality, 67 percent reported they wanted to bring about social change, 60 percent reported they wanted to spend time doing something outside the mainstream, and 42 percent stated they thought VISTA would give them skills useful in school or in a job. Furthermore, 13 percent reported they had a friend (or family member, 4 percent) who was applying to or had already participated in VISTA. Study participants were also asked many questions about training, location, and activities related to their experience while in VISTA. Forty-one percent of former VISTA members reported the training was very effective, while 42 percent reported it was only somewhat effective.[52] Fifty-three percent of former VISTA members reported that they were placed far away from their home community, while 17 percent were placed nearby, and 28 percent were placed in their home community.

Former VISTA members were also asked about the frequency in which they had specific experiences while in VISTA. Seventy-one percent of former VISTA members reported that community members helped them adjust to and deal with their service experience on a regular basis, 44 percent felt challenged by their experiences, and 33 percent felt emotionally challenged by their assignment on a regular basis.[53] Surprisingly, 41 percent of respondents stated that they regularly thought they were personally at risk of violence or exposed to other danger. Only 11 percent of former VISTA participants felt appreciated by community members on a local basis, while 58 percent reported never feeling appreciated by community members.

When near VISTA members (the comparison group) were questioned about their primary reason for leaving, many reported multiple reasons. Twenty-five percent reported they left for personal or health reasons, 23 percent said they left due to dissatisfaction with the program, 10 percent reported they were asked to leave, and 7 percent reported they left in order to take a job. Fifty-seven near VISTA members reported that they left because they were dissatisfied with the program. Among this group, 63 percent reported it was not what they expected, 18 percent reported having a disagreement with a supervisor, 9 percent said they felt the service projects were not that interesting, and 5 percent reported the service program was too physically demanding. Former VISTA members were asked about the time it took for them to feel comfortable as a VISTA volunteer. Thirty-four percent reported it took them one to three months to feel comfortable, 26 percent said they felt comfortable immediately, and 25 percent reported it took less than one month. The rest of the former VISTA members reported that it took four months or longer.

Since leaving VISTA, many former participants have remained engaged in their local community. For instance, 41 percent have been active in collecting signatures for a petition, 51 percent have participated in a rally, boycott, march, or demonstration, and 50 percent have been active in religious organizations. Voting in state, local, and federal elections is high among former VISTA members. In addition, many former VISTA members pursued additional education. Since leaving VISTA, 61 percent enrolled in a degree-granting program. When asked if they would apply and join VISTA again, respondents gave favorable reviews. Eighty-seven percent of former VISTA members and 67 percent of near VISTA members responded that they would apply again. Twelve percent of near members and

3 percent of former members reported that they would not join. The remaining respondents were unsure.

The Starting Line

In sum, what do we say about the young people who take part in AmeriCorps State and National, NCCC, and VISTA programs? There are several important facts that emerge about each of these special groups. First, they tend to have a high level of political and civic engagement prior to entering the programs. Second, those who take part in national service are generally well educated, with more than a quarter of those in AmeriCorps and almost half of those in VISTA having a college degree. Third, they are mostly Caucasian, though the programs do have significant minority representation. Finally, a majority have significant volunteer experience prior to service, meaning they enter national service with some sense of what it means to help others. The question that we attempt to answer in the balance of this book is what happens to these people during and after their service. To begin framing our response, we turn to the first three visions of national service and look to see if members left national service with gains in the areas of civic engagement, personal growth, and social capital.

— 4 —

Civic Engagement

National service can be a portal into civic life and a way for participants to learn about and engage community needs. The form of engagement may vary from short-term volunteer participation in community associations to lifelong involvement in political movements and parties. Whatever its form or duration, national service aims to immerse the individual in public life. Before looking at what the data tells about how successful national service is in growing the appetites of members for civic engagement, it may be useful to outline one person's actual experience in national service and how it shaped a lifelong commitment to politics and public service. It is a direct and personal account of transformation, which represents in some ways a best-case scenario of the way the program is intended to work, regardless of how systematic the civic engagement effects of service turn out to be once the broader data are scrutinized.

Michael's Story

For one former volunteer, the experience of helping and organizing the poor was so powerful and rewarding that it led directly to a career in politics and a forty-year commitment to social justice. The volunteer in question, Michael, ended up spending a year working along the Texas-Mexico border, serving very poor families and developing social service programs. There, working against all odds and with little resources, Michael met and was inspired by a local community leader who taught him about organizing. Later, he earned degrees in social work and law and then served as a state official. After working in politics and helping in various campaigns, Michael is now serving his fourth term in the state assembly. He has maintained a progressive political orientation throughout his life. He never married and has no children, but instead has focused his entire life on public service aimed at increasing social justice.

Michael grew up the son of a lawyer in New York and attended quality public schools. He was eventually politicized at Queens College in the 1960s. As the war in Vietnam divided American society, Michael knew he did not want to serve in the military. He applied to law school, but his deferment was not granted because he had part-time student status. Volunteers in Service to America (VISTA) was the only thing keeping him from being sent to war, and his enrollment in the program was a last-ditch effort to avoid the draft. While he entered into service without any real sense of what he wanted to get out of it, Michael described a profound learning experience during his training for VISTA in which he was taught organizing skills in a way that would stay with him for the rest of his life. He was told he would serve in San Francisco, but was later informed that he would be sent to a desolate rural area in Texas. There, his team worked to build programs and services for the local community, including a teen activity club. Michael recalled the dire conditions in the area and the solemn nature of the work, which led others to nervous breakdowns, resignations, and even beatings of fellow VISTA volunteers.

Still, Michael made it clear that he had a wonderful experience. He focused on building a community organization through grant writing and launched the teen program. The VISTA experience was a life-changing moment that taught him organizing skills and ways to get things done against all odds. These skills eventually allowed him to win an election in which few thought he had a chance. Looking back on his entry into politics, Michael noted: "I was approached by a bunch of people who said, you ought to run. At first, I was very reluctant because I was convinced there was no way I could win. I'm a New Yorker; this is [the South]. I'm Jewish. I'm an ex–VISTA volunteer, so others would accuse me of being a communist and mainly not being from here." Drawing on his VISTA training and experience, he jumped into the race: "I ran and I worked hard and I used all the organizing skills I had developed over the years. I had consultants come to me after I decided I would run and they all said, for $15,000 we'll organize and run your campaign, and maybe you'd have a shot at beating the three-term Republican incumbent who I ran against. I didn't have any money and I thought, well, what would the consultants do that I can't do? So I organized and ran my campaign, hired someone to run the office and coordinate the volunteers, and it was like a major grassroots VISTA project to get me elected. It worked."

National service also instilled a belief that public service was the highest calling. In looking back on the career choices he has made over many decades, Michael allowed: "I've always opted not to do what would generate reasonable amounts of money. I've always opted to do what I wanted to do and what would somehow directly or indirectly be an extension of what I wasn't quite able to do as a VISTA volunteer, which was eliminate poverty. So everything I've done has been geared to putting me in a situation where I can help people who need a little help and who are a little bit less fortunate than I've been." National service not only instilled in Michael a desire to serve and an ethic of political engagement, it also formed his personal politics in a lasting way: "I don't think I've had any changes of view. As a legislator, I've had to become more knowledgeable about issues, but my perspective has always been geared towards social justice and providing people opportunities, trying to level the playing field for people. And I often tell people I'm in the legislature now, but I'm working on the same issues I worked on as a VISTA volunteer. It's a different ballpark, a different battlefield, but everything I do in the legislature and have done is to make life better for the vulnerable populations. Needless to say, I'm a liberal Democrat."

While Michael's experience in national service was life-changing and led to a deep commitment to service and politics, we still need to look at trends of the broader impacts of national service on civic engagement to determine how universal this experience might be and what the average corps member actually gets out of service in terms of subsequent political and community participation.

Looking for Evidence of a Civic Engagement Impact

Earlier studies have investigated how participation in national service contributes to future civic engagement. Some research has tested the impact of national service on civic responsibility, political engagement, and effective citizenship,[1] generally addressing the success of national service programs in strengthening democracy by inspiring youth and creating future leaders.[2] In two 1999 reports by Aguirre International,[3] significant effects were found in the areas of civic involvement, with volunteers reporting greater interest in public service and improved leadership skills upon completion of service. Furthermore, alumni surveys have demonstrated clear linkages between the social justice experience in high school and civic engagement and social commitment later in life.[4] Other studies tracked voting behavior and community activism by young people who have either volunteered or completed structured community service programs. While the prior literature is suggestive, none of it has at once a quasi-experimental design, a large sample, and a broad array of testable outcomes.

To redress this shortcoming, we turn to our AmeriCorps longitudinal and VISTA retrospective study data. These data sets include quantitative data from the AmeriCorps member surveys collected shortly after service was completed and then again almost eight years after entry into the program, along with the VISTA participant interviews we conducted in towns and cities across the country.[5] During the program periods covered in these studies, both AmeriCorps and VISTA engaged their members in almost a year of full-time national service. While AmeriCorps members generally were more actively engaged in *direct service*—working in schools, food banks, and national parks—VISTA participants were charged with *building capacity* within local nonprofit and government organizations through such activities as recruitment and management of additional volunteers and program development. In reality, the activities of many VISTA members varied over time. In particular, volunteers enrolled in the early days of VISTA (the 1970s) were often very active in political and social advocacy, while those in later years were more oriented toward service delivery and community capacity building.

We used six main measures to represent participants' civic engagement: volunteering participation, neighborhood obligations, community problem identification, grassroots efficacy, and national voting participation. First, *volunteering participation* indicates whether the respondent served as a volunteer at any point during the two years following fall 2000. Second, *neighborhood obligations* represent the respondent's opinion about the importance of being active in his or her neighborhood, including reporting crimes, keeping the neighborhood clean, and participating in neighborhood organizations. Third, *community problem identification* tracks the respondent's knowledge and grasps the pressing social issues and public needs in the local community. Fourth, *grassroots efficacy* measures how confident the respondent feels about his or her ability to design and implement community projects. Fifth, grassroots activity tracks participation in community affairs.

Finally, *national voting participation* represents whether the respondent voted in the 2000 national election.[6] In each of these five areas, we use our data to examine the effect that participation in national service had on participants' subsequent civic engagement.

Volunteering

In speaking with former VISTA members around the country, we found that VISTA often invigorated people politically and led them to both volunteer locally with charities and run for local office when no pay was associated with the position. The reasons people volunteer are complex,[7] but service can awaken in people a sense of civic responsibility and a commitment to serve on a voluntary basis. For Margot, who served in a very poor community in the 1970s, helping children with emotional needs was a compelling experience because the stakes were high and the results noticeable. She recalled one memory of her service: "There were two young boys that will never go away from my mind. One of them was a little boy whose mom was in prison and his grandmother used to drive him to school every day. She was quite elderly and they had a very struggling relationship and he would come into the classroom every day and if I wasn't right there to greet him, . . . he would walk into the room and put his hand out and just take every single thing that was on the shelf and knock it off, and we went through this little routine of behavior modification of trying to get that to change." Over time, Margot started seeing results and changes in the people she served. While these results were not dramatic, sensing that service actually was related to changes in the human condition made an impression on Margot: "It made you feel like you had some positive impact."

The spirit of service has remained with Margot, years after her time with VISTA. Through work with United Way, she has maintained a sense of connection to community programs: "I've gotten pretty involved through the years with educational-related issues. I've spent lots and lots of time at State Departments of Education all over the country. But I've also gotten very involved with the United Way and have focused particularly on their work." Building on her earlier VISTA experience, Margot gravitated toward programs that helped disadvantaged kids: "They have a set of programs that they refer to as 'Success by Six,' and it's all the community agencies that they fund that focus on early childhood. And I've run United Way campaigns for my company. This last year we brought in $40,000 for them."

For others who perform national service, the experience can plant the seed of wanting to give later in life through unpaid service with local government bodies and volunteer work for political campaigns. A former Boy Scout raised in a strict Catholic family, Rick found VISTA to be an exciting and liberating experience. It energized him politically and he has been involved in campaigns several times during his post-VISTA life. Rick traces some of his appetite for politics to his time as an idealistic VISTA member and then later as a recruiter for the program. During that time, he learned about the world of politics and patronage: "When I moved to Chicago to be a recruiter for VISTA, I said [to my roommate], 'Well, let's go watch them count the votes,' and so we went. This was our experience: We walked in and there's no one there except four burly guys up in front. And they said, 'What do you want?' We said, 'We're here to watch you count the votes.' So they huddled in the back of the room and one of them comes out and says, 'Yous guys got to leave now. We just read the rules and the rules say, when the polls close everybody's gotta get outta here.' That was politics in Chicago." This experience did not discourage Rick, but rather got him more interested in elections and the electoral process.

While Rick remained interested in politics and volunteered to work on campaigns, his interest in actually running for public office was low until he got a call: "There is a guy in town, his wife is our state rep. He's more active locally and she does the state politics. He called me one day and he said because of redistricting, all town meeting members have to run. He said, 'There's a good chance you could get elected.'" After some thought, Rick decided to give it a try and began to campaign. "I went around the neighborhood and I worked pretty hard at it. The night before the election, I called a lot of people. And it was fun, too. I did extremely well. Out of sixteen candidates, I came in fifth highest. And this was my first attempt, so I felt good about that." Rick took his work seriously after he won a seat: "I try to vote as an informed member of town meeting. But I've also learned about a lot of things I wouldn't know about otherwise, like what does the town spend its money on? Well, most of us know in a general sense, and I've learned in a more specific sense. So it's been a good experience and I'm glad I'm doing it. I have indicated that I'd run again."

Perhaps the most important measure of the effect of national service on participants' subsequent civic engagement is the extent to which members continue to contribute their time as community volunteers. While this is clearly an important objective of the AmeriCorps program, it should be noted that until VISTA was formally incorporated into the Corporation for National and Community Service (CNCS) in 1993, the development of members' civic engagement was not a priority for VISTA. Instead, the focus was on building community capacity in poor neighborhoods. Nevertheless, it is reasonable to expect that common VISTA experiences, including community organizing, delivering services to clients from diverse backgrounds, and helping to develop organizational capacity in communities may have in fact promoted members' continued civic engagement, including volunteering. We certainly found this effect among the many VISTA members we encountered during our research.

There are many plausible reasons to suspect that participation in national service could lead to increased volunteering with community organizations: Members may experience positive psychological benefits directly related to seeing their work make a difference in the community, and then seek to recapture this feeling later in life through volunteer work.[8] They may experience increased self-confidence and a heightened sense of efficacy in their ability to influence policies and procedures. Doing good work may thus build self-esteem and confidence, something that people often search for throughout life. Members might also simply develop the habit of helping, which lasts beyond formal service programs.[9] At the same time, there are plenty of reasons for one to expect that the level of volunteering will dissipate after participation in a year of national service. Some individuals may believe that by contributing a year of intensive service, they have fulfilled their duty to their country or community. They may experience "service fatigue," and become psychologically or physically exhausted or tapped out from their service experience. After a year of focusing on community, they may feel it is time to refocus on themselves, perhaps pursuing more education by using their education award. Given the meager financial resources provided during their service year, members may feel a need to get their finances back in order and turn their focus to more lucrative activities. In the end, there are many possible reasons why there might be—or might not be—a link between national service and volunteering.[10]

What does the evidence show? The results are mixed. Two years after the treatment group enrolled in AmeriCorps, both participants and comparison group members reported volunteering at comparably high rates (see Figure 4.1). We found that there was not a statistically significant difference between State and National members and the comparison group members. In contrast, National Civilian Community Corps (NCCC) members

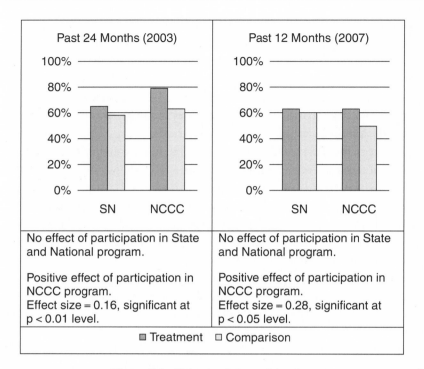

Figure 4.1. Volunteering participation

were 16 percent more likely to participate in volunteer activities, reflecting a statistically significant difference between the groups. Seventy-eight percent of NCCC former members participated in volunteer activities after service, as compared with 63 percent of NCCC comparison group respondents, reflecting a positive impact of NCCC participation on volunteering.[11] The same results were observed eight years after service, with former NCCC members—and not AmeriCorps State and National members—volunteering more than the comparison group.

This is a somewhat surprising finding in that the postprogram transition might be expected to be more challenging for NCCC members, most of whom leave the residential program to return to a community that is different from where they did their national service. This would require NCCC members to identify new resources and locations for contributing their services. Yet it is clear that they succeeded in finding new avenues for volunteering. When it comes to the larger group of AmeriCorps members, the data suggest that, in the short and long term, their year of national service was a period of high commitment, but one that did not prove to have a significant impact on postprogram volunteer behavior. This is disappointing because many who promote service believe the experience should have a long-term impact within communities in the form of greater levels of volunteer engagement.

All is not lost for AmeriCorps members when it comes to volunteering after service. When we altered the test related to volunteer activity to take into account volunteer work before service, the results were more encouraging for AmeriCorps members. While we did not observe a significant difference between the postprogram behavior of members compared to the near members in the comparison group, for the subgroup of AmeriCorps State and National members that did not volunteer in the five-year period prior to AmeriCorps, we did discern a significant increase in post-AmeriCorps volunteering. Members of the treatment group volunteered at a rate 25 percent higher than individuals in the comparison group. (See Figure 4.2.) For these previously disengaged members, the AmeriCorps experience was a catalyst for postprogram volunteering. Additional analyses indicate that, two years after enrolling in AmeriCorps, 31 percent continued to volunteer between six and ten hours a month. Volunteer participation is a function of the participants' reports of whether they performed volunteer work two years after entering the AmeriCorps program.[12] Thus, we can conclude from the data that there may well be an argument for focusing AmeriCorps recruiting on people who do not have a history of volunteering, particularly in attempting to admit to the program those who might get the greatest benefit and in prioritizing volunteerism as a component of civic engagement.

There is a deeper question that lies beneath this more positive finding of national service's capacity to spur volunteerism among those who have no previous experience helping others. What personal characteristics and attributes are connected to a person's commitment to volunteer? While controlling for other factors among AmeriCorps State and National members, three factors stand out as good predictors of volunteering after service. First, religious attendance during one's youth is connected to volunteering years later.[13] This finding is consistent with past research that finds a positive relationship between religious involvement and volunteering.[14] Second, working in teams positively predicts volunteering after AmeriCorps service. Third, among the NCCC group, when controlling for all other factors, female participants are overall more likely than males to volunteer

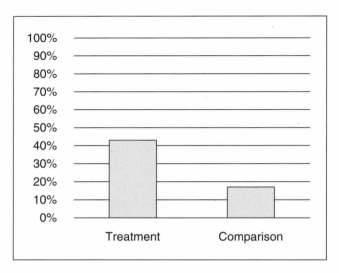

Figure 4.2. Participated in volunteer activities after fall 2000
but did not volunteer in five years before baseline

after their service. These explanatory factors may be useful to bear in mind when we explore possible ways to reshape and reform national service programs by changing their marketing and recruiting strategies.

We were curious about how those who had completed national service had located volunteer opportunities shortly after they completed their service. We asked if the member had been recruited by someone to volunteer, whether a friend or family member had told them about volunteer opportunities, or if perhaps they had heard of volunteer opportunities at work or had gotten a lead from an AmeriCorps service site. One clear pattern emerged. For both AmeriCorps State and National and NCCC members, there was little recourse to information about volunteering from "outsider" sources (friends, family, or work) and more of a dependence on "insider" information about volunteer opportunities from AmeriCorps itself (see Table 4.1). This suggests that the capacity to do volunteer work is enhanced by the information networks within the national service movement, and that members upon graduation do not make significant use of external sources of information.

Based on the data reported above, participation in national service appears to lead to subsequent increases in volunteering, though the results

Table 4.1

Reasons for Volunteering since AmeriCorps

	State and National			NCCC		
	AmeriCorps Participants	Comparison Group	Z^a	AmeriCorps Participants	Comparison Group	Z^a
Learned about volunteering by being asked to volunteer	35%	38%	1.1	30%	35%	.88
Learned about volunteering from a friend or family member	26%	32%	2.3**	25%	34%	2.10*
Learned about volunteering from an organization or group at work	38%	46%	2.9**	34%	50%	3.50**
Learned about volunteering through AmeriCorps service site	20%	2%	−10.6**	10%	2%	−3.10**

^{a}Results are from the Wilcoxon-Mann-Whitney test.

*p < .05   **p < 0.01

are not uniform and consistent.[15] The positive effects we found were focused on individuals who did not have prior volunteer experience before enrolling in national service, and for those enrolled in AmeriCorps NCCC. To broaden our understanding of how service might lead a young person to choose a life in which volunteer service figures prominently, we asked our subjects to reflect on their lives since VISTA and to share their thoughts on the issue of community engagement and volunteering. In our field interviews, we found in many cases that participation in VISTA apparently led to increased volunteering in the years—and in some cases decades—after leaving the program.

One example was Kate, a VISTA volunteer who reported a long-term commitment to civic engagement and community affairs after VISTA.[16] The experience of working with desperately poor people in the South in the 1970s also set Kate's political views in place for a lifetime. A career as a social worker allowed her to carry over a social awareness from her VISTA experience that would last her adult life: "I saw a lot of poverty and people living on the edge. Those people's lives, it's kind of hard to forget that, living your little middle-class life. But I have to say how it's changed me. I'm much more politically involved and probably aware and vocal than I ever was in VISTA." Kate was careful not to attribute too much to service and preferred to think of it as a critical trigger: "VISTA started the process. I think it was already there for me, but it sort of confirmed for me that there's just a lot of social injustice in our country. You have to work in small ways to try to correct that [and do] whatever you can do." The influence of service does not begin and end with the member. We heard many VISTA members describe how their commitment to volunteering in their local community had been passed on to the next generation. Several VISTA members reported that their children regularly accompanied them on volunteer activities.[17]

In our survey, 96 percent of all VISTA and near VISTA members reported volunteering since service in the program. Recall that the follow-up period is from ten to forty years after VISTA enrollment. Among former VISTA members, of those who have not volunteered since VISTA, less than 1 percent reported it was due to "burn out," less than 1 percent reported they haven't volunteered due to family responsibilities or child care, less than 1 percent said they haven't volunteered due to health or medical problems, and only 1 percent reported they had not volunteered due to lack of time. VISTA members continue to outpace their near VISTA counterparts on other measures of civic engagement.[18] Among former VISTA members, 26 percent reported that their VISTA experience strongly influenced the amount or kind of volunteering they have performed since leaving VISTA.

Neighborhood Obligations

The extent to which individuals feel an obligation to improve their community is an obvious indicator of their level of civic commitment and engagement. After all, how can someone want to be involved in the community if he or she does not feel a sense of obligation and connection to that same community? Data from the AmeriCorps survey measured changes in this outcome, which is defined as the respondent's opinion about the importance of being active in his or her neighborhood, including reporting crimes, keeping the neighborhood clean, and participating in neighborhood organizations.

The data are encouraging when it comes to the question of whether service cultivates in members a real sense of obligation and commitment to community. Figure 4.3 illustrates changes in the perception of neighborhood obligations for the AmeriCorps sample. On average, the State and National members showed an increase in neighborhood obligations, while the State and National comparison group showed no change. The net effect of participation in a State and National program on this aspect of civic engagement is small but positive and statistically significant (effect size = 0.27). The NCCC has no significant short-term effect on members' attitudes toward neighborhood obligations, though over the long term there is a positive effect.

Reporting is based on surveys given one and eight years after the completion of the AmeriCorps program. Lack of statistically significant findings for the NCCC program may be attributable to the structure of the program (members moved from one community to another over their service year and may not have had time to establish strong connections to a single neighborhood) and the fact that members would have had limited time to connect to their new (or rejoined) community after the end of their NCCC experience.

Regression results also confirm a positive, statistically significant increase in neighborhood obligations for AmeriCorps State and National program members and no significant change for the NCCC. Among former AmeriCorps members in the State and National group, when we controlled for

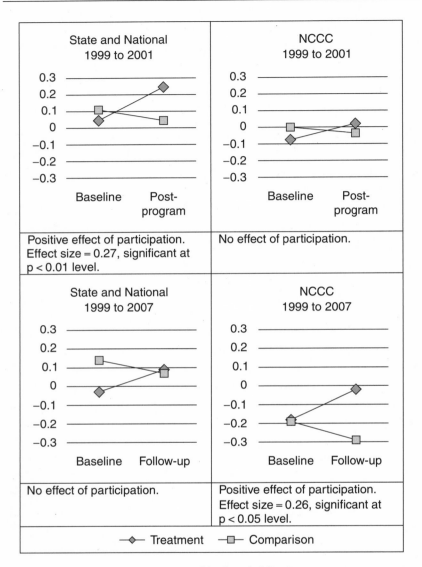

Figure 4.3. Neighborhood obligations

other factors, having volunteered twelve months prior to joining Ameri-
Corps was negatively related to gains in neighborhood obligations, and
this finding is statistically significant at the p < .01 level. One explanation
may be that those who volunteered prior to joining AmeriCorps already
had a strong sense of neighborhood obligations. Therefore, the AmeriCorps

experience did not matter in this area as much as it did for those without prior experience. When adding controls for members' AmeriCorps program experiences, growing up "at risk" was significantly and positively related to gains in neighborhood obligations. However, these findings only explain a small portion of the variance in neighborhood obligations (3 percent and 4 percent, respectively). Furthermore, among former Ameri-Corps members in the NCCC group, there was no relationship between participant and program characteristics and respondent perception of neighborhood obligations.

Community Problem Identification

Civic engagement has the potential for many different dimensions. Another way to assess whether national service participants have been oriented and motivated to be more engaged with civic life is to ask at the end of their service experience how confident they feel in being able to diagnose public problems. The assumption here is that it is hard for participants to become more engaged if they do not feel more confident in their ability to figure out what needs to be done. To measure the extent to which members were able to look out into communities and identify problems worthy of collective action, they were asked to assess their own ability to do this diagnostic work. To gather data, members of the treatment and comparison groups were asked: "How much do you feel you know about problems facing the community?" The question was posed for each of the areas of the environment, public health issues, literacy, crime, and lack of civic engagement; and a composite measure of community problem identification was created.

In both the short and the long run, the results indicate that AmeriCorps State and National members were more confident that they could identify community problems than members of the comparison group who did not have the benefit of a service experience. In the short run, AmeriCorps members were 30 percent more confident, and after eight years they were 26 percent more confident. For NCCC participants, the results were robust in the short run but were not significant over the long run from 1999 to 2007. While there are many possible reasons why confidence can erode over time—lack of practice, distance from the problem, and change in career orientation, among others—in this case, the effect seems to have been reduced by the fact that over eight years, those in the comparison group simply appeared to gain experience and confidence in this area at close to the same rate as those in the NCCC. (See Figure 4.4.)

When we spoke to VISTA volunteers about being able to understand and define community problems, several remarked that their experience taught them to be clinical and precise when looking at public problems.

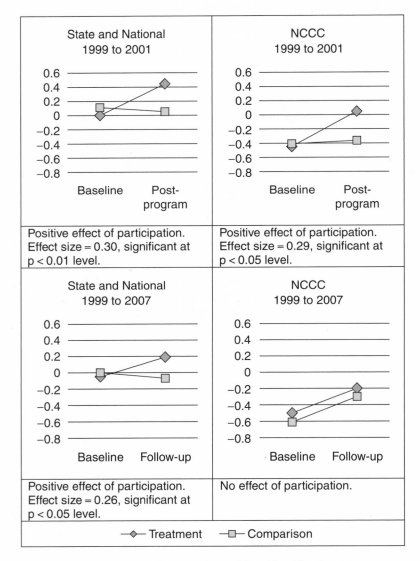

Figure 4.4. Community problem identification

One example was Marissa, who was born in Puerto Rico. She came to live in Boston when she was thirteen and served in VISTA when she was in her fifties, about ten years ago. She was interested in housing issues and found an opportunity to work on them through a VISTA position. The assigned task was to help a group of tenants get organized: "It involved visiting them frequently, generally understanding their problems, getting them interested in participating, and engaging them in this work. It was hard because the conditions [in the housing development] were terrible, sometimes there was no heat." Marissa worked with the tenants on "drafting bylaws, helping them develop committees, motivating them constantly to participate, and rewarding them by saying thanks to them or just being there for them." Her work changed over time: "It evolved from very simple and just visiting and inviting them to meetings, to really becoming very, very involved in every step . . . sitting down with them, writing articles, and writing bylaws, interpreting them." By the end of the project, Marissa felt a pretty deep mastery of the issues in public housing and commented that she could step into a community now and have a good sense of whether its public housing was on the right track or in trouble.

Serving in the late 1960s, Herman was assigned to Chinatown in New York City for a year and a half. He tried to improve a low-income community, in part by setting up a health clinic there. He remembered his VISTA service as being eye-opening and described a difficult task that involved understanding what kind of health care Chinese immigrants needed. Herman noted that the goal of his project was not very well defined, partly because no one knew what was needed for the health clinic, and a large part of the job was analyzing and figuring out what exactly needed to be done. The ambiguity of many early VISTA assignments may have inadvertently helped participants learn to step back, collect information, and then move to proposing a solution—a process that cannot help but teach community problem identification.

Herman explained the way he learned to size up a community's needs: "I got assigned to Chinatown and it was my job to go into Chinatown to meet people and introduce myself. I was trying to find out what the health-care situation was. Trying to find out what things were not being dealt with and what things were being dealt with, and figure out how to ease access to what health care was available." By talking with people and listening to their framing of the problem, Herman learned "how to get the health-care institutions to understand more of what Chinese people needed in terms of language and cultural understanding, and to make health-care services accessible to them." One reason Herman learned the skill of problem identification was that VISTA largely left it to the volunteers to shape the projects they worked on: "There was no understanding of what to do in Chinatown. Nobody knew—never been done before. So nobody knew how to organize Chinese people and to get them better health care." The response to this uncertainty was "to basically make up your own rules." This meant operating without a script or a clear endpoint in sight: "Community organizing is a very inquisitional process of discovering who was there and what was going on. Trying to figure out what they felt the important things to do were, where the holes were, and whether you could do anything to fill those holes."

While the structure of national service projects has been tightened up over the years from those early VISTA days, there is still a fair amount of ambiguity in service assignments. With no clear mandate, the need for a careful framing of the community's challenges remains a valuable part of the service experience. By learning to listen and diagnose complex community needs and desires, national service volunteers do indeed build their civic skills.

Grassroots Activity and Efficacy

While we looked at the issue of volunteerism among postservice members, there is a different way to frame the issue of civic activism that may well shed light on the issue of civic engagement. To get a somewhat different take on how service shapes civic engagement in the years after AmeriCorps and NCCC, we asked both members and nonmembers about their level of activity in community affairs and their perception of their own efficacy in contributing to local problem solving.[19] First, we took a behavioral measure of how much respondents were involved in community affairs. This included questions about how often they participated in events such as community meetings, celebrations, or local community-wide activities. Second, we took an attitudinal measure of how confident respondents in both the treatment and comparison groups felt about being able to accomplish tasks such as organizing a benefit for a charitable or religious group, starting an after-school program for children, or organizing an annual cleanup project for the local park. With both measures, our aim was to identify any effects in the area of grassroots activity and perceived personal efficacy in this domain. For both measures, we also considered the survey data from VISTA volunteers about their level of involvement in community affairs and its perceived efficacy.

In the short run, AmeriCorps State and National and NCCC both moved members to become more active in community affairs. In both cases, the comparison groups became less active over time while the treatment groups became more active. The effects over the long run were—as they were for community problem identification—significant for State and National, but not for the NCCC. Why the behavioral effect of the NCCC in the area of civic activism would decay over time is hard to know for certain. One speculative answer is that the program's residential nature, which can create an intense environment, may lead members to connect civic activism to group action. Once the strong group dissolves and members disperse around the country for their postservice careers, the commitment to participate in community activities may dissipate. (See Figure 4.5.)

Our survey of past VISTA volunteers provides some insight into the level of commitment and the type of community affairs former participants were likely to choose in the years following enrollment in the program. When respondents were asked about their involvement in key community organizations, former and near VISTA members participated in each type of community organization at roughly the same level, plus or minus 3 percentage points. The effects were thus not particularly robust. In the case of civil rights and other noneducational organizations, VISTA volunteers engage at a slightly higher rate. For religious and educational organizations, such as the Parent-Teacher Association (PTA), near VISTA members get involved at slightly higher rates. Participation in neighborhood groups is at the same level for both groups. (See Table 4.2.)

To get a better sense of whether service increases one's confidence in doing grassroots organizing, we asked about whether members and nonmembers felt that they had the ability to organize a local fund-raiser or community cleanup project. After serving in a team and getting support on a range of community projects, we wanted to know if there was an increased sense of personal efficacy in grassroots activism. In the short term, we found that there was indeed a significant increase in grassroots efficacy among AmeriCorps State and National members, but that NCCC members did not reap this same benefit. In the long run, we found that both groups had significantly increased confidence in their ability to design and deliver neighborhood programs (see Figure 4.6).

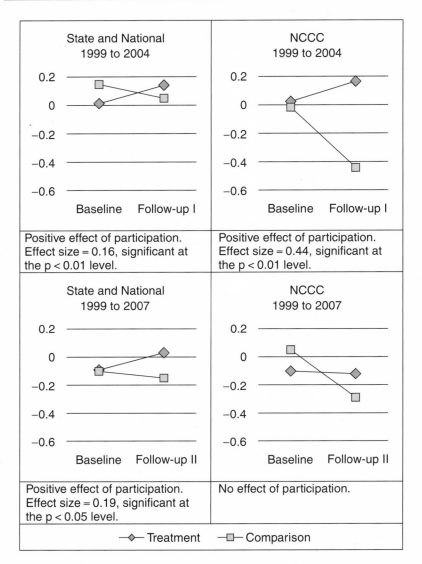

Figure 4.5. Active in community affairs

The sense that grassroots activism and community participation matter was reinforced by VISTA members, who in some cases had decades to reflect on what this kind of work actually meant. In the survey of former VISTA volunteers, 39 percent were members of groups and reported taking local action for social or political reform in the past 12 months.[20] Even

Table 4.2
Community Engagement since VISTA*

	Been Active in Civil Rights Organizations	Been Active in Religious Organizations	Been Active in Neighborhood Associations	Been Active in Educational Associations or PTA	Been Active in Noneducational Organizations	Total Sample Size
VISTA Group	24%	49%	37%	52%	40%	985
Near VISTA Group	21%	51%	37%	55%	37%	554

*Percentage involved in at least one organization.

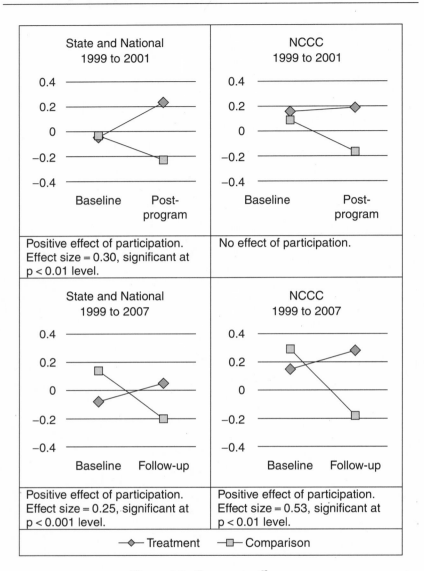

Figure 4.6. Grassroots efficacy

with a lot of perspective on their service, 44 percent of former VISTA
members reported that people like them had a big impact in making their
community a better place to live, indicating that both optimism and belief
in civic engagement still hold sway among those who did their service in
poor communities. These findings, along with those related to both the

behavior and beliefs of AmeriCorps members, indicate that there is not only a commitment to grassroots action among those who serve, but also a sense that it makes a difference.

Political Participation

Having considered four different ways to construe attitudinal and behavioral changes in civic engagement, we conclude with perhaps the most tangible and concrete measure, namely political participation, and examine the relationship between serving in AmeriCorps or VISTA and subsequent voting. Although there is no requirement that members vote in elections while they serve, there are reasons to expect that the community service might be associated with members' assuming increased responsibilities as citizens. Chief among these reasons is that, during the program year when Ameri-Corps members in the study were enrolled, many of these young people received in-service training on democratic principles. For some members, this training served as an introduction to the political process and the critical role that voting plays in our political system. In addition, the process of being around other people who are committed to community and political participation may also have had an effect on members who had not taken voting seriously prior to joining AmeriCorps. Since many AmeriCorps members come into the program energized and ready to serve, it is natural to assume that some of this enthusiasm for participation will rub off on members who may be less oriented toward political participation.

Conversely, there may be competing reasons why participation in national service may not affect political participation outcomes. While doing national and community service, AmeriCorps members are explicitly precluded from participating in political activities, including campaigning for candidates or lobbying. There is thus a programmatic separation between service and politics, designed to shield AmeriCorps from charges that its allocation of positions and use of volunteers has partisan political dimensions. Beyond this wall that separates service and politics, the experience of members may be so powerful in terms of bringing about significant change at the local level and getting one's hands dirty in the process, that members may come to view voting in national elections in contrast as detached, linked to the status quo, and perhaps even irrelevant.

For the AmeriCorps study, voting participation was assessed during the 2000 and 2004 presidential elections, and the results are shown in

Figure 4.7. For the 2000 election, participation in AmeriCorps State and National did not affect voting rates. For the treatment and comparison groups, the rates were 77 percent and 76 percent, respectively. Both rates are considerably higher than the 59 percent national average for that particular election. NCCC members were more than 10 percent more likely to vote in the 2000 election than comparison group members. However, this difference was not statistically significant. The results for the 2004 election were worse. Not only were there no significant gains in terms of voting behavior, but national service participants in both AmeriCorps State and National and NCCC voted less than their comparison group counterparts. We also tested whether participation in State and National programs had an effect on voting for respondents who had not voted in the 1998 national election. Specifically, we tested whether 1998 nonvoters participated in the 2000 national election any differently than members who had voted in 1998. For both State and National and NCCC, we found that there was no significant difference in the voting behavior of previous nonvoters in the two elections.

To understand more about the lack of a link between service and voting, we probed the data deeper. For the AmeriCorps State and National program,

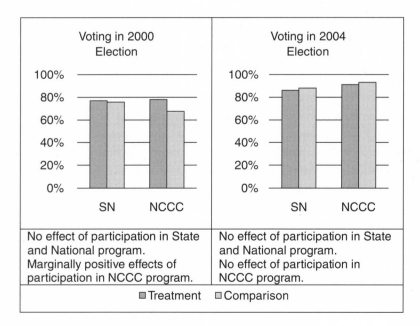

Figure 4.7. National voting participation

when controlling for other factors, females, older respondents, and college graduates were more likely to have voted in the 2000 presidential election than their counterparts.[21] Among AmeriCorps members in the NCCC group, age is negatively related to voting. In addition, those with some college experience and college graduates were more likely than those with a high school diploma (or less) to vote in the 2000 presidential election.

The more interesting results relate to race and voting. Among AmeriCorps members in the State and National group, African Americans and Hispanics are more likely to have voted in the 2000 election than their white counterparts. When adding members' AmeriCorps experiences to the model, working with members from diverse backgrounds is positively related to voting. This is an interesting finding because it may help address a long-standing issue in voter participation. According to previous studies of race variations in political participation, African Americans are less likely than Anglo-Whites to report voting. African Americans are more likely to say they have worked in a campaign, but less likely to say they have given money. In each case, Latinos are less active than other groups. However, in assessing these findings, socioeconomic status is often cited as the primary factor accounting for variations in rates of political participation across racial and ethnic groups.[22] Still, the fact that national service can close the participation gap between Anglo-Whites and African Americans and Hispanics is intriguing given the broader and deeper issue of ensuring equal political participation in America.[23]

Given the long-standing problem of voter apathy and low turnouts for elections, it is particularly interesting whether national service affects political participation and how it does so. One past study examined the influence of national service on the political orientation of participants. Researchers tested the hypothesis that AmeriCorps is biased toward liberal participants, and that such participants become more politically liberal by the time they complete the program. Based upon research involving the participants in fifty-six major AmeriCorps projects in four Pacific Northwestern states, participants do not change their political ideology as a result of their service experience, and that both self-identified liberals and self-identified conservatives emerged from their AmeriCorps service experiences significantly more likely to become engaged in whatever their agenda might be in their own communities.[24]

While the AmeriCorps data set only covered voting behavior for two elections, the VISTA data spanned a much longer time frame—at least ten and potentially up to forty years postprogram. VISTA data also allow us to examine the type of political activity engaged in by members after program participation, compared with their near VISTA counterparts. As seen in Table 4.3, 91 percent of the VISTA group voted in the first post-VISTA presidential election, while 83 percent of the VISTA group voted in the first state or local election post-VISTA. These percentages are 6 and 9 points higher than the near VISTA group, respectively.

VISTA members reported participating at higher levels than the near VISTA members in all activities they were asked about: volunteering for local government boards or councils; collecting signatures for a petition; participating in a rally, march, boycott, or demonstration; being politically active or working on a campaign; and voting in the next national and state or local election immediately after VISTA.

Moreover, findings suggest that participation in VISTA had especially important effects on political participation for persons of color. In the ancillary analysis we conducted, results from a chi-square test of independence showed that a statistically significant relationship exists between serving in VISTA and having volunteered for any local government board or council ($\chi^2 = 2.7$, p < .10); having collected signatures for a petition ($\chi^2 = 2.7$, p < .10); and having participated in a rally, march, boycott, or demonstration ($\chi^2 = 9.4$, p < .001). Among Hispanics, 82 percent of the VISTA group voted in the first presidential election post-VISTA, while only 53 percent of the near VISTA group voted in the first presidential election post-VISTA. Similarly, among African Americans, 88 percent in the VISTA group voted in the first presidential election post-VISTA, while the same was true for only 76 percent in the near VISTA group. These findings parallel those for the broader sample, which also supports the influence of national service on voting participation among minorities.

Conclusion

For some of the young people who complete national service programs, the experience can imbue them with civic enthusiasm and commitment. For Dianna, service during the Clinton years was part of a political awakening and commitment to helping others. Looking back now, the public mood seems different to this young woman. VISTA was about helping, and her perception today is that government is not as oriented as it might be to broad ideals: "Right now, I will say that I have a concern. I do think that,

Table 4.3
Political Engagement since VISTA*

	Volunteered for Any Local Government Board or Council	Collected Signatures for a Petition	Participated in a Rally, March, Boycott, or Demonstration	Been Active in Politics, Working on Campaigns	Voted in the First Presidential Election Post-VISTA	Voted in the First State/ Local Election Post-VISTA	Total Sample Size
VISTA Group	31%	42%	54%	41%	91%	83%	985
Near VISTA Group	28%	38%	46%	38%	85%	74%	554

*Percentage involved in at least one engagement.

I would say that I feel like political discourse and how people invest themselves in the society is in a negative place right now. It bothers me how consumerist we are and how that continues to manifest itself and [how] the social discourse really is kind of selfish. People are out for what is theirs." Dianna was struck by how different things felt when she was in the midst of her service: "When I started my VISTA service, I really was energized by the fact that it was the Clinton administration because there was something larger, more sustaining. I was really invested in wanting to make an impact on society and just give back to society. I needed to volunteer."

VISTA created in Dianna an enduring sense of connection to the public realm and a commitment to service. While the demands of family and work life take their toll, Dianna reported an orientation to community that started in VISTA and carried forward from there years later. "My husband is a pastor at a church and . . . I feel a part of my community in the neighborhood in which I live. I talk with my neighbors. I do some volunteering through the church." Still, her ability to translate the civic skills she built in VISTA into consistent civic engagement throughout her life has been imperfect: "I'm intending on becoming even more actively involved in community activities but [it is hard] right now, with two small children and working full time. That's kind of a crutch to fall back on, but it just does kind of seem like at the end of the day I'm falling into bed shortly after they go to bed." Nevertheless, she reported being involved in neighborhood groups and local politics, even though she regularly feels exhausted.

Dianna's thirst for civic connection stemmed from the language and zeitgeist in which she found herself during her service year: "For me, one of the things that I remember about [Clinton's] inaugural, Maya Angelou read a poem and I just thought that was a beautiful metaphor for society. And so that always kind of stuck with me. Now, it seems to me that we're really in a place where people are not really concerned about their brothers or sisters anymore." Energized and committed back then, Dianna threw herself into her organizing work and felt part of something bigger. While her family commitments weigh on her and while times have changed, there was little doubt that national service kindled a sense that she should do something in civic space and, even when her commitments at home seem overwhelming, she still thinks about this obligation and worries about the broader political context in which she lives.

In the end, those who serve in national service programs are getting significant civic engagement gains—though not consistently across all the measures we took or across all three of the service programs. AmeriCorps State and National, NCCC, and VISTA are nevertheless creating a sense of obligation to community, helping people learn to identify public problems and to become more active and competent community actors. While the impact of service on volunteering and voting in national elections was not significant, this should not overshadow the civic engagement benefits that were observed—both in the short term and long term—across many crucial behavioral and attitudinal measures. National service programs attract people who are seeking a door into community and civic life. And the evidence in total suggests that the first of the four major visions of national service—national service as a catalyst for greater civic engagement—is generally supported by the large volume of both quantitative and qualitative evidence we have collected and analyzed in our research.

— 5 —

Personal Growth

National service programs have a very ambitious goal when it comes to shaping the lives of young people. In constructing programs like AmeriCorps State and National, National Civilian Community Corps (NCCC), and Volunteers in Service to America (VISTA), there was, from the start, a desire to create a crucible in which learning and personal growth might be forged. While schools provide a set of valuable learning experiences for children, there has long been a need for a vehicle to ease the transition of young people from school into the workforce. This transition can be difficult, and many young adults struggle to define their identities and interests once the structure of school is removed. From multiple perspectives, we studied the question of whether national service actually succeeds in shaping the lives of young people and helping them build the skills and confidence to pursue healthy and productive lives. We begin with an account of what service meant to one woman's journey in life and then probe our data to see how broad and significant the effects of service turn out to be on the personal growth of members.

Ellen's Story

Although VISTA is not a job training program, it does aspire to build work skills, prepare people for employment, and shape their identity by showing them a direction they may follow for a lifetime. One national service member, Ellen, joined VISTA after law school to learn how to be a lawyer. She wanted to get into public interest law, so she secured a placement in a legal aid clinic. What was supposed to be a one-year volunteer experience turned into a full-time job, then into an entire legal career. Ellen became director of the clinic and stayed for thirty years until the clinic was consolidated with a larger one nearby. VISTA, therefore, was not just a transition from school to work, but the start of a life of activism and commitment to social justice causes. Today, Ellen continues to fight for social justice as the director of a health clinic for the poor and uninsured.

Ellen grew up in a middle-class family in which her father worked and her mother stayed home. She went to synagogue regularly and attended public schools. As a child, Ellen had conflicts with her mother over her decision not to work outside the home and not to become involved in community affairs. She remembered being angered by the fact that, in her social circle, all the families were white and all the household help was black. Though she had been sheltered, she became immersed in a social justice movement while at the University of Michigan in the late 1960s, where she became active in antiwar causes and community organizing. "I chose to go to law school. Out of 500 students in my class, maybe 50 were women, if that. I mean I went through law school thinking that what I would do when I graduated was be a movement lawyer until I realized that that meant criminal defense work, and criminal defense work wasn't what I was interested in. I was exposed to legal aid in law school and the [law school] clinic kind of brought together all of the things that made sense to me. I decided what I wanted to do was go into legal aid. So it wasn't that I wanted to go into VISTA per se. The way to get into legal aid was through VISTA." National service was thus Ellen's point of entry into the world of public interest law, a way to start a legal career aimed at helping those most in need. She started off as a volunteer, then became VISTA program director at the clinic, and years later became executive director. In short, VISTA turned out to be the starting point for her development as a lawyer, a place where she learned legal skills at a time when women often struggled to find a way into the legal profession.

Working in a national service program can become a breakthrough employment moment for young people. As Ellen recalled: "Everyone was thinking about how do you get a job? What do we do? Most of the people I knew were not interested in corporate practices of law, so they weren't looking at the big law firms or corporations. I had never actually held a job. I mean I had held summer jobs. So I still wasn't confident that anybody would pay me for anything. VISTA was a group that wanted me. There was a sense of acceptance, that this was a community of people who shared similar interests and views. As a VISTA lawyer, I was to start learning how to be a lawyer. One of the projects that I worked on had to do with access to small claims courts and trying to gather information on how to better use the small claims court to resolve issues."

National service also can be an attractive career starting place because it gives young people real responsibility. Often, the responsibilities come quickly and much earlier than in business or even government. Ellen continued: "By and large, it was learning to be a lawyer . . . Soon, I was the VISTA supervisor at legal aid for the region. Two years out of law school and I was a manager. Talk about the blind leading the blind. I was the VISTA supervisor, and what did I know?" The work done by VISTA and other national service volunteers varied greatly, from community organizing around critical needs to advocacy and service delivery for the poorest and most desperate populations to legal work aimed at increasing equity and social justice. For Ellen, the work started with being assigned clients: "We were all young new lawyers who had been given a couple of clients to try to work on, to do research, maybe a couple of community projects to work on . . . I think we all had the sense that we were trying to figure out how to use law to help end poverty and that was kind of the overarching belief system, that somehow we could use the legal system to, in a grandiose way, end poverty. The path that would actually lead to those goals wasn't that well thought out, however."

Ellen's first client as a legal aid lawyer was a housekeeper who worked her entire life but was turned down for Social Security benefits because she lacked employment records. Ellen realized that "people could work all their lives and not have Social Security because she was working as a housekeeper." Based on the feelings of discomfort that she had experienced as a girl with the treatment of household helpers, Ellen quickly identified with the client: "My parents probably didn't pay Social Security for [our maid], but it would never have dawned on me when I was growing up that they should have. And, so, it was only with hindsight and looking at this woman that I realized the injustice of working all your life and then having no retirement . . . Ultimately I got her benefits based on her deceased husband's record." The ability to help people and to redress injustice led Ellen to spend the next three decades doing legal work and running a large human service nonprofit that helps the most vulnerable population. Ellen's entire career and her personal identity were both shaped by her VISTA experience in deep and lasting ways. VISTA helped Ellen to grow, to build skills and confidence, and to enact her values.

Looking for Evidence of Personal Growth

Service can shape both the personal growth and the skill set of participants. Still, many researchers who study the effects of community service do not focus much on the intrinsic psychic rewards, but rather on the acquisition of practical work skills. They see the potential of Ameri-Corps in terms of workforce development, providing participants with training in both hard, technical skills and soft, interpersonal "workplace" skills. Service not only exposes young people to a skill set but also provides supervised opportunities to practice those skills. In principle, this kind of broad skill development results in more informed career choices, makes members more attractive to employers, and creates a stronger, better trained workforce. Given the costs associated with offering national service opportunities, there is a natural tendency to look for concrete "returns," and job readiness thus becomes a central consideration in assessing the impact of service.

An earlier study by Aguirre International found that national service participants who considered their own life skills to be deficient achieved substantial gains in all skill areas, except the use of information technology.[1] Benefits occurred for all AmeriCorps members, especially those with the least-developed skills at the time of program entry. Members of all ethnic groups reported gains in their skills. Significant effects were also found in the areas of educational attainment, with volunteers reporting greater interest in public service upon completion of their term. Here we revisit some of the issues and deploy out data to see just what kinds of effects service might have on the personal growth of members, construed a bit more broadly.

When we spoke with program managers and thought leaders in the national service movement, one of the most consistently articulated visions for national service was that it promotes the personal development of its participants through exposure to a wide range of perspectives while providing members with opportunities to take on leadership roles. This vision coincides with the core mission statement of the Corporation for National and Community Service (CNCS): AmeriCorps members in the longitudinal study enrolled in the program at a time when the CNCS identified "developing members" as one of its highest priorities. During the 1999–2000 program year, when participants in the longitudinal study were enrolled in AmeriCorps, many programs routinely devoted a day or half day each week to member development. Activities often included guest speakers, reflection on their service experience, and (toward the end of the program year) review of a curriculum designed to prepare members for "life after AmeriCorps." Given the design and program content of AmeriCorps, one would expect that members might experience several different forms of personal growth during their term of service and beyond.

We use five outcomes to measure the effect of AmeriCorps participation on the personal growth of members, spanning both psychic benefits and skill acquisition. *Personal growth through community service* represents the respondent's assessment of the impacts of his or her prior volunteer activities during the previous year with respect to personal growth, including exposure to new ideas, changing beliefs, and learning about the real world. *Personal effectiveness of community service* represents the respondent's opinion about the impacts of his or her prior volunteer activities during the previous year with respect to making community contributions, developing attachments to the community, and making a difference. Educational behavior is measured as *educational progress* and indicates the level of education attained three and eight years after baseline (during fall 2002 and winter 2003, during 2007; not a gain score). *Basic work skills* identifies the amount of experience respondents have with fundamental work skills including gathering and analyzing information, motivating coworkers, and managing time. Additionally, *public service employment* indicates whether the respondent was employed in the public sector during subsequent surveys. Public service employment was defined as work in education, social work, public safety, the arts, religion, or full-time military service.[2]

Personal Growth through Community Service

For the longitudinal study, AmeriCorps members were asked to assess their personal growth through service after a year.[3] This outcome tracked respondents' assessment of the impact of their service activities during the prior year on their own personal growth, including exposure to new ideas, changing beliefs, and learning about the real world. For those in the treatment group, this year corresponded to their time in AmeriCorps. To gauge the complex issue of personal growth, a number of questions were asked about whether respondents reexamined their beliefs and attitudes about themselves, whether they were exposed to new ideas and ways of seeing the world, whether they learned something about the "real world," whether they did things they never thought they could do, and whether they actually changed some of their beliefs and attitudes.[4] With the answers to these questions, we hoped to understand whether those taking part in service gained a broader perspective and deeper self-awareness.

As illustrated in Figure 5.1, in the short run, both State and National and NCCC members reported positive, statistically significant impacts on

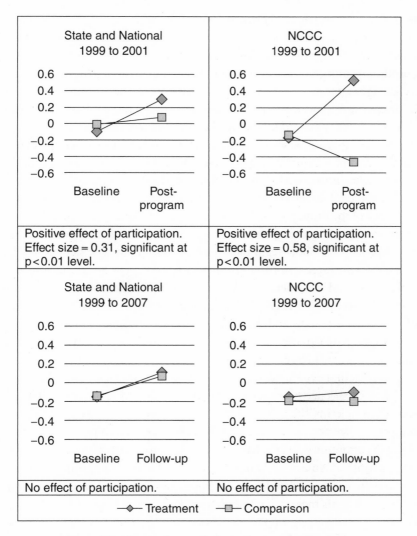

Figure 5.1. Personal growth through community service

their personal growth as a result of their AmeriCorps experience. For State and National, the treatment group experienced growth during the study period, while the comparison group experienced little change, resulting in a medium-sized effect (effect size = 0.31). The NCCC members also showed positive gains while the NCCC comparison group members regressed, reflecting a larger effect of participation (effect size = 0.58) for this first personal growth outcome.

When the time horizon is extended and we consider the long-term effects of service on personal growth, the effects we saw in the short term fade away. For both AmeriCorps State and National and NCCC, there were no statistically significant gains between 1999 and 2007. These are disappointing results given the encouraging personal growth data that was collected right after program completion. Still, one can only conclude that the feeling of having been exposed to new ideas and having reexamined one's beliefs does not extend far beyond the initial glow of service. This may be due to the intensity of some national service experiences where members are thrown into very stressful environments and told to adjust and find a way to help. Immediately after emerging from this experience, members may become introspective about what has just happened. Over eight years, the shock of the immersion appears to fade and attitudes and beliefs become more set with the passing of time.

We probed the short-term data further to find out whether those who had not volunteered prior to enrolling in AmeriCorps State and National had experienced more personal growth through service than members with prior volunteer experience. While controlling for other factors, AmeriCorps members in the State and National programs who had not volunteered prior to AmeriCorps did indeed gain more from the experience than those who had prior volunteering experience. We also found that AmeriCorps members' actual experiences in their programs were clearly related to their ability to experience personal growth through community service. For instance, completing the program fully and becoming involved in the planning of service activities were each positively related to personal growth through community service. More counterintuitive is the finding that working with other AmeriCorps members with diverse backgrounds turned out to be negatively related to gains in personal growth through community service. This means that members who were put in programs that involved a very diverse group of individuals left their year of service reporting a lower level of personal growth.

When we turned to the NCCC, we also uncovered some interesting results. While controlling for other factors, female AmeriCorps members in the NCCC program scored higher on personal growth through community service than males. NCCC members who worked with members of diverse backgrounds scored higher on personal growth through community service compared to NCCC members who did not work with members of diverse backgrounds, a result that runs contrary to what we found for the State and National program. One interpretation of this result is that the residential nature of the NCCC gives members a greater amount of time to get to know one another in the program and this allows for greater levels of personal growth.

Among former AmeriCorps members who completed one year of service, 55 percent reported that their AmeriCorps experience was very transformational, while 38 percent reported it was only somewhat transformational. Among the former group, 70 percent had never volunteered prior to AmeriCorps, while 30 percent had volunteered in the past. This would suggest that if one is looking to have a real effect on the personal growth of members, finding individuals who have not been engaged with their community prior to joining AmeriCorps may help increase the odds that the program will lead to substantial levels of personal growth.

Personal Effectiveness of Community Service

For members to feel good about their service and to feel as though they are learning and growing, they need to believe that their service made a real contribution to the community, that they forged new relationships, and that they made a difference. Seeing their work translate into meaningful change is both satisfying and empowering to young people. And while it is entirely possible to learn something from failure, we believe that when it comes to personal growth, being effective is ultimately more associated with personal growth than frustration, isolation, and ineffectiveness.[5] The personal effectiveness outcome we tracked represents the respondents' opinion about the impacts of their volunteer activities in the year after completing AmeriCorps (and a corresponding period for individuals in the comparison group) with respect to their assessment of the following three statements: I felt I made a difference in the community. I felt like part of the community. I felt I could make a difference in the life of at least one person. Taken together, these three items give us a sense of how members interpreted the efficacy of their service and how good they felt about their year of service.

What did the data reveal? Participation in AmeriCorps State and National has a positive effect on members' perception of their personal effectiveness in service. In the short run, the State and National treatment group experienced gains, while the comparison group did not change much, resulting in a medium-sized impact of participation (effect size = 0.38). For NCCC, the data collected soon after program completion showed no gain for members. In the long run (after eight years), the tables were turned and the results inverted: NCCC members believed their work made a difference and that they forged new relationships, while State and National members did not achieve gains. This tells us that opinions about what actually happened during the service year did in fact change over time, and that the results were far from stable. (See Figure 5.2.)

We examined some of the short-term drivers of members' perceived effectiveness of community service and found that prior service experience was a significant factor. When controlling for individual characteristics, members who reported volunteering in the twelve months prior to enrollment in AmeriCorps State and National reported lower gains in their perceptions of subsequent effectiveness in service. One programmatic feature—planning—seemed to be positively correlated with personal effectiveness of service. Program participants who reported that they were able to plan their service activities reported higher levels of personal effectiveness.[6] It is useful to reiterate that not all community service projects have built into them a careful planning and project development component. Indeed, many programs are invented on the fly and are launched even when the ends are ambiguous and the means not fully specified. Finally, AmeriCorps State and National members who actually completed their national service program year reported higher levels of personal effectiveness in service. To appreciate service and to leave with a sense of having done something, we conclude that members need to complete the program without giving up or moving on to something else in midstream.

Our analyses also pointed to some interesting findings for NCCC members: Latino members were more likely than white participants to report increases in personal effectiveness. Religious diversity and participation in religious services as a youth were negatively related to their perceptions of effectiveness in service. Moreover, the more NCCC members attended team meetings while in the program, the higher they scored on personal

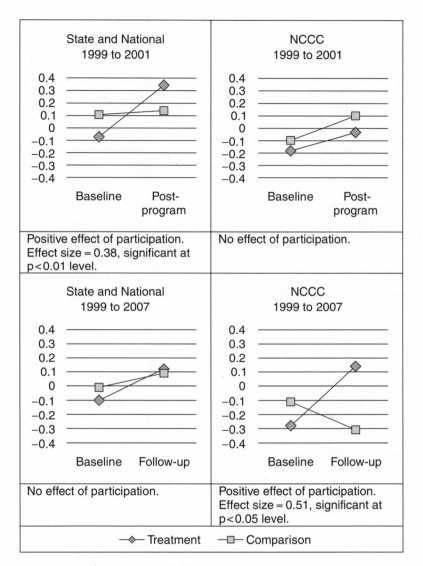

Figure 5.2. Personal effectiveness of community service

effectiveness of service. This factor explains 11 percent of the variance in the outcome for NCCC members. Even though the NCCC is a team-based service model, formal team meetings, in which participants have a chance to discuss the work and plan next steps, appear to be an important element in promoting perceptions of effectiveness in service.

To broaden our understanding of how members grow and build confidence through the accomplishment of service objectives, we surveyed VISTA volunteers on what they got out of service and whether they felt they made a difference. During the program period covered by the retrospective VISTA study (1965 through 1993), VISTA was primarily a poverty eradication program and it did not have a deliberate intent to benefit its participants. Nevertheless, the retrospective study enables us to examine whether participation in VISTA influenced long-term goals and life decisions. The survey findings indicate that the program had a fundamental influence on former VISTA members. Seventeen percent of former VISTA members reported that their term of service fundamentally transformed them, while 34 percent reported that it changed them in important ways and only 7 percent reported their term of service had only a moderate impact on their lives. Forty percent of respondents said that it helped to reinforce their own basic values and beliefs. When asked in what ways the experience transformed them, 40 percent said it transformed them both personally and professionally.

For those who made it through VISTA, we found that the program left a strongly consistent but not universal imprint. Ninety-two percent of former VISTA members agreed or strongly agreed that they "were exposed to new ideas and ways of seeing the world." Eighty-nine percent agreed or strongly agreed that they "learned more about the effects of poverty and social injustice." Finally, 76 percent of former VISTA members agreed or strongly agreed that they "re-examined their beliefs and attitudes about themselves." VISTA participants were asked about their service while enrolled in the program. Ninety-three percent agreed or strongly agreed that "they made a contribution to their community," while 88 percent strongly agreed or agreed that they had "felt like part of the community (where they served)."

We noted above that completing AmeriCorps was strongly related to feeling that one had accomplished and learned something. Dropping out of national service can be an important catalytic event, leading in many cases to the rethinking of career objectives and even to some wheel-spinning as a search begins for a new direction. In one striking case, leaving VISTA had catastrophic long-term effects in terms of life course. Jody grew up in Upstate New York and moved to San Francisco in the late 1960s rather than attend college like all her friends. The victim of sexual abuse at home, she decided at eighteen to try to make a fresh start by doing something for others. She read about the work of Cesar Chavez and the organizing of farmworkers and was moved by this effort. With an eye to doing something like this work, Jody applied to and was admitted to VISTA. She recounted how during her training, role-playing that was focused on cultural differences brought out some of her immaturity. The VISTA trainers thought she needed a couple more years of growing up and asked her to leave the program. For Jody, this was the start of a two-decade-long nightmare involving drugs and prostitution. Many of her problems were traceable to a fateful decision to seek a shared car ride soon thereafter: "I was nineteen then and I went down to the university and to the ride board and got a ride. The guy was a psychotic. He drugged me and tied me up and beat me up and put a gun to my head and had me call a relative and ask for money. I was a prostitute for eighteen years . . . He was crazy. So the older daughter is the daughter of a pimp. He sexually abused her from the age of four, so she's a mess. I haven't seen her since she was eighteen." While it is unfair to pin all this sorrow on one decision or one moment in her life, Jody did think that her dismissal from VISTA was a critical turning point that led to a horrible downward spiral from which she only recently emerged, through a religious conversion and by finding a partner who was supportive and caring. Rather than learning how to interact with others in a respectful way, which is what her VISTA trainers told her she needed to work on, she made a series of bad choices and was the victim of some terrible circumstances. It took her more than twenty years and a huge amount of pain and sorrow to get her life back on track.

Educational Progress after National Service

A central premise of AmeriCorps is that individuals who engage in full-time domestic national service deserve an educational benefit, similar to the GI Bill for those who serve in the military. There are several aspects to AmeriCorps that are intended to encourage members' educational progress. The emphasis on education starts in the service program itself. Members who do not have a high school diploma are strongly encouraged to work toward a diploma or general equivalency diploma (GED) while they are enrolled in AmeriCorps. After completing a year of service, AmeriCorps State and National and NCCC members receive an education award of $4,725 that can be used to pay for postsecondary tuition, to cover the costs of educational training, or simply to repay existing college loans. Currently, seventy colleges and universities match the AmeriCorps education award for their students. Members have up to seven years to use the award after they leave the program so they are not forced to make quick decisions once their service year is complete. VISTA members who complete a year of service can either receive the AmeriCorps education award or an end-of–service cash award of $1,200. Educational benefits were not provided to VISTA members who served in the periods covered by the retrospective study. To understand better whether service is connected to educational progress, we use survey and interview data from the two studies and try to see whether this core human capital building function of service is being fulfilled.[7]

In the AmeriCorps study, data on educational progress was collected in 2003 (rather than 2001) to give members a chance to use their educational award. Three years after program completion, members who entered the program without college degrees were surveyed to see whether they had completed at least some college course work. As shown in Figure 5.3, a smaller percent of both State and National and NCCC members reported completing some college than those in the pertinent com-

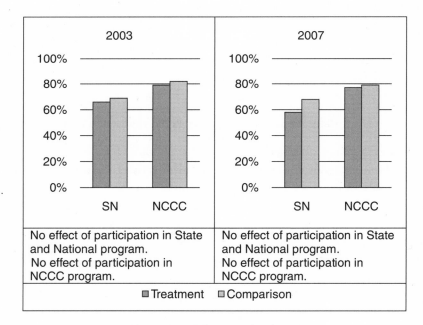

Figure 5.3. Educational progress

parison groups. By 2007, State and National members still lagged, while NCCC members had drawn closer to even. In both cases, the long-term effects of service on educational progress were not significant. When the measure of educational progress was changed for the collection of 2007 data to having a bachelor's degree or greater, the results remained insignificant: AmeriCorps members were simply not getting any meaningful long-term education benefit from their service.

Further analysis of the issue of educational progress revealed interesting facts. After leaving AmeriCorps, respondents were asked to indicate if they continued their college education or pursued graduate school. Some noticeable patterns emerged for AmeriCorps members in the State and National programs. Older participants were less likely to continue their education than younger participants. Those who had completed some years of college were likely to continue their education after completing their term of service in AmeriCorps.[8] Additionally, successful completion of AmeriCorps was associated with educational progress for those in State and National programs.[9] Among NCCC members, neither the demographic characteristics of participants nor their experiences in the program were related to their educational progress after completing their terms of service.

We looked further into our negative findings about educational progress after service by analyzing the life stories we heard of those who had served in VISTA and who had years—or even decades—to reflect on its meaning and impact in terms of their education. A number of the former VISTA volunteers we spoke with recounted how their service led them to seek out graduate and professional degrees in fields such as psychology, social work, and nursing. In some instances, VISTA was the exposure young people needed to see that social problems were complex and required educational preparation. In more cases, however, the effect of VISTA on educational aspirations and attainment was weak and indirect.

Rick is a professor who cautioned against the kind of qualitative research that was at the heart of the VISTA study. After warning that his account was subjective and not subject to external validation, Rick described VISTA as a turning point in his early life, during which he was able to discover what his passions were and to take his ideas and put them into action. He said that VISTA gave him a lot of responsibility for someone as young as he was at the time. He described the southwestern city where he served as alien as a foreign country. A member of one of the earliest VISTA cohorts, Rick got involved with many community projects that simply needed doing, rather than carving out one particular problem area to work on during his term of service. He characterized the work he did as amorphous and confusing rather than narrowly circumscribed: "The ultimate goal [was] not at all well specified. I'm not sure I would have wanted it any other way. Some people did have jobs and they went someplace for six hours a day and did something—in the hospital or school. But in my neighborhood we didn't have that structure." Still, there was a lot of freedom to improvise and Rick did that often. He helped a church set up a credit union and also worked on a range of smaller neighborhood projects, usually at the request of local residents.

While Rick saw a new world and worked on lots of projects, he was unsure how it all added up in the end: "There were a lot of interesting experiences. How could there not be? But nothing that changed the course of my life, nothing that dramatic." Nevertheless, Rick said the experience left him with plenty of vivid memories that ranged from jailhouses to dance halls: "I remember this small town; it was the first time I ever was inside a jail. One of the local guys was picked up for a drug-related offense. And the police let us in to talk to him. And I thought, I couldn't survive on the other side of this door." Later, Rick tried to socialize with local residents: "I remember one time they had one of these dances and I was getting friendly with one of the local girls. Some of the local guys resented that, so we had to leave . . . These are just experiences, not something that changed the course of my life. It just said, you need to be more careful, about what you're doing in public, who you're doing it with." Even if his VISTA experience was fragmented and uncoordinated, Rick still left with a seriousness of purpose that led him to get his PhD and become a university professor for many years before leaving academia to start a company. Through VISTA, Rick learned that many public problems are extremely complex, and this brought out his curiosity. By getting a doctorate, Rick tried to get the deepest formal understanding he could of the issues that mattered most to him.

For another person who left VISTA without completing the program, pursuing additional education was never really a priority. Sam grew up in a diverse neighborhood in Baltimore. In the 1950s, his school was integrated and so was the community he played in. His mother was an activist, spent time in jail as a result of her penchant for protests, and was involved in the McCarthy hearings. His father, a labor organizer, was just as politically committed. Sam enrolled in VISTA right after high school and, after two trainings, "washed out" of the program. Sam was told by his trainer that he was not yet mature enough and that VISTA would call him in a year. When VISTA did call back, he was already on to his "next adventure" and did not serve. Sam ended up dropping out of college after one year and has worked for both the state and nonprofit organizations that provide services to people with disabilities. Sam reported that being sent away by VISTA pushed him to seek more adventure and travel. Lacking patience and regularly seeking change throughout his adult life, Sam did not feel as though he would have completed college had he done a year of VISTA service. His rambling ways were more of an obstacle to completing his education than anything else.

While educational progress on the AmeriCorps longitudinal study was only tracked for eight years following program completion, the VISTA retrospective study allowed us to examine this outcome over a much longer time frame. Since leaving VISTA, 59 percent of former VISTA volunteers (like Rick) entered a degree-granting program, while 64 percent of near VISTA members (like Sam) enrolled. Interestingly, the VISTA sample was more educated at the time of enrollment compared to those in the AmeriCorps study. Fifty percent of the VISTA participants were college graduates, compared to 48 percent of AmeriCorps members in NCCC programs, and only 28 percent of AmeriCorps members in State and National programs. Moreover, study respondents reported somewhat different patterns of educational degree pursuit, as indicated in Table 5.1. While slightly more near VISTA members pursued a bachelor's degree (24 percent compared to 17 percent for VISTA members), more VISTA members sought a master's degree after leaving the program (26 percent compared to 20 percent for near VISTA members). Overall, it does not appear that participation in

Table 5.1
Degree Earned since Leaving VISTA

	Associate's Degree	BA	MA	PhD	JD/MPP
VISTA Group	7%	17%	26%	6%	2%
Near VISTA Group	9%	24%	20%	7%	1%

VISTA had an important effect on participants' postprogram educational engagement.

In the end, national service may contribute to the personal growth of members, but this effect does not measurably manifest itself in educational progress. AmeriCorps State and National, NCCC, and VISTA members do not appear to leave service with a commitment and determination to pursue more education. They may learn a great deal about human relationships, the dynamics of communities, and the challenges facing the poor, but these programs are not significantly changing attitudes and behavior related to education.

Basic Work Skills

Beyond inspiring members to seek more education, national service can promote personal growth by imparting basic work skills. If these skills are built during service, participation in AmeriCorps could influence members' subsequent employment in many ways. It could energize and equip members with the skills to thrive in a variety of workplace settings, especially if the skills taught are broad enough. Skills learned through service could also help members overcome real or perceived barriers to employment by showing them that they can indeed function effectively in the workplace. Finally, basic work skills could simply give members greater competency that will enable them to pursue jobs that maximize their potential. To get a sense of whether members learned work skills, a battery of ten different questions about skill acquisition was developed that covered such things as problem solving, collecting and analyzing information, listening to others, resolving conflicts, leading teams, learning from others, adapting to changing circumstances, meeting deadlines and managing time under pressure, and dealing with difficult work conditions. Because these skills can be acquired through work outside of national service, data on basic work skill acquisition during AmeriCorps was only collected in the first postprogram survey in 2001. (See Figure 5.4.)

We found that participation in AmeriCorps had positive, significant effects on members' assessment of their basic work skills. The average treatment effect on State and National members was small, positive, and statistically significant (effect size = 0.15). State and National members showed a mean gain in basic work skills, while comparison group members showed no change in this outcome. For NCCC, the impact of participation on ba-

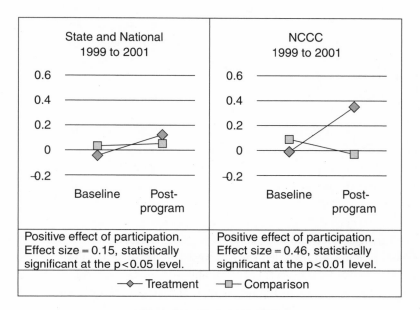

Figure 5.4. Basic work skills

sic work skills was medium-sized, positive, and statistically significant (effect size = 0.46). The NCCC treatment group showed an average increase in these behaviors between baseline and postprogram, while comparison group members showed no change. During their service, AmeriCorps members were thus picking up work skills either through formal training or through the lived experience of trying to make a difference in the community. To gain some understanding as to whether building basic work skills translated into employment advantage, we did some additional analysis. After completing the program,[10] 57 percent of AmeriCorps members reported they were working full-time. However, 57 percent of nonmembers also reported they were working full-time. A similar percentage in both groups reported working part-time: AmeriCorps members, 30 percent; nonmembers, 31 percent. In 2002, 26 percent of former AmeriCorps members reported being at home taking care of their children, while only 18 percent of nonmembers reported the same. Twenty-seven percent of AmeriCorps members stated they were looking for a job, while only 24 percent of nonmembers reported they were actively looking for employment. Less than 2 percent of both the former AmeriCorps members and nonmembers reported enlisting in military service or the National Guard.

Among the former AmeriCorps members working full-time in 2002, 21.4 percent pursued jobs in social or community work, 21 percent held jobs in teaching, 13 percent held jobs in business, and 10 percent pursued health-related jobs. Among nonmembers working full-time in 2002, 14 percent pursued social or community work, 20 percent pursued teaching jobs, 18 percent held business-related positions, and 10 percent went into health-related fields. This suggests that the AmeriCorps experience orients members more toward social and community work and less toward business. Smaller percentages of former AmeriCorps members and nonmembers pursued fields such as public safety, agriculture, performing arts, carpentry work, and computers.

We also considered the experience of VISTA members with both training during service and its effects on employment later in life. After a relationship went sour, Kate left the Midwest and drove to San Francisco with her girlfriends, seeking a fresh start. She worked as a secretary there, and saw an ad for VISTA in the newspaper: "I just saw the ad and thought it was an interesting job. It was for helping and it was in Idaho and I thought that sounded interesting to be going somewhere. I didn't have anything going on and it just seemed like a way to get started." Her VISTA assignment was in northern, rural Idaho to develop a program that assisted low-income families in obtaining federally funded Section 8 housing. The work taught her some important lessons. "It was Section 8 rental assistance, so it's federal funding and it's kind of twofold: One, you have to find the clients on assistance or Social Security. Two, you have to qualify them. Then you had to convince the landlord to accept the money directly, which wasn't easy because in Idaho they really don't like the government. So I would drive around and find these people and then I had to look for the place." One of the key skills that Kate felt she learned from the hunt-and-seek work was to be really organized. "I had to learn how to do paperwork, which in any social service job you have to get the paperwork done. And I learned . . . how to work within the bureaucracy because it's what's required and how far are you willing to stretch the rules to make it work. I've had to do that in every job I've had . . . not violate the rules but [learn] how to make it work. I had to do a lot of networking, which you have to do as a social worker on the job, figuring out where to find your clients and explain your program to them . . . it was definitely a career booster for me."

For volunteers with graduate degrees and skills, VISTA can be a place to hone and refine their craft. Several VISTA members from the 1960s entered the program after law school and were given a great opportunity to have real responsibility and develop their legal skills. Morris grew up in Queens, New York, and went to college and law school in New York. His VISTA placement was in New York City, he believes, because no outsider probably could have figured out how to live in the city on the modest stipend provided by VISTA. The VISTA work assigned to Morris involved helping to represent and correspond with prisoners and those accused of crimes: "My job was to go into court with these guys and try to convince the prosecutor and the judge that, yes, this guy may have actually done what was in this warrant, but the guy who did it is not the same person who is here before you, and society would not be best served if you take this guy, and disrupt his life, and send him to jail, and disrupt his family, and take away the job. Let's come up with something more appropriate, whether it's a long-term probation supervision, or restitution to the victim." By working on behalf of those in trouble with the legal system, Morris learned firsthand how the system worked. He also maintained an extensive correspondence with prisoners: "The other thing I would do, which was really incredibly moving to me, was we would get letters from people in prison, all around the country . . . They were suffering in prison, issues of brutality, things they wanted to let us know about, just a voice to share their stories with. Letters from prison are censored, but letters to lawyers are not. So basically, I held a correspondence with hundreds of inmates around the nation, advised them as I could about their rights, listened to their stories, and shared their stories when possible."

Morris reflected on the Attica riot and tried to explain the prisoners' perspective on this event. He considered carefully what his VISTA experience taught him and settled on something very concrete: "I learned to be a criminal defense lawyer. I learned to bring test case litigation." Morris eventually decided to leave litigation and spend much of his career doing broader advocacy and policy work, "but you know, I didn't really use most of those skills ever again . . . other than to remember and to know what prisons are like, and to know what the plight of ex-offenders is." Beyond imparting legal skills that eventually were turned into lobbying and policy skills, VISTA taught Morris something more important about the nature of justice.

Not everyone in VISTA felt trained or more ready for work upon completion of service. In thinking back on what skills she gained through VISTA,

Heidi noted that she felt as though she did not do a great job volunteering in a rural Kentucky community because she lacked specialized skills. Heidi reported not having learned any real new skills in VISTA, but was more concerned about the fact that she brought few concrete skills to the program. Concerns about finding a practical career and a diagnosis of cancer in her late twenties focused Heidi's attention in directions other than community organizing and social justice. She chose to be a nurse and married for the first time in her late forties, but has never really felt as though her VISTA service prepared her for the curveballs that life has thrown at her. While Heidi enjoyed the challenge of the work she did in Kentucky, she ultimately was swayed more by other events in her life and built a skill set in the years after her service designed to meet her lifelong needs. When asked about the big decisions in her life and major turning points, VISTA was not prominent: "Marriage was one. And just deciding to really get well. I had a choice. Did I want this treatment? I said, 'Give it all to me, I want to live.' That was big." In this sense, VISTA's influence on Heidi's skill development was overshadowed by bigger events in her life, particularly related to health and survival. VISTA was rewarding personally for Heidi, but she reported learning more in college than in the small Kentucky town where she helped others for a year.

As we listened to many people reflect on their VISTA service, the work of a member tended to be described more often than not as vaguely defined and constantly shifting. We heard of many placements that either started off with little focus or that simply became ill-defined over the course of the year. While many volunteers were assigned to positions designed to empower and assist residents in poor communities, the work skills that were needed to accomplish the tasks were general and often nontechnical in nature. Listening and taking initiative are skills that are very different from those needed for the fields of accounting or computer programming. Given its loose focus and flexibility, VISTA managed alternately to frustrate members and to impart some useful interpersonal and problem-solving skills.

Participants in VISTA had many opportunities to develop their work skills that would benefit them in future employment settings. Monique grew up in a large Catholic family, not particularly aware of diversity issues. She became interested in serving the community through a high school political program that allowed students to shadow officials in local government. After dropping out after her first year of college due to drug use, she took a VISTA position in a recreation program in her hometown in Connecticut. Her first placement in a youth service agency ended because the organization closed. A second placement in a program for juvenile delinquents was more successful and allowed her not just to help others but also to address her own drug abuse problem. Service may make people more idealistic, but it can also be a harsh reality check. Thinking back to her first client contact, Monique recalled a sense of surprise at how others thought about life and the choices they had to make:

> Her name was Jeannie. She was my first client, and she was getting out of jail. She had been in jail for prostitution, for maybe a year. I went to the jail and picked her up. I got her an apartment, got her set up with a community agency which was going to see if she could start going to school . . . I'm all happy, she's going to have a place to live, and she's going to get going, we're going to change this girl's life. And she had money. She had a check for maybe $50 or $100 or something for work that she did in the prison. She wanted to go see somebody or buy something, so I let her out on the main street in town and was going to pick her up in about an hour or something. And she comes walking out of this store and she's got on a hooker dress and these big hooker shoes. She bought this big ring, and she spent every dime that she had that she was supposed to survive on for the next month, on this stuff. That was my first experience with my first real client. I learned my lesson.

For Monique, the sense of shock and disappointment in this first effort to help was not crushing but rather a catalyst to measure her idealism against the realities of the constraints and impulses that drive the decisions of people with few opportunities. The real effect of VISTA on Monique was not how the program shaped her perception of others but rather in the way the experience held a mirror up and allowed her to see herself more clearly: "I walked in there and I thought I was going to learn about hard-core drugs [and] how I could help these kids in the youth program. I sat down and did a personality analysis, and talked to somebody, and really looked at my life and the fact that I was smoking pot, and I was drinking. And I'm like, I'm messed up!" Before helping others, Monique realized that she needed to listen to the warnings her friends were giving her and look more deeply at the choices she was making in her own life.[11] She did not like what she saw at the time: "I had dropped out of college because of drugs, and I had only a few people in my life who really [knew] how messed up I was." However, in the long haul, the epiphany of VISTA was needed to shake Monique up and lead her to redirect her energies toward building a real career: "I've been with [this organization] ever since, and I've gone from that [low point] to the executive director of the program, internationally responsible for fifty centers around the world. [This is] over a thirty-year history of working with this program, but that's where it started. And it was because of VISTA."

Public Service Employment

One of the possible benefits of a robust national service option for young people is that it could orient and prepare a whole new generation of public service workers. Recent concerns have been raised about the pending large-scale retirement of government employees. According to the U.S. Office of Personnel Management, over the next ten years, 60 percent of all government employees and 90 percent of the government's 6,000 executive employees will be eligible for retirement.[12] To assess whether AmeriCorps was orienting and motivating members for public service, broadly construed, we explored the effects of participation on the likelihood of public service employment.

The data indicated that there was a positive and statistically significant difference between State and National members and their comparison group, though the size of the effect was modest in both the short run (measured in 2003) and in the long run (measured in 2007). Forty percent of former State and National members were employed in public service, making them 7 percent more likely than their comparison group members to report employment in public service three years after baseline. The difference between the NCCC and the comparison group was not statistically significant (see Figure 5.5).[13]

Results from analysis on subgroups of AmeriCorps members again indicated important differences between members who had or did not have prior volunteer experience before enrolling in AmeriCorps. Participants in the State and National program who had volunteered prior to AmeriCorps were more likely to enter public service employment than those who had not.[14] Furthermore, religious service attendance as a youth increased the likelihood that members would pursue employment in the public service sector. When adding members' AmeriCorps experiences to

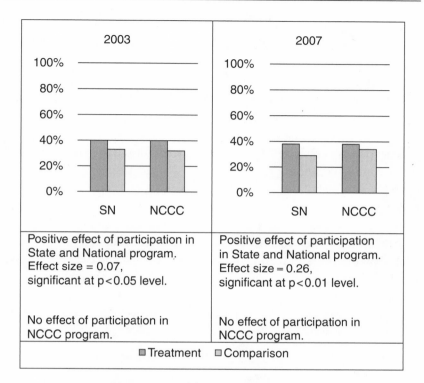

Figure 5.5. Public service employment

the model, the data showed that the opportunity to plan service activities increased the likelihood of participants entering public service employment after leaving AmeriCorps. When program characteristics were introduced into the model, we found that members who worked in teams were less likely to pursue public service employment post-AmeriCorps than those members who were not in programs that required them to work in teams, a finding that is highly statistically significant. Among participants in the NCCC programs, former members who worked with members from diverse backgrounds were more likely to enter public service employment than those who rarely worked with members from diverse backgrounds.

What about long-term orientation toward public service? When we interviewed VISTA members, we asked them to reflect on public service. We heard many stories about a possible link between service and a longer-term commitment to working on behalf of the public. Many of the VISTA members we spoke with went on to pursue careers in the helping professions. The chance to work with clients when they were young and to see their work make a difference was both inspiring and useful to them. One former VISTA member, Jack, saw in his service the start of a slow and career-long process of building workplace skills. While VISTA did not prepare Jack entirely for the thirty years that followed as an administrator in non-profit and public agencies, he did see the year he spent in the South helping local leaders get organized as the starting point for much of what followed in the coming decades.

Sheila, a former VISTA volunteer with a real social conscience, credited private school for raising her social awareness and kindling her interest in helping those in need. National service may have given her a chance to act on her commitments, but Sheila was clear that she brought to the program a lot of preexisting social and political commitments and did not discover them in the program. Looking back to a high school field trip, Sheila heard her social conscience speaking to her. The trip exposed her to racial disparities and began to plant in her mind the challenge of taking local action to change things:

> We knew that Washington, D.C., and the area around it in Virginia were technically in the South. We saw so many black people waiting on us. We were embarrassed, as a group of girls. There were ninety girls and four nuns. We were embarrassed, because the only black people that we saw were waiting on us. They were in the hotels. They were busboys. You know, they're grown men and they were busboys. They were sweeping the streets, and we didn't see any black people doing the stuff that white people were doing. We didn't see any black men in suits.

The legal aid work that Sheila was assigned was difficult and challenging, but geared toward a goal of empowerment that resonated with her: "The idea was to give people of color, poor people of color in the community, the same kind of power, the same kind of perception of power, as people with money who could hire an attorney. And by doing that, our goal was to give people vigorous defense, and because we didn't work for the public defender's office." A key attraction of the work was being able to give defendants concentrated attention and support: "We would have sufficient time to explain stuff to them so they could follow what was going on, and give them the feeling that they weren't being just ground up in little bits. And giving people that kind of power, being instrumental in letting people take that kind of power, and have that kind of involvement, really matched with my personal goals."

Looking back on her long career in nonprofit and community organizations, Sheila saw her VISTA work as a critical first step toward her goals: "It gave me a good feel for the community, so that I actually knew people. I had my own law practice for a time, and then I was a referee, which is like a judge, in juvenile court. And I knew people. I knew the community. I think it made me much more effective, much more credible." Since she stayed in the Minneapolis area after her VISTA service, Sheila built up a reservoir of trust and credibility upon which she could draw: "I didn't have to guard what I said or how I said it, because I'd had some experience. I knew who I was working with, and they knew me."

Employment interests played a role in influencing why many former VISTA members had enrolled in the program. To some extent, participation in national service may serve as a "tryout" for the real world, providing members with a way to test their interest and capabilities in various occupations. Forty-three percent of former VISTA members reported that the activities they were involved in with VISTA were very related to their career goals at the time, while 38 percent reported they were only somewhat related, and 18 percent reported they were not at all related. This tells us that many of those who entered the program had an interest in public service and were taking a year to explore what it felt like to actually do a specific job.

At follow-up, in some cases up to forty years after enrollment in the program, employment patterns were largely consistent for VISTA members and their near VISTA counterparts. Members spent time in a variety of settings after VISTA. Twenty-six percent of former VISTA members reported being hired as an employee by their VISTA program or sponsoring organization where they did their service project. Respondents were asked about their current employment. Slightly more VISTA members were employed, compared with the near VISTA members, although the figures for unemployed, retired, and keeping house were comparable. (See Table 5.2.)

Current employment patterns were similar for both VISTA members and near members. Thirty percent of former VISTA members and 28 percent of near VISTA members were working in the private/for-profit sector. Nearly the same percentages were working in the government or public sector: 30 percent of former members and 28 percent of near members.

Table 5.2
Employment since Leaving VISTA*

	Full-Time	Part-Time	Unemployed	Retired	Keeping House
Near VISTA Members	57%	12%	3%	12%	6%
VISTA Members	62%	13%	2%	10%	5%

*See Markovitz, Schneider, et al. (2007).

Finally, 16 percent of former members and 12 percent of near members were working in nonprofits. The most common fields of current employment for the two groups were similar: Teaching, social and community work, health-related occupations, business, and law were the careers most frequently reported. Together, these five occupations accounted for 72 percent of the jobs held by former members and 74 percent for the near members.

Respondents in the VISTA study were also asked about their total household income in the previous calendar year.[15] As shown in Table 5.3, income levels are quite similar for both groups, although a higher percentage of VISTA members reported income in the highest bracket, more than $90,000; 36 percent reported incomes in this category, compared to 29 percent of near VISTA members.

Although employment patterns for VISTA members and near members are similar, slightly more members were employed at the time of follow-up. The fact that more members report household incomes in the highest wage bracket may reflect partially the earlier persistence of members continuing with the VISTA program, seeing it through, and entering and advancing in their chosen fields earlier.

As we look across the many measures we took of personal growth, our analysis indicates that AmeriCorps members in the State and National and NCCC programs scored higher on one out of five measures of personal growth compared to those matched study participants who did not enter the AmeriCorps program.[16] In three areas, the results were mixed. And in one critical area—education—there were no gains. These results suggest that when it comes to building human capital and developing the capacity of members, AmeriCorps produces results, particularly in the areas of work skill acquisition. The results related to educational progress sug-

Table 5.3
Household Income since Leaving VISTA

	$1,000– $9,999	$10,000– $19,999	$20,000– $29,999	$30,000– $39,999	$40,000– $59,999	$60,000– $89,999	$90,000+
VISTA Members	3%	8%	8%	8%	16%	20%	36%
Near VISTA Members	5%	10%	7%	10%	16%	20%	29%

gest that AmeriCorps still has room to improve in motivating people to maximize their educations. This suggests that we need to think through more fully how AmeriCorps can both capitalize on its notable successes and address some of its visible shortcomings in the areas of promoting the personal growth of members.

— 6 —

Social Capital

In a perfect world, all young people would possess a deep commitment to tolerance, an abiding trust in their fellow citizens, and a willingness to set aside egocentric impulses and to work closely with others toward shared goals. In the world we know and live in every day, few young people fully possess the wisdom to appreciate the centrality of social capital and community connectedness to their own success and the success of their communities. This is why national service has long been considered a critical tool for cultivating an appreciation of social capital in the form of trust, teamwork, and tolerance. But do AmeriCorps programs really serve as laboratories for the development of these characteristics? Before sorting through the data we collected, it is useful to hear how Dorothy learned a powerful lesson through service.

Dorothy's Story

Dorothy applied to Volunteers in Service to America (VISTA) in 1968 with the man who would become her husband, and they were assigned to the same town in New Jersey. VISTA changed Dorothy's perception of people and broadened her horizons. Raised in Massachusetts as the daughter of a policeman, Dorothy had a sheltered and happy childhood, in which she saw her mother work in a range of community organizations. Growing up, Dorothy had little contact with people of diverse races, and she approached service as a way of broadening her horizons. Not only did VISTA expose Dorothy to people very different from those she grew up among, it helped her build new relationships and connections that deepened her understanding of the world. National service led to a set of bonds that built social capital within her member peer group and across the community in which she served: "It was the camaraderie. It was really the camaraderie of the group. We were very embraced and welcomed in the neighborhood, again, for what we could do for them. But you know people liked us. We all became friends. We VISTAs were invited to homes all the time and it was a real sense of community."

When it came to actual work, Dorothy recalled working on conceptualizing projects and helping to write grants to turn them into reality. Sometimes successful and other times not, Dorothy's work in a community group gave her a chance to build relationships across racial boundaries, which was a new experience for her. It also gave her the opportunity to translate local aspirations into concrete project plans: "There was a large community center. It was a large building that had been an arsenal. But we didn't go in and sit in an office in there. We were kind of out . . . doing the research to write the proposals. We were always trying to bring together community-based people. Even though they were receiving federal money, a lot of them were church based. The black community was there and we were always working on finding partnerships within the broader community of people who would be interested. We were, in some ways, the link to the white community." Beyond writing grants, Dorothy and her fellow VISTA volunteers were deeply involved with implementing the new programs and initiatives, ranging from a training program for mechanics to a tutoring program for young children.

Working with low-income populations left an impression on Dorothy. Helping children with emotional needs was a compelling experience because the stakes were high and the results noticeable. Dorothy told of how she forged relationships through the tutoring program with children who came from very different backgrounds than hers, which made her realize how narrow her social network really was. Within a group of VISTA volunteers, national service also has the ability to bring people from different backgrounds together and transcend boundaries. Dorothy's experience was typical: "There were probably about six of us from the major group that all got assigned to the Community Action Program. And it was a great, it was just a great agency, a great group of people. They were all very smart. There were two white Jewish guys from New York and several black guys who had been union organizers. The county we were in is one of the wealthiest counties in the state but it has big pockets of poverty." Dorothy learned to work with a wide variety of individuals and to focus group effort on common goals.

The sense of connection and community, and the feeling of bridging boundaries, led Dorothy to extend her commitment: "We joined VISTA for the year, but we ended up staying with the agency for almost four years. They offered us jobs once our year was over. And a couple of the other people stayed, as well, so I think there were six of us at the beginning and probably three or four stayed for more than the single year . . . And friendships happened. We had dinner probably less than six months ago with a high school girl who is now a teacher, but she was a high school student who was in our program." Dorothy also related how several of the VISTA members had remained in touch and maintained friendships over the decades as their lives went in different directions.

If national service is about building trust, social capital, and tolerance, Dorothy left with all three: "It was a fabulous experience, very fulfilling and enabling. I think that folks kind of bonded right at the beginning; everyone reached out to stay in touch with each other and we had one of the most successful stories. I've always really said that I felt that my VISTA experience was much more educational and enlightening for me than college ever was. You know, on an intellectual plane, but as well on the plane of being in a position where you really understood collaboration and the power of people working together. I'd never really been involved in anything quite like the VISTA program."

Weighing Evidence of Social Capital Effects

Teamwork, building trust, and understanding group dynamics are all important "soft skills" needed for success in life and the modern workplace. We examine next the relationship between participation in national service and the development of social capital and related life skills. Social capital refers to the set of networks and reciprocal relationships (or capital) that are often cited by business leaders as crucial for accessing jobs, conducting successful business transactions, and just getting along better in the workplace. In researching social inequity, sociologists such as James Coleman have posited that societal privilege is not only related to financial capital but also to social capital.[1] More popularly, Robert Putnam documented the decline of social capital in the United States in recent decades.

Putnam's claim was that vibrant and effective communities need social capital to remain strong.[2]

Efforts to build or increase our nation's social capital have been stepped up dramatically in reaction to September 11 and the disasters of Hurricane Katrina and Hurricane Rita. Communities across the country have realized they need to establish networks of citizens and community leaders to prepare for possible terrorist attacks or natural disasters. During the hurricanes, the traditional sources of government emergency support failed in many instances. In contrast, teams of AmeriCorps members came to provide aid within the first twenty-four hours after Katrina slammed into the Gulf of Mexico. Government bureaucracies have slowed the Gulf rebuilding efforts and much of the reconstruction continues to be done by volunteers. Recognizing the fragility of our national emergency and social support infrastructures, the White House established the USA Freedom Corps to encourage individuals to volunteer and make it easier for them to connect to local service opportunities. In times of emergency, a network of ties and a reservoir of trust at the community level can be the difference between quick, effective, and coordinated response and one that languishes in negotiations and turf struggles.

AmeriCorps programs are encouraged by the Corporation for National and Community Service (CNCS) to provide training, team-building, and reflection opportunities to members. A key goal of the national service movement is to support AmeriCorps members' ability to interact in team settings with groups of diverse individuals. Our findings in this chapter are organized into four broad themes: social trust and connection to community, constructive group dynamics, appreciation for diversity, and interpersonal networks. In each area, we probe to see how AmeriCorps State and National and NCCC perform.

One conceptual concession is needed before we turn to the data. The concept of social capital operates at both the community and individual levels. Communities possess aggregate stores of trust, goodwill and interorganizational ties that make community progress possible. At the same time, individuals also possess stocks of social capital in the form of attitudes and behaviors that are either conducive or threatening to the existence of networks and relationships within a community. Each of the measures we take of social capital resides in the members we surveyed. While it would have been useful to take broader community-level measures of social capital construction, we were unable to do so given the parameters of the study.

Hence, the construct of social capital here is measured at the individual level, though we believe that the concept of social capital resides at the intersection of community and individual.

Connection to Community

The reciprocal networks of relationships constituting social capital require individuals to feel connected to their communities and trust their neighbors. The connection to community outcome is based on the perception of respondents regarding their feelings of attachment to their community, the frequency that they think about how larger political issues affect their community, their awareness of ways to meet public needs in the community, their sense of being able to make a difference in their community, and their willingness to try to make a difference in their community.[3] By combining these five measures into an index variable, we can test the effect of service on the sense of community attachment following service. As illustrated in Figure 6.1, there were positive, statistically significant effects regarding connection to community for both AmeriCorps State and National and NCCC members a year after their enrollment in the program. For State and National, the average change for program members was positive, while the average comparison group members showed no change, reflecting a medium-sized effect of participation (effect size = 0.51). For NCCC, the average change for members was positive while the comparison group showed a decline, reflecting a medium-sized effect of participation (effect size = 0.39). The positive findings for the NCCC members are especially interesting. Despite having just spent a year moving around from one community to the next, NCCC members still increased their connection to community.

After eight years, the connection to community is still present for both State and National and NCCC. The effects remain of similar magnitude. These consistent results indicate that during service something significant happens at the level of forging an attachment and connection to community. It is hard to imagine social capital existing without this kind of connection and commitment. After all, trust and interpersonal ties can only flourish when the members of a community feel a sense of personal investment and linkage to the larger collective.

To understand the drivers of connectedness, we examined whether certain participant or programmatic characteristics are associated with changes

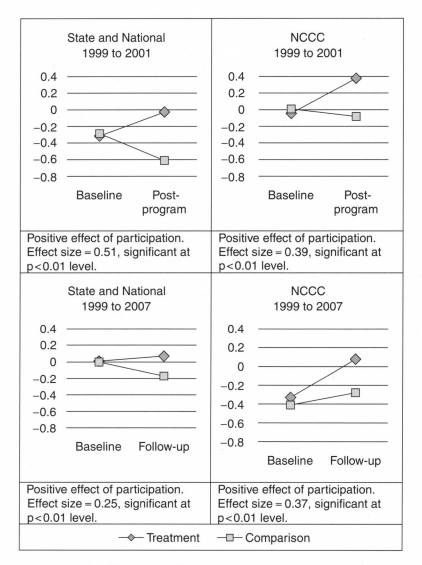

Figure 6.1. Connection to community

in reported connection to community. Among participants in State and National programs, older members gained in their connection to community. Here, again, the findings mirror some of the results reported in the analysis of civic engagement and personal growth: Those who had prior volunteering experience did not gain in the area of connection to community as much as those who had no prior volunteering experience. Increased connection is thus easier to achieve when someone comes into national service without having had prior service experience. We found a connection between planning and connectedness to community: The more participants were able to plan their service activities, the more gains they experienced in the area of connection to community.[4] When controlling for program-level factors, faith-based organizations increased members' connection to community more than organizations not based on religion. This is an interesting result given that one might expect faith-based organizations to be more inward and believer-focused in their work. In practice, a religious dimension simply deepens the broader connectedness of the member to the community. Members enrolled in larger AmeriCorps programs— programs enrolling larger numbers of members per service site—increase in their connection to community compared to smaller programs. Among participants in NCCC programs, neither member demographic characteristics nor program experiences are related to postprogram perception of connection to their community.

One other question we pondered was whether social capital flowed from family background rather than from service experience. We thus examined whether AmeriCorps members came from families who had high levels of social capital. Forty-two percent of AmeriCorps members and 38 percent of nonparticipants reported that their family was very strongly connected to their neighborhood. Forty-six percent of AmeriCorps members reported that their family was very strongly connected to the schools they attended, compared to 41 percent of nonparticipants. Thus, while there was some difference in social capital entering the program, the differences were modest.

Data from the VISTA study also provide evidence of the relationship between participation in national service and development of social capital networks. In the decades since they served in the program, VISTA members maintained many of the connections they established while enrolled. Since leaving VISTA, 43 percent had stayed in contact with their fellow VISTA volunteers and 24 percent had stayed in contact with their VISTA team leader or immediate supervisor. Beyond the immediate work team, 12 percent of former VISTA members reported staying in touch with program administrators, and 17 percent had stayed in contact with service site administrators. Because many VISTA volunteers were thrust into complex situations and given only minimal training, mentorship was important as members learned by doing. Thirty percent of former members reported that they had stayed in contact with someone who served as their mentor during their VISTA service.[5] Remarkably, 28 percent reported that they had stayed in contact with former clients who had received VISTA services.

When it comes to ongoing networks and belief in the power of individuals to make a difference in communities, former and near VISTA members reflect similar patterns. Respondents were asked about the frequency with which they talk to or visit with their immediate neighbors. Sixteen percent of former VISTA members reported talking to their neighbors every day, while 30 percent reported several times a week. Near VISTA members reported a similar frequency of connection to their neighbors. When respondents were asked how much impact they think they have in making their community a better place to live, 47 percent of near members and 44 percent of former members reported they have a big impact. Forty-three percent of former members and 38 percent of near members reported they have a moderate impact.

Trust is a critical ingredient in social capital.[6] It allows relationships to form and patterns of cooperation to emerge in communities. Trust makes getting work done easier and it represents a critical bank of resources on which communities can draw in times of stress and need. When asked if people in general are trustworthy, a majority of former and near VISTA members reported that people can be trusted (72 percent and 70 percent, respectively). Eighteen percent of former VISTA members and 22 percent of near members stated that they "can't be too careful" when it comes to trusting people. Both groups reported high levels of trust in neighbors. Sixty-five percent of former VISTA members reported that they trust their neighbors a great deal, the same percentage as near members. Twenty-nine percent of former members and 29 percent of near members reported they somewhat trust their neighbors. Fifty-seven percent of former VISTA members reported that they trust their police a great deal, while 60 percent of near members reported that they have high trust in their local police force. However, these patterns of high trust do not apply to government. Only 2 percent of former VISTA members and 3 percent of near members placed a high amount of trust in the federal or national government to do what is right.[7]

Due to limitations related to sampling, the VISTA data does not allow for testing the statistical significance of these trust effects. However, a question included in the AmeriCorps survey in 2007 (not included in the short-term postprogram survey) about the respondents' general level of social trust is pertinent. When asked whether they believe that other people can be trusted, there was no significant difference between the Ameri-Corps State and Local treatment and comparison groups. This is disappointing for those who are deeply committed to the vision of national service as a healer of rifts and a builder of social trust. After eight years of other experiences, a year of community service does not contribute to greater levels of social trust. For NCCC members, we did discover a social trust benefit. A year of living in close quarters and working together built a significant and lasting reservoir of social trust (see Figure 6.2). This effect

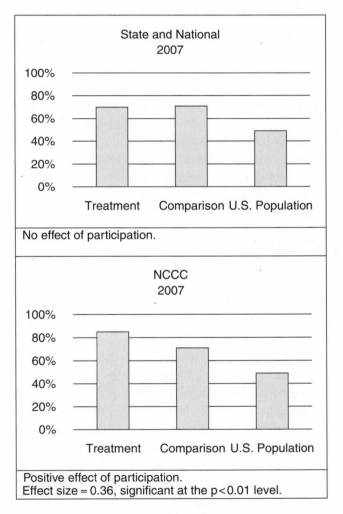

Figure 6.2. Social trust

might be attributable to the intensive nature of NCCC work, which requires a great deal of collaboration and communication.

Constructive Group Dynamics

The development and persistence of social capital requires individuals to work well in groups. As solutions to community problems are sought, coalitions, teams, associations, and groups of all kinds must work cohesively together if progress is to be made. About half the AmeriCorps programs have their members serve in teams, and many programs devote considerable time to the building of group skills through member development and reflection. Data from the AmeriCorps longitudinal study allowed us to examine group behavior from two perspectives: (1) constructive group interactions and (2) constructive personal behavior in groups. Constructive interaction in groups is a series of behaviors such as including team members, avoiding favoritism, and working out conflicts among individual team members.[8] These outcomes are critical components to successful team dynamics and building social capital.[9]

Measured one year and eight years after completing AmeriCorps, the first construct, constructive group interactions, tracked the frequency with which respondents reported being in group settings in which people discussed issues and shared ideas, involved everyone and avoided favoritism, disagreed with one another without fear, and took time to work out any conflicts. The questions all aimed at capturing the extent to which AmeriCorps members felt the group interactions they experienced were characterized by openness, consideration, and tolerance. In both State and National and NCCC—over both the short term and long term—we found no significant difference between those who had served and those who had not. (See Figure 6.3.)

To probe this issue further, we turned to the second construct, constructive personal behavior in groups, which included a battery of questions about the actual behavior of members and nonmembers in group settings. Respondents were asked how often they did each of the following: tried to understand the ideas and opinion of others before stating their own, presented their ideas without criticizing those of others, encouraged different points of view in groups, considered all points of view before forming an opinion or making a decision, encouraged the participation of others, and helped find solutions when problems arose. Constructive per-

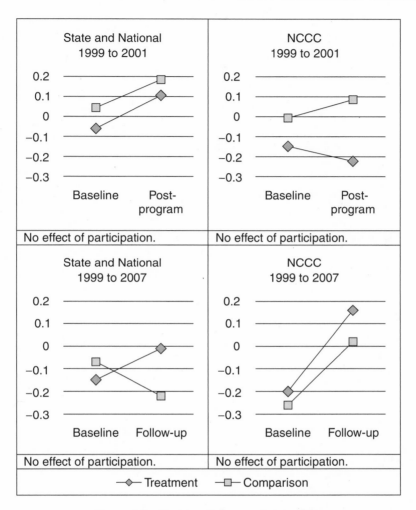

Figure 6.3. Constructive group interactions

sonal behavior in groups thus measures individuals' behavior in situations where they must interact with others while trying to get something done. Again, over the short run across both programs, we found no significant effect of service on constructive behavior in groups. Over the long run, there was a small improvement for State and National members of marginal significance. (See Figure 6.4.)

Looking at the short-term results in more detail, we found some differences in the two group behavior outcomes based on State and National

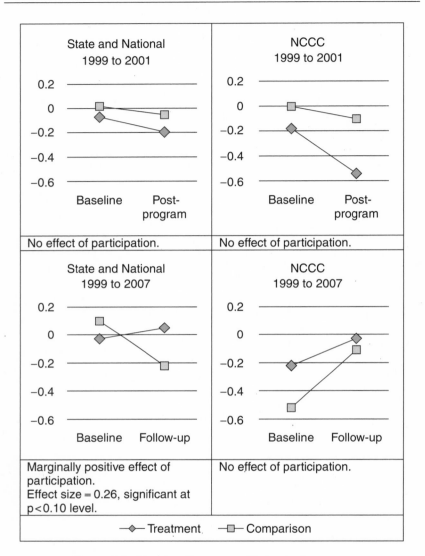

Figure 6.4. Constructive personal behavior in groups

member characteristics. African Americans, Hispanics, and those of other races did not gain in either of the constructive behavior outcomes, compared with whites. However, working with members from diverse backgrounds did lead to gains for both group behavior measures. Members serving in faith-based AmeriCorps programs had weaker gains in constructive group interactions compared to members serving in organizations not based on religion. Other significant differences worth noting include: College grads or members who obtained at least some college experience at the time of program enrollment showed increased gains in the area of constructive group interactions, compared with members who only had a high school diploma or less. For the outcome measuring constructive personal behavior in groups, at-risk youth gained more from service, as did members in programs that included working in teams. Members whose AmeriCorps State and National program placed priority on member development had weaker gains. For NCCC members, we noted that only a couple of participant and program characteristics appeared to influence group behavior outcomes: For constructive group interactions, there is a statistically significant negative relationship between religious attendance as a youth and constructive group behavior. However, it should be noted that members who attended services frequently in their youth also scored high on group behavior measures at baseline. Finally, past volunteering was negatively related to constructive personal behavior in groups.

In sum, the effects for both measures of group dynamics suggest that national service is not having much of an impact on developing the ability of members to function effectively in group situations. While the advocates of national service would like to believe that service builds interpersonal skills and an increased ability to work effectively with others, the data do not support a conclusion that this aspiration is being fulfilled.

Appreciation for Cultural and Ethnic Diversity

For most teams to function effectively, including those formed in AmeriCorps programs, participants must display an appreciation for diversity. The changing nature of the American workforce will require a sensitivity and appreciation of the varied backgrounds, identities, and perspectives that together make up the modern workplace. However, as Putnam points out,[10] while it is more difficult to establish *bridging networks,* those formed among members from diverse backgrounds, they are perhaps more valuable than *bonding networks,* which bring together individuals with similar characteristics. A critical aspiration of national service is that it will serve as a vehicle for the construction of bridging social capital, grounded in a deeper understanding of cultural and ethnic diversity.

During the time that participants in the AmeriCorps longitudinal study were enrolled, the CNCS encouraged leaders of the State and National program to recruit and enroll diverse members who reflected the many demographic and socioeconomic characteristics of the local populations within which the programs operated. The study measured members' appreciation for diversity through a construct that assessed agreement with the following items: if people from different backgrounds took the time to understand each other, there wouldn't be so many social problems; some of my friends are of different backgrounds than me; racism affects everyone; and multicultural teams can be stimulating and fun. (See Figure 6.5.)

When looking at the short-term results for State and National, we found that there were no significant gains in the area of appreciating cultural and ethnic differences. The program did not succeed in building the kind of tolerance and understanding that would be so valuable. When we looked at the way member and program characteristics shaped these outcomes, we found that among participants in State and National programs, those who were college graduates scored lower on the measure of appreciation of cultural and ethnic diversity than those who had a high school diploma (or less). When accounting for program-level characteristics, three findings stood out: (1) being in a faith-based organization was positively related to gaining in the area of appreciation of cultural and ethnic diversity; (2) the frequency of training was negatively related to appreciation of diversity; and (3) if members were given a chance to plan their service activities rather than simply being told what to do, they gained in their appreciation of cultural and ethnic diversity. That faith-based organizations did a better job of building appreciation of difference is interesting because some believe that the infusion of religion into service delivery cannot help but balkanize communities. In fact, a faith component seems to introduce a context within which appreciation of cultural and ethnic diversity can flourish. When interpreting the negative, significant effect of training, one speculative reading of this finding is that efforts to bring members together through structured training efforts appear to be less successful than approaches that give members the chance to define their own relationships with other members within service programs. It might also simply indicate that current training approaches are more than ineffective; they are counterproductive. By contrast, giving members control over their work appears to help open their minds.

The short-term NCCC results were striking. We found that participation results in a medium-sized statistically significant negative effect for

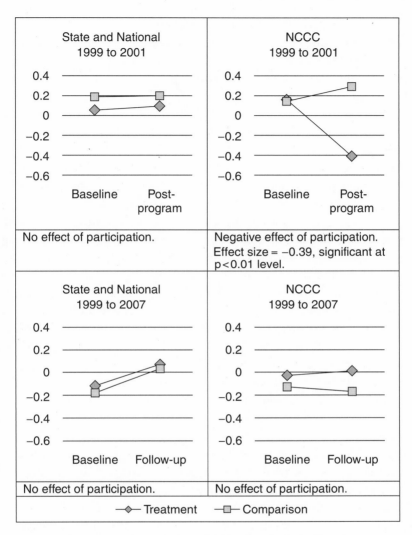

Figure 6.5. Appreciation of cultural and ethnic diversity

this outcome (effect size = −.39). On average, the NCCC treatment group became less positive in their appreciation for diversity during their participation in the program, while the comparison group's mean score did not change significantly. Given the unexpected nature of this result—the only significant negative finding in the entire study—we need to explore some possible explanations.

First, this negative finding on appreciation of diversity resonates with the pattern of difficulty with constructive group behavior in the NCCC that is described earlier. On a daily basis, the intensity of the NCCC experience is high—members live and work together, away from home for almost a year. They work in teams with individuals who do not know each other prior to their meeting on the NCCC campus. Members do not have a voice in choosing the teams to which they are assigned. While on extended periods spent away from their regional campus, they live together in even closer proximity in a variety of circumstances—camping in state parks, cramped with little personal space in church or school basements, or with even more rudimentary shelter while serving at disaster or emergency sites. Living conditions are generally far from optimal. The harsh nature of their service experience may therefore include challenges that feed interpersonal conflicts by putting special pressures on members. We suspect that these stressful environmental challenges can easily shorten fuses and create conflicts that may lead to short-term disillusionment with the reality of working within diverse groups. One might question whether it is reasonable to expect that such experiences would promote tolerance and understanding for anyone, let alone relatively inexperienced young adults who enrolled in the NCCC.

Another possible explanation for this finding may be found in social identity theory, which holds that individuals categorize or classify themselves in specific ways in relation to what they perceive as the classification systems in use around them.[11] Through a process of social comparison, individuals who are deemed similar to the person forming a social identity are categorized and labeled as the "in-group," while persons who are different are labeled part of the "out-group." The consequences of this process of self-categorization can be ethnocentrism and stereotyping.[12] The stereotyped perceptions of out-group members can be amplified by identification with the in-group. In all these cases, social identity theory predicts that formation of an in-group will substantially heighten suspicion and separation from the out-group. NCCC members may construct strong "in-groups" because members live and work in extremely close proximity to one another.[13] This dynamic may lead to challenges in the form of tension among NCCC members and citizens in the community where members serve. We suspect that these challenges may lead to short-term disillusion with the concept of working in diverse groups,[14] which is reflected in the present analysis.

One other fact requires acknowledgment. As a whole, the NCCC members were much less diverse than their counterparts in the State and National program. Members participating in the NCCC program are between the ages of eighteen and twenty-six, while members in State and National programs are between seventeen and eighty-eight years of age. NCCC programs are less ethnically diverse in comparison to State and National programs. Thus, there may not be a "critical mass" of members diverse in life experiences or ethnicity to allow for an appreciation of diversity to develop. Without sufficient member diversity, the NCCC may encourage the development of bonding social capital rather than the more complex and elusive bridging social capital.[15]

The one encouraging result is that the negative effect in the area of diversity disappears after eight years. After NCCC members have years of life and work experiences, the negative effect is no longer present. NCCC members achieve a small positive but statistically insignificant gain in the area of appreciating cultural and ethnic diversity compared to the comparison group. Still, the findings from the NCCC analysis raise questions about whether it is reasonable to expect positive changes in appreciation for diversity from the intensive residential and close-proximity service model.

Social Networks

We had one limited opportunity to study how friendship patterns might be altered by service. In the short postprogram supplemental survey conducted three years after exit from the program, former AmeriCorps participants and nonparticipants were asked about the closeness of their circles of friends. In addition, measures were created to understand how close the people in the respondents' friendship networks were to each other.[16] Ironically, the comparison group had closer networks of friends as compared to former AmeriCorps members ($\chi^2 = 10.7$, p < .05). It is important to understand that 31 percent of AmeriCorps members moved away from their community to join the program and may not have been as in touch with their network of friends as nonparticipants were.[17]

AmeriCorps members and nonmembers varied in other areas of their social networks. Both AmeriCorps participants and nonparticipants have similar percentages of friends in their social networks who are employed and who attend the same school as the respondent. Some unique characteristics of AmeriCorps members' social networks are that they are slightly older and more educated than the social networks of nonparticipants. Furthermore, AmeriCorps members have known their friends slightly longer and they tend to consider friends within their social network to be mentors. Two-thirds of the friendship networks among former AmeriCorps members who served in the NCCC program were limited to persons of the same race as the respondent, while the friendship networks of participants from State and National programs were more racially heterogeneous.

To take a deeper look at social capital construction, our interviews with VISTA members included many questions about the extent to which they had built strong social networks and friendships through service and whether they had continued to build these networks throughout their lives. National service programs take people from across the country and inject them into new and challenging contexts with the goal of building social capital. Tolerance is a critical precursor to the forging of friendships and connections that are so important to the maintenance of social capital.[18] The experience of difference and the challenge of becoming more tolerant may be related to the newness of the community in which the volunteer is placed or it may be connected to the experience of working with other volunteers in teams. Exposure to people and places that are outside the comfort zone of the volunteer can have one of two effects. It can disorient and alienate the volunteer and lead some to abandon service if the cultural disconnect is too great. It may, however, change the volunteer's worldview and lead to a greater understanding of others. The VISTA volunteers we spoke with, particularly those who served in the 1960s and 1970s, often reported that the experience made them less judgmental and forged deep connections to people living in poverty.

VISTA experiences are conditioned by the political context in which they unfold. Nadine's experience occurred near the apex of social and racial tensions in the United States. VISTA thrust her into an environment with high levels of distrust and even anger. Part of doing the work of a VISTA volunteer is a willingness to build bridges and reach out to people that Nadine never would have encountered otherwise. She recalled the time of her service: "In 1967, the biggest race riot in Milwaukee occurred and it was the summer. I worked for the Department of Corrections and I would go to all the kids who were at foster care; someone from the state had to go to all the doctors' appointments with them, to buy clothing, everything. And I was a student intern, I guess it was called . . . I was in the inner city all day long and there was a curfew at five o'clock and I had to make sure to be in." Beyond working with a curfew, Nadine recalled the mood of the times: "There was a lot of tension, a lot of stress in the community, and of course it didn't help that people had prejudice. My parents just were not happy that I was doing this. I really felt strongly that our generation was responsible for helping to turn things around, and that things weren't going to change unless we took responsibility."

While volunteers may initially view VISTA as being about getting concrete tasks accomplished in communities, its real value often resided in the process. Nadine learned about listening, searching for a way to make a connection with people, and honoring the felt needs of community members as the starting point for effective community action: "I think one of the things that was exciting about our project [was] the whole concept of listening to what community people were needing. We didn't go in with this idea like we're going to do this or that. We just went to the community center where leaders in the community were, talked with people and their neighbors, and asked what's important, what worries you?" Listening to others and not projecting their own values and expectations is challenging for volunteers, many of whom come with strong commitments and beliefs. Nadine made friends in the community based on her listening skills and she soon built a strong network of connections throughout the neighborhood. For Nadine, the process of accepting and trusting the truth and authenticity of another person's representation of their community's problems was a critical lesson of VISTA: "That's how we came up with some of the things that we worked on and that was exciting . . . I think I've used that for the rest of my life."

Eliza was raised on a Minnesota dairy farm and had what she described as an idyllic childhood. Hers was a sheltered life and she reported seeing no ethnic or racial diversity in her community as a child. Eliza's main recollection of discrimination was the ridicule that was heaped on poor people in her small town, where hard work was seen as the solution to all problems. When Eliza encountered a black person for the first time—an exchange student from Africa who spoke to her school group—she recalled checking the back of his shirt collar to see if his skin color had rubbed off. During her childhood, she was active in community service projects through the 4-H Club. Trained as a licensed practical nurse, Eliza wanted to join the Peace Corps but was unsure about the safety of traveling to another country without a companion. Despite her parents' protests, she joined and served in VISTA after seeing an ad in a nursing magazine. She wanted to experience life outside Minnesota and was eventually placed in rural Arkansas.

Working with a retired eighty-five-year-old doctor, she and another VISTA volunteer operated a medical clinic for local people twice a month. Eliza made home visits and organized outreach programs. In her work, she encountered desperate poverty and need. She developed a network of friends while on-site with other Arkansas VISTA volunteers. Thinking back to the first few weeks of her experience, Eliza recounted how her training was essential because it taught her "how to communicate with people, and how to trust people."[19] She also learned through her VISTA training "different ways of understanding the cultures that we were going to be working with. We did exercises [in which] we would have to be blindfolded and trust the person that was our partner. We would go to downtown Dallas, Texas, with these blindfolds on," and then working with a partner, "we had to eat and walk the streets, take the buses." After this training, Eliza dove into her work and felt as though she had gained a much broader perspective and a greater level of understanding of inequality: "VISTA taught me to speak out for other people, and to make disadvantaged people my priority. The experiences with other VISTAs really opened up my worldview, more than anything ever has. It was my first experience in knowing what went on in the rest of the world." Eliza ended up building strong friendships within the VISTA group and eventually within the small community where she worked.

While we sought to learn from interviewees about their VISTA experiences, we also asked regarding their current concerns about society and culture and how they might or might not be connected with the VISTA work they did. Iris grew up in St. Louis and served in VISTA in her hometown. She worked with children who had severe learning disabilities, mostly organizing experiential learning opportunities for them. This work continued experience she had with children in Head Start and was the catalyst for greater involvement with education, field trips, and nonprofit work later in her life. Iris helped start a multicultural school when her son was young and she could not find good options for his education. When we talked with her, Iris was thinking about what her involvement in the community would be over the next few years until her husband retired. Three decades after VISTA, she reflected on her biggest concerns and aspirations for society and her focus was on bridge building and acceptance: "I think justice, you know, just basic justice and fairness, and tolerance. It feels like we've become so intolerant of people who are different from us, people who don't think the same way we do. I think there's so much more gray than there is black and white, and it feels like people are so strident both ways that there's just no room for [compromise], gentleness, or caring. It scares me. Everyone is just so angry all the time, and I feel like that's just a destructive emotion. I wish really we could not be so angry, you know, so uncompromising." VISTA showed Iris a constructive way to act, and ultimately left her wanting a more accepting and supportive world. Today, when Iris looks back on VISTA, she sees the seeds of a lifelong commitment to being less harsh, less judgmental of others, and, in the end, more tolerant.

VISTA influenced Ronald's life significantly. While he was involved in antiwar and civil rights work in college, Ronald developed a passion for working with communities during his time in VISTA. He was an architect for a housing development organization in upstate New York, learning the important lesson that he needed to build what would be useful to the people who would live in the home, not what the architect might think was interesting. VISTA training laid the groundwork by teaching Ronald "people" skills that have lifelong relevance to someone who had technical skills but not much more: "A lot of it was the kind of labor organizing training that you get from Alinsky. How do you begin conversations with strangers? How do you show respect? How do you contact people? What are the legal levers you can pull? What should one avoid doing? Those kinds of things. It was really practical hands-on stuff, along with a bit of consciousness raising. And anger mongering, of course."

On many occasions during his time with VISTA, while working with clients who had little money, Ronald would listen to clients describe their ideal home. Often they would ask for layouts and finishes that Ronald knew were less than optimal. However, he let a lot of small things go rather than trying to get his clients to make what he knew to be the smart design decisions. Ronald had already decided on a career in architecture before entering VISTA. The experience still influenced the kind of architecture he practiced and the way he perceived his role in the community. Most important of all, exposure to people who have different tastes and different perceptions of their relative needs enhanced Ronald's tolerance: "I think [VISTA] cured me of being judgmental. I just can't a priori say that's wrong. It's funny; it made me aware of how I can know somebody else without really knowing them well, and how dangerous it is to presume you do. It's I think made me able to operate in a lot of different realms. I lost all sense of pretense, I think, in VISTA. I got to prefer the gritty to the glittering." Accepting others who simply see the world differently or who have different life goals has been liberating for Ronald. Rather than trying to convert everyone to his view, he has learned to be tolerant and accept difference.

Social capital may manifest itself in terms of increased trust and teamwork. By serving those who are less well-off and who are suspicious of outsiders seeking to render aid, VISTA volunteers may be able to increase trust in communities. Trust is important because it is necessary for so many other things, ranging from collaboration to communication. In addition, the nature of VISTA service may also build teamwork skills, helping young people learn how to work together on complex projects and get along with others. The ability to work in teams is often critical in VISTA placements where projects are long and require the effort of many to reach fruition. After a sheltered life, VISTA was a breakout strategy for Hannah. The program thrust her into a situation that was totally alien and demanding to her. Part of the initial alienation that members often experience stems from the fact that many assignments are in isolated areas, where VISTA volunteers stick out like sore thumbs. Hannah was surprised at what she found: "The VISTA place where I was stationed was 70 percent Appalachian and it was in Kentucky . . . The steel mills closed down. All of these people were stuck in the city and they were poor and there was nowhere to go. So the cash registers were full of food stamps rather than money and you saw a lot of poor people around. We unfortunately saw a lot of that. But what was important was there was a movement going on to take control of the city by the people, to build it up and make it a good thing." For Hannah, exposure to rural poverty was an eye-opener, which made it possible to see her own circumstances very differently.

While some VISTA members reflected on their experience primarily in terms of what they were able to accomplish for others, Hannah saw a clear link between her experience and the way she understood the world later in life. The VISTA experience gave this volunteer a perspective on poverty and inequality that many people do not have. Participation rendered poverty and need more real, while its causes were shown to be more complex: "People would talk to me about economic issues and I would have something to say because I had experience that other people might not have had. I was enriched, I think, by that experience. I hear ignorant things like 'people make their own choices' and 'they do this to themselves.' Yes, sometimes that is true, but sometimes there are the children of a crack addict in the inner city, and they do not do that to themselves." For Hannah, VISTA increased both her tolerance and her empathy for those less well-off. She became less judgmental and more open-minded when it came to understanding that life outcomes are not always equal and that not all differences are a function of character faults.

Sometimes the work of VISTA volunteers focused on building social capital in the form of new relationships within the community. One VISTA volunteer who served in the late 1970s, Benjamin, recalled playing the role of a matchmaker in his community: "They would give me lists of people that needed a big brother or a big sister, and that was my job to try and find big brothers and big sisters for these people." In the interim, as the VISTA volunteer, he would "spend a little time with them; maybe take them bowling and that sort of thing. So I would have to go over my list and try and match up people. They might say, 'Well Jane says that she wants a big sister. Tommy, he would like somebody to play checkers with.'" Beyond this sort of community relationship brokering, Benjamin actually tried to make connections among all the various civic groups: "I had a projector and a screen and all this kind of thing. I would go out and I would make presentations to the various civic organizations in town like the Elks. And, so, I would make a presentation in the morning, then I would come back and I would have to write an article for the newspaper on what we were doing. I would have to call up some more civic organizations to schedule some appointments for more presentations." To cap off this network and relationship-building process, Benjamin recounted that he spent a fair amount of time organizing parties for the community so that people could get to know one another better on a personal level.

In the end, the qualitative and quantitative data suggest that national service builds connections between people and between people and communities. The results for connection to community were strong across programs and over time. While we found that members were not acquiring usable group interpersonal skills upon completion of AmeriCorps or the NCCC, there were some gains in the area of social trust for those in the more intensive residential programs. Participation in the NCCC led members to have greater levels of social trust once time had passed and the service experience was contextualized against other work and life experiences. The most disappointing result was in the area of tolerance, where we found a significant short-term negative effect on appreciation of cultural and ethnic diversity among NCCC members. This troubling effect faded away over the long term, leading to no effect of the program—either positive or negative—on NCCC members.

Social capital can be a complex and elusive concept that incorporates the characteristics of both the individual and the community. It supports bonds of trust and reciprocity. For this reason, we placed the construct of social capital at the intersection of individual- and community-level effects in our general theory of change model for national service. AmeriCorps would dearly like to construct social capital through service, both as a way of supporting member development and as a way of building lasting community capacity. The evidence we examined suggests that the program is an imperfect but not implausible tool for social capital construction. National service creates not just a sense of connection to community but also a set of enduring friendships and relationships upon which the creation and maintenance of social capital ultimately depends. Still, more could be done to strengthen the program and ensure that these effects are amplified and made more consistent.

— 7 —

Public Work

"Getting things done" is the motto of the Corporation for National and Community Service (CNCS). This touchstone phrase, prominently featured on the stationery and materials of the CNCS, has focused attention on the public work that AmeriCorps, Volunteers in Service to America (VISTA), and other service programs accomplish.[1] These projects are the concrete and visible artifacts of national service and serve as proof that these programs do actually address real community problems. Traditionally, the CNCS has identified four main areas in which public work takes place: public safety, education, environment, and human needs. In addition, there is a crosscutting "other" category for work that either spans these four areas or is in allied areas. In its four main forms, public work serves as the most concrete and easy-to-explain rationale for national service, especially when researchers worry about the more difficult to assess objectives of promoting civic engagement, supporting personal growth, and increasing social capital.[2] When public work is done by AmeriCorps members, it can be seen by everyone and it leaves behind a trail of evidence in the form of community crime patrols, tutoring programs, park conservation and cleanup projects, and parent education classes.[3]

AmeriCorps' Models of Public Work

To understand the nature of the public work dimension of national service, we begin by presenting here four case studies, one in each of the four focal areas of service, to illustrate just how national service programs deliver on their claim of getting things done in communities. These cases are illustrative—and by no means exhaustive—of the many ways public work is carried out. In each of the accounts, the work started out clearly within one of the specified fields, but over time expanded into others. These accounts of local attempts to render concrete the charge of "getting things done" still provide real-world examples of how the nature of public work has been interpreted and rendered real in communities around the country.[4]

Addressing Education Needs

In Texas, things are "getting done" in the field of education. Literacy AmeriCorps-Bayou City is a program that helps Houston's adults improve their reading and writing skills.[5] The West Side of Houston has a number of high-poverty neighborhoods and has long been an underserved area. The East Side of Houston has many low-income areas, along with mostly older, established neighborhoods and pockets of upper-middle-class developments and gentrification. The area is diverse and its population includes white, African American, and Hispanic neighborhoods. In addition to a large number of homeless individuals, there are many parolees and probationers in the area. The Houston area job market has been good even during downturns, with many jobs available in food service, construction trades, health care, and the computer field. While entry-level job opportunities are abundant, many city residents are unable to participate in the labor force due to a lack of basic skills, low literacy, lack of transportation, language barriers, or criminal records that prevent individuals from being bonded.

The majority of literacy agencies in Houston belong to the Houston READ Commission (HRC), which includes approximately 137 partner agencies. The requirements for membership are that agencies be nonprofit and actively involved in literacy education. As members, agencies have access to monthly networking meetings with other literacy providers, training activities, technical assistance, fiscal agent services, mini grants, and other resources provided by HRC. Of the 137 member agencies, about 23 participate in the Literacy AmeriCorps program and have members placed on-site. The mission of Literacy AmeriCorps-Bayou City is "to engage individuals of diverse backgrounds as leaders in their communities and as effective providers of literacy and support services to adults and youth, so that they all have the opportunity to achieve their full potential." As such, the state program fits well into HRC's overall mission, which is "to enrich the lives of Houstonians and their families by helping them achieve their full potential through literacy." One of the top priorities of the AmeriCorps program is to provide increased literacy instruction in the community for parolees and probationers. By one estimate, there were at least 100,000 persons released from prison living in Houston.[6]

As the original umbrella group receiving AmeriCorps slots in Houston, the HRC staff works to allocate these slots to member agencies. From 1 September 2005 through 1 June 2006, fifty-three full-time literacy tutors were placed in thirty-six sites throughout Houston and Harris County. More than 47,000 service hours and tutoring was provided to over 1,334 adult learners and 375 families. Member agencies include community learning centers, missions and churches, family centers, elementary schools, women's centers, parole offices, correctional facilities, and other local community agencies. The agencies complete a member request form, which describes the agency and its need for AmeriCorps members, and the HRC chooses sites based primarily on need. Other criteria include having space for services, possessing some resources to support the members, providing supervision for members, and having the capacity to conduct on-site orientation for members. The HRC staff tends to take the word of applicants when it comes to how many AmeriCorps members they need. There is no elaborate preassessment of need, only a part of the application in which sites must detail how they will use each member. All sites sign a cooperative site agreement, which spells out their responsibilities. In recent years, the program has had an abundance of applications from agencies and has not been able to fulfill all requests.

The program recruits local residents from the neighborhoods where service activities take place. The HRC's goal is to recruit members who have graduated from community literacy programs. In general, they seek members each year who are over the age of seventeen, preferably with teaching or tutoring experience, and holding a high school diploma or general equivalency diploma (GED). The HRC prioritizes members who are newly released from the criminal justice system, with exceptions when it comes to those with histories or convictions related to violence, sexual assault, or abusive behavior. The program is marketed as an opportunity to gain work and literacy instruction experience as well as a way to give back to the community. At one point recently, the members had education levels ranging from a doctorate in math to less than a high school diploma, and four members did not have a GED or high school diploma. Approximately 50 percent had volunteer experience and all had some work experience. On average, 90 percent were African American, with most coming from the east and west sides of Houston. All of the members were full-time.

Like many other AmeriCorps programs that enroll disadvantaged people, the Literacy AmeriCorps program struggles to combat member dropout, which has averaged about 50 percent a year. A small number of members are terminated each year for disciplinary reasons. The main problem lies in the low living allowance paid to members and the burnout that can result from intensive engagement with the work. Members are expected to deliver 1,700 hours of work, and when they fall behind in their work schedule, they either give up or work harder. Some members have left the program because they found employment offering more generous pay. When members drop out, the program sometimes transfers a current member from another agency or the slot is left unfilled.

What is the exact nature of the work done by members in this large multiagency system? The program provides a variety of literacy services such as basic skills, English as a second language (ESL) and GED instruction, tutoring, some case management, family literacy, computer instruction, curriculum development, and learner recruitment. Members serve adults and youth in underserved urban areas of Houston. Thus, they work directly with clients through a full range of literacy programs, with supervision coming from the staff of the sponsoring agencies. Members are trained on how best to deliver these services.

To link up some of the work going on across the participating agencies, the HRC organizes some joint service activities. The members coordinated an all-day read-a-thon on Martin Luther King Jr. Day. The event resembled a carnival and was held in a local mall. It was attended by the AmeriCorps members and their families and friends, adult learners and their families, and interested people living in the area. Members constructed the booths needed for the event and began planning the activities during a team-building exercise months earlier. Activities included members reading books to children, face painting, puppet shows, a break-dancing show, and other activities that related to or promoted literacy. In addition, members spent a day working at the Houston Food Bank where they inspected, packed, sorted, and distributed food. Other joint service activities have included an AIDS walk and a Cinco de Mayo celebration, during which members helped raise community awareness of the importance of education by distributing and posting flyers and posters.

While community projects are part of the Literacy AmeriCorps program in Houston, the main element of the effort remains one-on-one tutoring and teaching. A typical example of the work that is done through these efforts is the project at Ruth's House. As part of Lutheran Social Services of the South, Ruth's House is located in a storefront office on a highway access road in a low-income area in north Houston. The agency provides a variety of services such as clothing, a food bank, literacy classes (GED, ESL, basic reading), job referrals, and assistance with rent, utilities, housing, and transportation. With a small staff, the agency struggles to meet the demand for its services. The addition of two AmeriCorps members enabled the agency to increase the number of literacy classes held on-site and to serve more students. The agency director is located on-site in the mission office, several feet from the desks of the members, and is responsible for their supervision. One member focuses on teaching GED classes, while the other member offers ESL instruction. In addition to the orientation provided on-site, the director is available to answer questions on a daily basis and provides regular training for members and staff in areas such as communication skills, anger management, and recognizing different learning styles. In many ways, this is a typical use of AmeriCorps members within the HRC system. The members add capacity to small local agencies and work alongside staff in key program areas. Program staff at Ruth's House and other participating agencies report that the AmeriCorps members have helped the majority of sponsoring agencies to provide more services and classes than they would have been able to offer otherwise. The program supervisor explained that the introduction of AmeriCorps members allowed their agency for the first time to achieve consistency in the delivery of their literacy services.

One reason why there has been a high level of satisfaction with the performance of members is that agencies in the HRC invest time and effort in preparing members for their service. Orientation includes eight days that focus on an overview of the AmeriCorps program and the HRC, member responsibilities, paperwork, leadership, diversity, contracts and compliance, team building, work styles, conflict resolution, journal writing, budgeting, and survival in AmeriCorps. Following this, members focus on literacy techniques in adult education, ESL and GED, how to work with adult learners, lesson planning, instructional methodology, classroom accountability, reporting, and discipline. Training is done individually, as well as in small and large group formats. Members also receive a manual containing all the materials covered during the orientation. Some members are ready to get into the classrooms as soon as training is completed, but some are still unsure of their skills and need support and coaching at the beginning of their service. In addition to orientation, the program requires sponsoring agencies to provide four to five days of initial site-specific training for its members. Once the members begin their work, they receive supervision and support from roving trainers and local agency field supervisors.

When national service is focused on education and literacy, it operates in a range of different ways. While the HRC program is a large-scale example of how AmeriCorps works to improve adult literacy, there are countless other educational initiatives driven by national service workers. Notable examples of school-based programs include Teach for America, which places recent college graduates in public school classrooms, and the national network of charter schools operated by the Knowledge Is Power Program (KIPP), which uses AmeriCorps to supplement its educational programs. In many of the cities in which it operates, City Year deploys its AmeriCorps volunteers in schools as classroom assistants and tutors to students. Early childhood education groups like Jumpstart also rely on AmeriCorps to boost their capacity. Across the many different educational domains in which national service operates, the one constant is that these efforts are focused on creating educational opportunities. And when public work is focused on creating opportunities, it reaches for one of the oldest and most universal goals.

Increasing Public Safety

While the idea of public work is broad and all-encompassing, one area where national service focuses a fair amount of community effort is public safety.[7] By engaging members in towns and cities struggling with crime and delinquency, national service programs have forged community partnerships aimed at solving visible and pressing problems. The forms of public safety interventions are many and varied. The Greater Holyoke Youth Services Corps (GHYSC), located in Holyoke, Massachusetts, began operations in 1995. In partnership with the Holyoke Police Department (HPD), the organization secured AmeriCorps support to meet the city's need for improved public safety. The GHYSC program, which focuses much of its attention on crime prevention, is committed to using corps members to serve the city through community policing and organizing community projects and safety initiatives. An additional objective of the program is to provide its members with opportunities to advance their educational and workplace skills. The GHYSC has tried to combine public work with personal growth objectives because Holyoke's economy has struggled as a result of the failure of the local paper industry. With the loss of jobs associated with an economic downturn, the program was designed from the start to curtail growing crime while giving young people a chance to gain work skills.

The Holyoke community is composed of a substantial number of low-income households, many of which rely on state and federal assistance. Holyoke has long suffered from a litany of urban problems that include poor city management, local citizen apathy, lack of resources, high crime and drug use rates, and a large number of gangs. According to the program director, William Hynes, these problems are exacerbated by the lack of local government representation for the large Hispanic population, which makes up approximately 25 percent of the total population of 44,000 people. AmeriCorps members have been thrust into this mix with the imperative to help turn things around by getting crime more under control.

This AmeriCorps program did not appear in a community bereft of other efforts to improve the quality of life. Other local programs that address the wide range of issues facing Holyoke include several Latino grassroots community organizations, which engage the community in gardening projects and neighborhood cleanups. These organizations also provide free programs to the public such as photography, martial arts, dance, computer training, and ESL. Before developing its national service program, the GHYSC worked with these organizations on a safe neighborhood grant from the U.S. Department of Housing and Urban Development (HUD) in which they jointly held community meetings to improve neighborhoods, gut buildings, and create community rooms.

The GHYSC is located in the center of Holyoke, just a block and a half from a nearby bus stop. Many members walk or take a bus to the program, and some drive. Project leaders drive members to projects in police vans donated by the police. A top priority for the GHYSC is to build its program into a model for other neighborhoods, to inspire residents, and to drive neighborhood change. Tapping the resources of the Police Department, the owners of apartment buildings, and local residents, the program strives to find ways to improve daily living conditions in Holyoke and to reverse some of the years of decline the area has endured. The nature of public safety work can be quite broad. The program in Holyoke was designed to include a range of activities that include after-school programs for children, juvenile diversion programs for first-time offenders, drug elimination programs, and community meetings.

Through its work with the Police Department, the GHYSC has developed a name for itself in the community as a program committed to making changes. Since its inception, a growing number of organizations have expressed interest in working with the program. Partners have included the Agricultural Center, the Council on Aging, the public school system, and the Holyoke Children's Museum. To increase their visibility and community involvement in Holyoke, the Youth Services Corps holds a one-day City Serve event in the fall, modeled after Boston's City Year serve-a-thon, which attracts up to 250 volunteers a year.

During its early years, the GHYSC received approximately half of its funding from the HPD through a block grant from its community policing program. One of the major objectives of the HPD's partnership with the GHYSC was to involve members in their community policing effort and ultimately enhance the HPD's outreach to the community. The community policing program includes the establishment of substations (community rooms located in a storefront, an apartment, or a room in an apartment or housing complex), assignment of a police officer to a community, and community meetings. The HPD provides members with forty hours of First Aid, CPR, and First Response Training, which lays the foundation for member activities with the HPD. Members spend ten hours a week in substations, usually in pairs, where they are immediately available to the community and where people can go to report a crime. Normally, HPD officers patrol the community in which they are assigned, leaving the responsibility of manning the substation to the corps members.

As part of their duties at the substations, members organize activities for neighborhood youth and encourage them to talk to the police about any suspicious behaviors they have seen. They also organize community meetings for the residents to learn how to implement crime watches and hold gang awareness workshops with police, who occasionally give canine demonstrations for the community. The HPD and the GHYSC hold joint crime watch community meetings and make presentations on crime reporting. Getting residents to attend these and other community events involving police has been difficult, though. Some residents are concerned about appearing to be closely allied with the police. This all points to a broader challenge for community service in the area of public safety: While volunteers can add capacity to local law enforcement agencies, the affiliation can make it harder to build and maintain community trust and participation. For the Holyoke police, the relationship is largely beneficial. By involving AmeriCorps in community policing, members provide a link to the community that traditional patrols cannot always establish. Most corps members are bilingual and are able to effectively communicate the nature of the changes that the HPD is making in the community to improve safety and decrease drug use and gang activity. In return, members learn the value of responsibility and being resourceful, while also having a chance to gain work experience and advance their education.

Members work with first-time offenders on Saturdays and do community service activities with them, including neighborhood cleanups, making cards and cupcakes for the elderly, and helping with other community projects that arise. Over time, the GHYSC has expanded the services it offers and is now addressing other public needs. Feeling some frustration at the amount of "downtime" associated with working at Police Department substations, members decided to seek out additional sponsors to increase and broaden their activities. Six new projects were developed, including providing elementary school classroom assistance to students in math and science, outreach programs for the elderly, conservation and gardening projects, and after-school programs for kids. In addition to these sustained efforts, members also take part in a whole range of short-term efforts that involve one or two days of service. In addition, within the police substations, members volunteer on Friday to provide entertainment for children in their early teens. Events include movies followed by discussions, organizing a dominos tournament, and a dance. Even though the GHYSC was founded as a public safety program, it has expanded its work into the areas of education, environment, and human needs. In this sense, the traditional categories of public work are somewhat artificial since many programs operate across boundaries and have multiple programmatic elements. The program in Holyoke is grounded in public safety but works through many different areas, in part because it must recruit a large and diverse group of young people each year, many of whom need to be engaged in a range of challenging activities to hold their attention and commitment.

To recruit members, the GHYSC places ads in area publications and local papers, on radio stations and community bulletin boards. The two most successful draws have come from flyers hung in local barbershops and from a local church whose pastor has referred members to the program. Recruiting for the program has been challenging. While the GHYSC receives plenty of applications for the twenty positions it seeks to fill each year, many applicants cannot meet the requirements of having a clean police record, showing up on time, and being able to work in a team. Full-time members receive the benefits of health care and vouchers for day care that pay for 75 percent of the cost. Members also receive two long-sleeve and two short-sleeve AmeriCorps shirts, two pairs of pants, and two AmeriCorps sweatshirts. Leaders at the GHYSC believe that the biggest draw of the program is the offer to assist members in obtaining their GED and the education award that is conferred on those who complete their service. Members can attend classes during their normal service time for two hours each weekday.

Even though these perks are attractive, the GHYSC's rate of attrition has been high over time. Corps members have quit because of in-staff fighting that polarized members, personal issues such as needing to care for younger siblings or their own children, the need for a higher level of income, or simply because the program was too stressful. To avoid problems, GHYSC staffers look at the applicant's motivation, try to assess if the education award would be used, and if the applicant is inspired to change and grow. Many of the applicants who are chosen are interested in a career with the Police Department, and the program can provide the experience and an education award to help them reach that goal. However, the program has not seen many members enter the Police Department, which requires a college or associate's degree, though several have gone on to study criminal justice. At one time, two candidates were on the waiting list for jobs and another member had an administrative position with the Department.

To foster personal development, members write personal goals for the year, such as obtaining a GED, developing a resume, getting a better job after the program, and improving their skills. Within the first week of the program, staff and members attend a three-day off-site retreat where they participate in icebreakers, team-building exercises, and a communication workshop. The members also set group goals, which include doing a good job, showing the community that youth can make a difference, increasing acceptance of diversity, and reducing conflict. Later in the year, another retreat is held where everyone reflects on progress toward personal and group goals. Member development also includes keeping a personal journal. Journals are intended to promote reflection about what the members have learned, how they are managing various situations, and whether and how they are reaching their goals.[8]

One thing is apparent about the program in Holyoke. Though it began anchored in public safety, the work has evolved so that it cuts across the four fields of public work. Members are doing more than just working directly with the police on crime issues. To be sure, public work is completed that benefits the community and that aims to eradicate the conditions that lead to crime in the first place. The program has a second distinctive feature, however. It also crosses the boundary between the competing conceptions of national service as public work and as personal growth. While members are focused on getting things done for Holyoke, a fair amount of time and effort is devoted to building their personal skills and awareness. There is also a social capital dimension to some of the work, in that it seeks to build bridges and connections in a community bereft of trust. In this sense, the story of Holyoke's national service program shows how service is hard to contain in neat programmatic and conceptual boundaries.

Protecting the Environment

The Maryland Conservation Corps (MCC) is a statewide program initiated in 1984 as a summer-only residential program as part of the governor's Save the Bay program. At that time, the Chesapeake Bay watershed was badly polluted and in need of restoration. In 1992, the MCC expanded to include a year-round, nonresidential program aimed at focusing young people's work on reversing the environmental damage in the bay. Funding for the year-round program continued under AmeriCorps.

Members are organized into six crews across different "curriculums" that reflect local environmental needs: tree forestry, wildlife, and fisheries management crews work in state forests, fish hatcheries, and wildlife management areas. Members learn forestry management and understand wildlife habitats. Service sites are in rural areas in the northern and northwestern parts of the state at the following locations: Potomac/Garrett, Elk Neck, and Morgan Run State Parks. The Chesapeake Bay Restoration crew conducts bay enhancement projects to assist in the restoration of the bay. Members specialize in watershed systems and conduct various surveys, assessments, and plantings. Service sites are throughout the watershed area, although the crew operates from a base on the outskirts of Annapolis. The Natural Resources crew is based at Greenwell State Park. They provide various projects, such as building and marking trails, restoring campgrounds, and other maintenance and light construction tasks. The Tidewater crew on the Lower Eastern Shore involves corps members in the tidewater ecosystem and in related environmental projects. This crew also designs and implements environmental projects that draw in local schoolchildren.

The eleven-month program operates much like a traditional youth conservation corps. Each year, the program seeks to enroll approximately fifty young people ages seventeen to twenty-five in its program. The program has tended to attract educationally and economically at-risk youth with little or no postsecondary education who are looking for a job. More recently, member demographics have shifted somewhat with about one-third of the members possessing college degrees. The majority of them are young women and the program is beginning to attract young people interested in environmental careers and in participating in community service. Under an agreement with the Department of Justice, the MCC has recruited from the state's boot camps, and one year enrolled five young men who had completed that program. These young men were the only nonwhite members enrolled in the program. The changes in member demographics have important implications for the scope and nature of member development activities. Each work crew is under the supervision of a crew chief, and some of the larger crews also have an assistant crew chief, often an MCC alumnus.

The MCC does not operate in isolation. It is embedded in a set of connected programs and initiatives. The state commission on service convenes regional, cross-program swearing-in sessions for AmeriCorps members and promoted the concept of the United Corps of Maryland (UCOM). Under that framework, three traditional youth corps—the MCC and two Baltimore-based programs—conduct joint training sessions and occasional joint service projects. Some MCC staff and members have expressed frustration regarding their involvement with UCOM. This is because the joint service projects have been conservation-related due to the need to find a project and a space large enough to accommodate the couple hundred members that comprise the three programs. As a consequence, much of the work connected to developing and managing the joint service projects has fallen disproportionately on the MCC. Moreover, members in the other two programs are primarily engaged in direct service that does not require extensive physical activity. These volunteers tend to be less interested in the outdoors and are not as ready to engage in physically demanding work.

Most Maryland AmeriCorps programs start with a statewide "launch" in which all of Maryland's members take the oath at the same time, with as many of them as possible in a central location.[9] Historically, members from all three UCOM programs begin their year of service with a week-long residential "fall project," typically taking place in a state park. One year, the project was in Swallow Falls / Herrington Manor State Park, home to Maryland's last remaining stand of old-growth hemlocks and white pine. Members were organized in cross-program teams comprising six or seven individuals. Under the direction of park managers and rangers, they completed a variety of projects that included repairing a trail damaged by erosion, building a railing along a sheer section, installing directional signs, and building a six-sided educational kiosk. The MCC also has occasional opportunities to interact with the Maryland-based National Civilian Community Corps (NCCC) programs, often on joint service projects that are usually conservation-focused. MCC members receive navy blue MCC hard hats, T-shirts, and sweatshirts from the program, along with project-specific safety gear. As state employees, they are also covered by medical insurance. The eleven-month program allows for weeklong breaks in December, February, and April.

The majority of the MCC's projects are conducted for the Department of Natural Resources (DNR) in state parks and other recreational facilities. Roughly a third of the work is fee-for-service. On these projects, a local sponsor pays for the crew's wages and materials in exchange for having the work completed. The MCC only agrees to fee-for-service projects that provide opportunities for member education and development. Sometimes, sponsors overestimate the time it will take crews to complete the project, and will pay for two weeks of crew time when the crew ends up needing only a few days to complete the assignment. When the project is completed in less time than planned, the work team still feels that it has to provide the labor hours purchased by the sponsor, and members occasionally perform less-interesting "make-work" projects, identified at the last minute by the sponsor. As this work sometimes frustrates and bores members, the situation ends up highlighting the tensions between getting things done and member development.

An important part of the MCC program involves taking a project from conceptualization to completion. One example of this kind of project was a stream survey effort that the Chesapeake Bay Restoration and Morgan Run crews contributed to on alternate days in Thurmont Mountain State

Park. The goal of the project was to collect detailed information about one of the streams feeding into the Chesapeake watershed. The information was then fed into a computer and monitored over time. The stream survey was an important part of the main project. Prior to starting it, members received two weeks of training from DNR biologists. During downtime, the team also did a series of smaller work projects, such as pulling stumps, clearing wood, and turning it into a usable firewood pile. Members met at their base at 7:00 a.m. and headed via the MCC van to the service site. After a day of hard work, they packed up to return to their base around 3:00 p.m. "Base" was a house in the middle of a state park outside of Annapolis. The house, previously occupied by a park ranger, served as an informal meeting space for the team. It also provided office space for the crew leaders, who spent most of their time at the base instead of at their smaller work spaces at the DNR.

The MCC's mission statement is direct and focused on its core objective, which—interestingly enough—is not defined as getting things done, but rather as developing the capacity of young people: "To provide for the youth and citizens of Maryland opportunities for personal growth and hands-on learning experiences through community and conservation service." Thus, even though the MCC is clearly doing public work within the environment category, public work is considered to be the vehicle through which personal growth is promoted. Public work in the field of conservation is the means, not the end, of service. Not everyone shares this exact conceptualization. The AmeriCorps program is viewed quite differently within the Department of Natural Resources, where it is seen as a cost-effective way to provide services that would probably not be completed by regular DNR staff. This difference in perception and conceptualization underlies the fundamental conflict of visions that often surround national service. One person's program of youth development and identity formation is another person's cost-effective service delivery mechanism.

Member development is still a critical objective of the MCC. The first day of each project is spent on environmental education related to the conditions of a specific service site focusing on its history, its ecological importance, and its current uses. Additional ongoing training is often provided throughout the course of the project. There are group training days for all members approximately once a month. Issues covered include teamwork, public speaking, workplace harassment, and conducting a job search. All members receive training in first aid, cardiopulmonary resuscitation

(CPR), drug avoidance, and AIDS prevention/awareness. Crew-specific training is provided to individual teams by DNR staff and consultants, based on the nature of the service projects undertaken. In practice, this means that the bay crew is briefed on wetland assessment and soil erosion control while the forestry crew hears about disease and pest control. The program also provides training that is indirectly related to, but not necessary for, accomplishing the service activities. For example, the Bay Restoration team underwent cold-water rescue training, which involved wearing wet suits and practicing to save drowning victims in the frigid waters of the Chesapeake.

Crew chiefs are responsible for recruiting members of their teams, usually targeting individuals in the immediate geographic area. Sometimes the MCC struggles to reach its recruiting goal. Program staff attribute shortfalls to competition from better-paying jobs, especially in the more urban areas that are the source for members in the Chesapeake Bay crew. Applications that come through the central office are referred to the nearest crew chief. The primary source of recruitment is word of mouth, although the program sometimes uses newspaper ads that emphasize the program's conservation focus. Recruitment activities take place in the summer, especially during the weeks prior to the program's startup. When recruiting, the crew chiefs look for willingness to learn, interest in service, and capacity to work in a team situation. Interest in conservation is not critical. More important is a willingness to get one's hands dirty, to try new things, and to work with others. Sometimes there are more acceptable candidates than there are slots; in this case, the crew chiefs ask all candidates to come in for a "tryout" day in which they work on a service project. The crew chiefs then select those who they think are most likely to thrive in the program.

The MCC program is in many ways fairly typical of the public work done in the area of conservation and environmental protection. It is hard work, often performed in isolated areas, which both makes a contribution to the community and helps young people find direction and build skills. Even though the MCC mission statement places the emphasis on member development, the public work component is still very significant. Given that many of the projects are paid for by sponsors who seek the achievement of specific conservation objectives, there can be little doubt that the work meets a market test. In addition, it is hard to dispute that members also grow from this work. Again, it may not be wise to see the conceptualizations of national service as conflicting or competing, but instead as reinforcing and overlapping, as they are in this case.

Meeting Human Needs

Aunt Martha's Home Instruction Program for Preschool Youngsters
(HIPPY) AmeriCorps program serves the adjacent communities of Ford
Heights and Chicago Heights, which are located just south of Chicago.
Ford Heights is a small, residential community of about 4,000 people. The
population is almost exclusively African American and has one of the
highest poverty rates of any "suburban" community in the United States.
Although suburban, the community suffers from the same woes as poor
inner-city communities: joblessness, teen pregnancy, crime, and drug ad-
diction. Chicago Heights is a larger, more diverse community in terms of
income and ethnicity, with a large Hispanic population that includes many
stay-at-home mothers.

The HIPPY AmeriCorps program is one of several dozen services provided through Aunt Martha's Youth Service Center.[10] This multiservice
nonprofit agency provides comprehensive services to more than 13,000
youths and their families in the area. It is comprised of more than 600 professional staff and 500 community volunteers and board members. Aunt
Martha's has thirty-eight offices and program sites in and around the Chicago metropolitan area. Its administrative office is based in Matteson, Illinois, about thirty miles south of Chicago. The agency is the main source
of support for the Ford Heights and Chicago Heights communities, and its
services include health care, foster care, parenting education, residential
services, and community outreach. As a private charitable agency, Aunt
Martha's relies on assistance from individuals, churches, private service
clubs, foundations, state, county, and federal contracts, and several suburban Chicago United Way organizations. Thus, when it comes to the necessary matching funds for the HIPPY AmeriCorps program, contributions
come from the local National Council for Jewish Women, the United Way,
Ford Motors, and from individuals on the advisory board.

Although Aunt Martha's has operated its HIPPY program for some years
independently of national service programs, it received its first AmeriCorps
grant in 1997. HIPPY is a home-based program with two primary goals: (1)
to encourage the educational enrichment of preschool children and (2) to
promote increased awareness of the parent's own strength and potential as
a home educator. Prior to receiving AmeriCorps funding, the local chapter of the National Council for Jewish Women sponsored three paraprofessionals (two volunteers and one paid staff member) for the program.

With this light staffing arrangement, the program could only serve fifteen to twenty-five families at any given time. However, as a result of an Ameri-Corps grant, there was funding for ten paraprofessionals, serving eighty to ninety families. As news of the program spread, more families became interested in receiving the service, and the waiting list grew.

The HIPPY AmeriCorps program is housed in the Family, Education, and Developmental Services (FEDS) branch of Aunt Martha's. The Ameri-Corps program shares facilities and resources with other programs in this division, including Head Start and Even Start. For example, the Ameri-Corps members participate in staff training events that are relevant across programs in the area. Other than training, there has been little interaction among AmeriCorps and other agency programs. Since Aunt Martha's HIPPY AmeriCorps program is so small, the management of the organization is quite simple. The director is responsible for all aspects of the program, in-cluding recruitment, member development, and training. The program has struggled at times to fill all its slots given the difficulty of the work and the potential danger of working in these communities. In addition, there have been only a limited number of Hispanic applications, despite the need for Spanish speakers in Chicago Heights.

The HIPPY AmeriCorps program provides two basic services: (1) con-ducting home visits focused on sharing child development curriculum with parents and (2) planning group parent and child activities that span households served by the program. Of these two activities, the primary service work is the weekly home visits using the HIPPY curriculum. Each member typically visits ten to fifteen families weekly. These visits take about one hour, during which the member prepares the client for a week's worth of activities with his or her child. The member provides the client with a weekly home activity packet; this is a highly structured les-son plan devised to facilitate the child's learning of new skills and con-cepts. The materials are designed to enable parents with even little formal schooling (including those who can neither read nor write) to teach their children successfully. The AmeriCorps member (called a parent partner in the HIPPY program) role-plays the activities with the parent and pro-vides support. Since the paraprofessionals are using the HIPPY material with their own children, they identify with the kinds of challenges parents face. The AmeriCorps members implement a Read for Success program with their clients as part of the visits. In this program, the parents set the goal of reading ten books to their child per month. The child is rewarded with a Pizza Hut gift certificate if they reach the goal. The AmeriCorps members took this program a step further by organizing teams of members and their clients. Each team has a door in the Aunt Martha's office, which is decorated with pictures indicating the books that have been read by the parents on the team. The members encourage the parents by bringing them different books each week when they make their home visits.

In addition to the weekly home visits, the members organize group activities for all of the families in the program twice a month. These usually consist of either a guest speaker or parent and child (PAC) interaction time. The members choose a theme for each PAC time, such as a popular children's book, and design activities centered on that theme. These type of activities include reading, singing (in both English and Spanish), and sharing in a group meal. The coordinator provides transportation for the families to encourage attendance, and usually between thirty and fifty families attend. Since all AmeriCorps members are recruited from Ford Heights and Chicago Heights, the corps members are able to connect easily with HIPPY clients who live in the communities. According to the HIPPY model, the members' knowledge of their community allows them to develop trusting relationships with the families.

Operating in these economically distressed communities involves overcoming some sizable obstacles. There is no library in Ford Heights, and city residents cannot check out books at libraries in other towns. This is of great concern to parents and educators in the community, who feel they are severely lacking in the resources necessary to educate young children in this poor community. To address this problem, the members established a small library in the office. They lend the books to parents so that they have the opportunity to read a variety of books to their children. The director and the members encourage organizations to donate books, including some in Spanish, on tape, and with pictures. The members check out books and bring them to parents on home visits, and they also encourage the parents to come in and pick out books themselves.

With the goal of building more group activities, HIPPY initiated a summer enrichment program at the elementary school in Ford Heights. By the start of summer, most of the clients have finished the thirty-week HIPPY curriculum, and the AmeriCorps members are able to focus more heavily on community-wide activities. The main purpose of the summer program is to get families out of their homes and give both the parents and the children opportunities to learn and play. Activities range from outdoor play to field trips to most of Chicago's children-oriented attractions, such as the children's museum, the zoo, and the aquarium. These activities and trips are organized and led by the AmeriCorps members. Recognizing the importance of getting parents out of their neighborhoods and exposing them to activities beyond their local community, the program took financial responsibility for these outings.

The HIPPY program was designed with the commitment that corps members be mothers from the community in which they are serving. In practice, many of the members have been former HIPPY clients. Others heard about the program through word of mouth or saw fliers posted around the community. The program does not strictly forbid males from participating, but thus far, none have ever applied for a position. In hiring, the program director looks for individuals with good people skills, and those who know the community well. Women who may not have much service experience, but who are ready and willing to work, are actively recruited. Upon receipt of an application, the staff checks references and the applicant must also complete two interviews before being hired. In assessing why people apply to and then join this program, it is important to note that none of the members report signing up because of a burning desire to do public work. Members tend to stress the educational award and the child care provision as major factors in their decision to join AmeriCorps. They express a desire to go to college and want to secure the needed financial support. Capitalizing on the flexibility of their schedule in AmeriCorps, many members take GED classes at Aunt Martha's. The staff supports the members in their GED efforts with child care for the mothers. While important human needs are being met by the program, its personal development aspect is a critical driver of commitment among members.

Members who are recruited at the beginning of the enrollment cycle begin their program year with a three-week-long orientation. The program director's goals for this training are to provide members with the necessary tools to serve their clients, to empower them to be leaders and organize activities, and to guide them to reflect on their service afterward.[11] Orientation covers information on the structure and mission of the program (AmeriCorps), the host site (Aunt Martha's), and the curriculum (HIPPY). This overview is an important first step because these three components interact to form the basic substance of their work. Members are trained in the HIPPY curriculum, with much of this training consisting in role-playing the HIPPY lessons, but it also includes rules and advice about going into clients' homes as paraprofessionals.

Over the course of their service, members tend to develop strong relationships with the families they serve. As a result, they often help their clients with registering their children for preschool and Head Start. This also requires them to become immunization advocates, since the children cannot register for school without complete immunization records. They also encourage ESL opportunities so that the parents are better able to understand and manipulate the nuances of the school system. In this sense, HIPPY is not simply an education program, but rather a general intervention aimed at meeting the many needs of poor families with children. One measure of the HIPPY program's value is that it has a constant waiting list of families wanting to be involved. Families must first fill out an application, and they are then selected via a need-based formula. Parents are required to attend orientation prior to their first home visit and they must show serious commitment to the program.

Meeting basic human needs such as improving parenting skills in the most disadvantaged communities is hard work. It requires commitment, caring, and local knowledge. By designing and implementing a program that draws on local mothers, Aunt Martha's HIPPY program represents the strategic melding of both the call to address serious community needs and attending to the development of members. Because the program relies on local residents, there is a social capital benefit as well, as neighbors meet and work with neighbors. With all of its other programs available to members, Aunt Martha's has the capacity to do public work while building the human and social capital of its members and clients.

Providing Other Community Services

The NCCC Capital Region program is a residential AmeriCorps program that serves populations in Washington, D.C., as well as Virginia, West Virginia, Ohio, and Pennsylvania. This program is located in southwest Washington, D.C., in a municipal facility, formerly a state nursing home. The economy of this area is varied, although the majority of its communities suffer from a lack of growth and higher unemployment than the national average. Communities are dominated by minority populations and face issues of poor school systems and a shortage of public and affordable housing. The NCCC Capital Region program is one of five regional NCCC programs in the United States. The NCCC headquarters are located in Washington, D.C., and the program maintains weekly contact with the AmeriCorps NCCC national director, as well as the other four regional campus directors. The Capital Region program began in 1996 at Fort Belvoir, Virginia, in response to unmet needs in Washington, D.C., but soon expanded to include four states in its service region.

The program has 110 corps members divided into nine teams of approximately twelve members each. In a typical year, the program implements fifty to sixty projects of four to six weeks each and twenty disaster-relief projects. Proposal evaluators attempt to find a balance between repeat and new business at local sites versus "spikes" across the region. Spikes are projects located in the region's states where corps members live and perform service activities for four to six weeks. Project sponsors usually provide housing and one or two meals per day. The remaining meals are paid by the NCCC through a food allowance. Local projects (in the Washington, D.C., area) allow a team to remain on campus where residents are responsible for preparing their own meals, for which they also receive a weekly food allowance. In general, the NCCC Capital Region strives for each team to participate in at least one disaster-relief project. The unique aspects of the AmeriCorps NCCC program, the residential component, and the "spike" experience, provide an opportunity for members to learn the necessity of teamwork, become sensitive to others' work styles and needs, and discover how to take advantage of the unique skills each individual brings to a project. From cooking meals and living together at the D.C. campus to traveling and sharing the heartrending experience of witnessing the devastation of floods and tornadoes on their spikes, the members learn to work together as a team and value each other's individual contribution.[12]

Applications are handled by the NCCC headquarters in Washington, D.C., and are then divided among the five campuses. In dividing the applications among the campuses, there is an attempt to place individuals at a distance from their homes and to have a corps of members from all over the country at each campus. This strategy is designed to expose individuals to both new environments and to people from many locations within the United States. The age range for the NCCC program is eighteen to twenty-four, and educational levels vary from only some high school to one member with a master's degree. Education levels in the NCCC in general are higher than in AmeriCorps State and National programs.

The members work on projects that cover all four areas addressed by AmeriCorps—education, environment, public safety, and human needs—along with the additional area of disaster relief, which encompasses responding to community needs as a result of floods, hurricanes, tornadoes, and wildfires. The local needs that the program fulfills include: assisting the District of Columbia Housing Authority (DCHA) with apartment renovations; improving homeless shelters; tutoring young children; acting as companions to the elderly in nursing homes; rehabilitating schools; building playgrounds; creating after-school programs; and assisting the Police Department with fingerprinting elementary school children for emergency purposes. Spike projects are similar in nature, although they tend to have more of an environmental focus.

Most teams participate in one disaster-relief activity, usually sponsored by the Red Cross or Federal Emergency Management Agency (FEMA). Teams are mobilized within twenty-four hours and spend six to eight weeks assisting communities with such issues as floods, earthquakes, and other natural disasters. Two teams we observed served on a one-month disaster-relief spike in North Carolina. Sponsored by FEMA, the project involved members in flood recovery activities that included gutting houses, food distribution, and community outreach. In addition to the standard recovery work, two members who were proficient in Spanish worked separately as translators for the FEMA relief guides. Upon their return, corps members were very emotional about their experience. Many remarked that the project "changed my life." Seeing the effect of a flood disaster on people's homes and infrastructure was emotionally trying, but caused the members to realize the important effect that their time and energy had on the community. Perhaps the most difficult aspect of this particular spike for members was returning to campus to work on their next project, clearing trails in a Washington, D.C., park, which to them seemed of little consequence and almost meaningless in comparison. Members also participate in several one-day service projects, such as the "Make a Difference Day" and "Raise the Roof Day." For instance, the NCCC led "Make a Difference Day" at East Capital Dwellings in southwest Washington, D.C. Members worked with 300 community members, gutting and painting apartments and creating a Boys and Girls Club from one of the apartments. For "Raise the Roof Day"—a HUD initiative that incorporated some NCCC teams in the D.C. area and one in Alexandria, Virginia—members gutted and framed walls and repaired steps in a development bought by a nonprofit agency.

Although member development activities are secondary to providing service, they are a focal part of program implementation. The program's theory on member development is that if a project allows members to take a role that will positively impact the community, the members will learn and develop individually as a result. The program attempts to tap and utilize what each member brings to a project, but this is difficult because of the team-based approach. NCCC members begin their program with the required three-week training session. Training is a time of preparation and readiness for the months of service ahead. The Capital Region's training, for example, began with six days of in-processing that included equipment issuing, review of campus policies, benefits, and a history of service. The second week was mostly composed of a standard physical exam that included drug testing, as well as tests for vision, hearing, blood pressure, and so forth. It also included First Aid CPR training and one full day of construction skills training. In the third week, members camped and did team-building exercises and team time with project briefings, in which members also received diversity training, disaster-relief training, chainsaw training, and training for working with at-risk youth, as well as team role training.

Individual Action Plans (IAPs), documents that set goals for the year, are considered an important part of member development. Members who have not completed high school are provided the opportunity to obtain their GED, and staff help obtain information about and applications for colleges or graduate schools that will accept the NCCC education award. This program tries to alleviate some of the cost of applying to college by requesting that colleges waive their application fees. To help members fulfill an IAP, the NCCC organizes career nights where they can gain knowledge about job opportunities and career choices, including the Peace Corps. The IAP requires that each member have a professional résumé upon completion of his or her NCCC year, as well as a personal portfolio of project experiences. To encourage members to become more involved in their community, the Capital Region campus requires each member to complete eighty hours of service outside of its program. These hours comprise the *individual service plan,* which can be accomplished during weekends or breaks during the year.

The NCCC is the generalist program within national service, spanning the four other areas and adding the disaster relief and residential experience components.[13] In some ways, this represents a bet that community needs are very diverse and that members develop best when working across multiple issue areas. The challenge of operating in this cross-cutting domain is that it is hard to develop member expertise and competence, given the rotation in tasks. In this way, perhaps more than in the other four areas of service delivery, the task of getting things done is interpreted and filtered through the lens of member development.[14]

VISTA's Vision of Public Work

In the AmeriCorps program, the meaning of getting things done has focused heavily on the critical areas of education, public safety, environment, and basic human needs. In VISTA, the nature of public work has long been far less well-defined, particularly during the first two decades of the program's implementation. If AmeriCorps has an emphasis on concrete tasks, VISTA work has been clearly concentrated on helping disadvantaged communities build capacity. However, the actual substance of the work done by volunteers for these disadvantaged populations has been much less clearly circumscribed.[15] It has traditionally revolved around empowering and organizing communities. In some cases, the work has demanded the delivery of legal, health-care, and educational services. In other cases, it has involved bringing people together, listening to their needs, and attempting to formulate solutions on the ground. Within VISTA there has thus been a dual focus on getting things done and building community capacity. What has this work actually entailed? Drawing on volunteers' own accounts, years later, of what they were working on during their service, we present below an illustrative array of the public work and capacity building accomplished by VISTA volunteers.[16]

Delivering Critical Services

Sometimes helping disadvantaged populations took the form of broad-based community organizing around interests and rights. Many VISTA volunteers in the 1970s were set loose in communities or cities and told to "make things happen." One volunteer remembered the freedom he was given to improvise and intervene as he saw fit across the area of welfare rights: "I did a lot of community organizing. I did a lot of interfacing with lawyers downtown in fancy offices, meetings with people in the welfare department at the highest levels. So it was sort of all over the place. It was more like a movement and a cause than a particular community." Within this flexible structure, VISTA volunteers were often asked to figure out what they could most effectively add to the collective work of the project. As one early volunteer recalled:

There was a chief organizer for the effort. And there was a small group of us, probably five or six, who spent a lot of time together. I had a fair amount of input into what I was good at, what I wasn't good at, where I was needed . . . It's probably more structured now than it was back then . . . I think I started out doing mostly sort of legal research. I transitioned from doing that sort of office work, if you will, to much more hands-on organizing and working with poor people of all sizes, colors, and shapes. We did a lot of training. I put together booklets, which I thought at the time were brilliant. They actually were quite good. You know, "Welfare Recipient, What Are Your Rights?" And we had somebody illustrate them, and they were just very good, down to earth, matter of fact.

Explaining to people what their rights were to public benefits was seen as a valuable and lasting contribution to a community in the early 1970s. Today, the emphasis might be on helping the poor transition from welfare to work, but back in the early days of VISTA, there was a clear and pronounced focus on rights and advocacy. This approach fit the goals of VISTA and drew on the abilities, interests, and commitments of the volunteers, who were called upon to deliver critical heath services to communities. We heard from one nurse about a roving community health clinic for the poor. The goal was simply to get services to those most in need. The nurses would go out into the community and encourage people to come to the clinic and draw upon its services:

They also had set up an eighty-five-year-old doctor who would help. He was a retired plastic surgeon who lived in the community. We had clinics in that town for the whole county twice a month. We would see probably close to a hundred people each time. They would just line up, we would see them as fast as possible. We would dispense medications as well. We also went to another county and had that same clinic once a month. People would be lined up for hours and hours to see this one doctor. The sick babies and old people, there was also a public health nurse that went with us to most of those clinics.

The doctor was able to see people for the first time at their roving clinic, and then VISTA volunteer nurses would go out into the community and make follow-up visits at people's homes: "We did outreach, that is what we did the rest of the week. We would go out to see people who were diabetic or had wounds that we would have to dress. We would follow up on people who had sores, anemia, people who were hungry." Sometimes, the work would involve helping people apply for assistance and make better lifestyle choices: "We identified them in the clinic and they did not have enough to eat. We would go help them apply for food stamps and welfare. We would even meet them at the store and show them how to make good food choices as far as proteins and vegetables and that kind of thing."

Getting things done meant sometimes trying to change public policy in order to affect broad change, rather than just diligently working with individuals in need on a one-on-one basis. For example, VISTA volunteers were involved in the fight for the health and Social Security benefits of coal miners. When the work that gets done is advocacy, it is harder to attribute causality to the changes that may result since policy making is influenced by so many different and often intangible factors. This did not stop VISTA volunteers from trying to focus national attention on the problem of black lung disease and the pressures it placed on mining families. Looking back on his work, one volunteer noted: "In some vague way, I think we had quite an impact. The rise and fall of the economy does more than anything to [shape outcomes], but we had some successes. We worked with the Black Lung Association and lobbied for changing the black lung laws." Seeking change on a national level, VISTA volunteers did everything from going to Washington to holding mock trials to hosting forums:

> We invited the president of the Black Lung Association from West Virginia, and we held a mock hearing on how the government program was going, with an empty chair for the Social Security Administration [representative], who was invited to attend but felt that there were security issues and didn't. We had a doctor who had been lobbying for the law to be passed in the first place, as one of our witnesses. And had miners testifying about their problems with it, and got a lot of news coverage for that, in about three or four magazines like *The Nation*.

Much to the VISTA members' delight, policy change occurred very quickly. The hurdles to getting qualified for benefits were lowered, allowing many to apply for and secure support. Ironically, the volunteer observed that "it almost reverted from being too difficult to being maybe almost too easy. And there were a lot of people who got the benefits, who certainly needed the money, but weren't all that sick." While something did indeed get done about meeting the needs of miners with black lung, the volunteer was clear that there was a sense at the time that VISTA's contribution to the policy change process was real, but it was also just one part of the very complex system. Other efforts by VISTA volunteers, like those to limit strip-mining, were much less successful, but they too aimed at broad policy and regulatory change.

Sometimes, VISTA volunteers were assigned to narrowly defined tasks and other times they were given a huge amount of autonomy and choice in the work they undertook. For one volunteer in Louisiana, a menu of options was presented from which one project stood out: "Opening the battered women shelter seemed very intriguing to me. I knew nothing about battered women. But it was disorganized. There was real conflict between the volunteers and the staff. So I wasn't there long." Getting this project off the ground created a lot of conflict and contention among the team members, with one person trying to take the lead and another leaving to take on other projects like a crisis telephone line: "It ended up just really being one person who dominated the dynamics. So much that it never got off the ground. The shelter never opened. Kind of sabotage. So, luckily, I was out of there before that. And then I just did the crisis line full-time. There were a whole lot of people in crisis." By defining a lot of different projects and allowing people to move among them, the VISTA efforts in Louisiana were able to hold on to its members: "Baton Rouge had so many [slots] available— you didn't have to leave. This was kind of good in a way and kind of bad in a way. I wonder if I had to leave VISTA [entirely] whether I would have stayed with [the shelter] longer. I tend to think I would not have because it had gotten that bad, but I don't know for sure. I know I didn't want to leave that group of people that you had made a little family with."

In Appalachia, the meaning of public work was focused on strengthening community ties before working on more concrete community issues and challenges. One volunteer who was part of the effort remembered: "The people who had been there before got the grassroots organization going and that was just to get communities to start talking to each other." After this groundwork was laid, the volunteers focused on helping women in the community sell the quilts that they stitched by hand for good prices: "We got the quilts doing better, financially. The women were paid more. But that's just a drop in the bucket. It's ten families, because there weren't any jobs." The goal of bringing change to the community was difficult to achieve given the depressed nature of the local economy. In this sense, the goal of doing meaningful and constructive public work ran up against the constraints of local conditions: "It wasn't as if you could do something about it. They had to move and they weren't going to move and why should they? Now that I have a lot more perspective on it, I guess we did what we could. We did change some lives, one person at a time and it was slow but we made some difference."

While opening markets for quilters may have been pleasant but only marginally influential work, VISTA members in other locations have taken on more challenging and difficult projects on behalf of communities. One VISTA volunteer explained: "The first thing we did was try to articulate what the community needs were. A primary need they had was to develop a sewer system. They had outhouses. They had septic tanks, but they also had some hepatitis epidemics. So they really needed a sewer system." Diagnosing a complex public problem like a sewer system was easier than meeting the need. It turned out that it would have taken years to get a sewer system in place given the local opposition: "I heard people say well, 'I've had a septic tank for thirty-five years and it works fine. I don't see why I should have to pay for a sewer.'" Part of the problem in trying to do major public work projects was that there was no real sense of community or solidarity. An idea to install a fire hydrant and thereby lower home owner's insurance rates in the community was also applauded until the financial costs and complexities of the process killed the effort. Residents were isolated and independent, and often resisted the ideas of VISTA members if they required a lot of collaboration. This led VISTA to focus on smaller and more actionable projects like trash pickup: "We set up the trash pickup with a man in the community. We were able to get that off the ground." Other smaller projects involved cleanups and demolition. One VISTA member recounted how a broken and leaning barn was taken down for a resident who was too weak and poor to do it himself: "We organized several of the neighbors and we got the fire marshal out there. We were able, one night, to ram a truck a couple times into what was left of the barn, collapse it, and pour some kerosene on it and burn it. We had the fire truck to take care of any problems that might develop. It was quite a bonfire. There were no problems and we got rid of the barn that way." The VISTA volunteers took pictures of the bonfire and got a positive story in the local newspaper about their cleanup effort, which continued on for a year, focusing on small, quick wins for the community.

In many cases, VISTA tried to help young people find direction and stay in school. In one project, VISTA members worked with at-risk youth and attempted to help them with their problems: "The people we worked with were the people who were dropping out of school, so our sponsoring organization was a youth service agency. Many of the people who were there were basically families in stress or teens in stress possibly living on their own, possibly living with their boyfriend, possibly in an open conflict with their parents." The work was difficult and involved taking on kids that other agencies and organizations were less than eager to work with: "I remember one person. She was like thirteen. She could pass for twenty-one. She was a handful. I mean, at the time in this state, you could still lock girls up for being incorrigible. She was trouble to have in a public school and there were lots of other kids that were everything from identified as learning disabled or special needs people." The nature of public work thus took the form of handling the most difficult human cases, and helping where philanthropy and government were unwilling or unable to intervene.[17]

In other cases, VISTA tried to intervene early on and help young children in poor homes get a good start in life. The work involved organizing an early childhood center for the community. The work of members was to set up the center and recruit children by talking to parents, not necessarily in that order: "We would just contact families and let them know that we were going to be establishing this center for preschool education. And then we had to find a building and then physically turn that building into a preschool program, purchase educational materials and toys and tables and chairs, and everything that it would take." While there was strong interest in the program, which was designed to run from 9:00 a.m. until noon every day, there were challenges with getting the physical plant cleaned and equipped: "We found a site within the first few weeks. It was an old Boy Scout hut, which had been abandoned. We just took that over and we would spend part of every day just cleaning and going to that site. Then we would make some home visits to families who had been identified as people with preschoolers who might benefit from the program." The work thus entailed everything from cleaning to planning to marketing to teaching.

Building Community Capacity

In many instances, VISTA volunteers described the painful process of trying to get local community members to take action for themselves, rather than simply allowing VISTA volunteers to do the work in question.[18] In one case, the work focused on housing issues. Rather than simply writing bylaws and creating structure, the VISTA volunteers tried to draw residents into the process and give them ownership. The temptation was strong to simply do the work for residents of the development, but this would have violated the spirit of the project, which involved creating community commitment and capacity that would outlast the VISTA program's presence in the community.[19]

> The goal was to help a group of tenants . . . This would involve visiting them a lot, knowing in general their problems and getting them interested in participating and fully engaged in this work. It was hard because people worked two or three jobs, and the conditions were terrible, sometimes with no heat and things like that. So it evolved into this very complicated effort to help them with their weekly bylaws, help them develop committees, motivate them constantly to participate and reward them by saying thanks to them, or being there for them. So it evolved from just visiting and inviting them to meetings, to getting them very, very involved in every step. It was really very, very time-consuming.

Part of the tradition of VISTA is a focus on organizing and empowering. Sometimes this was around rights, while other times it was around basic needs. In one case, a group of VISTA volunteers helped set up a wholesale food distribution system that would give residents better-quality and less-expensive food. This required a lot of coordination and collaboration among the volunteers. As one member recalled: "Every neighborhood where VISTAs [worked] had a preorder food co-op, so they came together to become part of this downtown food distribution warehouse. We were constantly in contact. We had periodic meetings, not sanctioned by downtown, but we just did it. We played softball together. And so there was a community of VISTAs. It felt comfortable." The work of organizing was not something that could simply be discontinued immediately after a year of service was completed. Building capacity in a community has its own schedule and timeline, which required some flexibility: "I stayed four months past my year and that was supposed to be forbidden. Because they wanted to get you in and out. You were supposed to accomplish everything that, you know, you set out to do in that year. Same thing as the Peace Corps." Of course, this was not always realistic, and one member noted with some sarcasm: "You imparted all your genius, knowledge, and skills to the people who needed it and then you were gone. Of course, very few of us bought that. We knew that we were there for a short period of time, but we all knew—some of us more than others—that organizing is something that goes on all the time and that neighborhoods can use outside help, as long as it's sensitive, as long as it's done in a way that it should be done."

In many cases, VISTA volunteers were brought into communities to help pull resources together and build organizational capacity. In a Colorado housing project, the member admitted that his role was ambiguous, but he noted that the overarching goal was clear: "The purposes and the goals of VISTA, when they were expressed to us, were to build infrastructure, which would remain in place after [we left] and which would carry on and move forward. I did a lot of mailing campaigns for fund-raising. I did what some would call volunteer coordinating, meaning I would be calling to try to enlist people to volunteer. I worked with the families. I guess, in some ways, I would call myself a sounding board." The member served as a floater in the broader project helping out where needed and trying to build local capacity. The housing group that was organized was able to get things done once it found its rhythm and independence: "It was chaired by quite a few movers and shakers in the community and they were in contact with the other communities in Colorado. They were very efficient in terms of building housing in the community. So there was an incredibly strong board in place." Even though the member was working alongside the board and trying to build a lasting organization, there was a sense of the limits of young volunteers. "I didn't have practical skills. I was not an architect. So it was like, 'Hey, we'll take a body.'" The housing group used the VISTA "body" to build its capacity and systems so that it could carry out the complex task of designing and building affordable housing.

The Nature of Public Work

National service programs come in many sizes and shapes. Most, like the ones highlighted here, focus in one way or another on the critical areas of education, public safety, environment, and human needs. While the CNCS also defines a catchall category of "other needs," more often than not, programs do not align perfectly with any of the exact subject categories. Service programs, like the one in Holyoke, may start off in the area of public safety, but tend to expand over time into education and youth services. One way to look at the trend toward broadening the service focus is to label it "mission creep" and to worry that it leads inevitably to a blurring of the nature of public work. Another way to look at the same process of mission broadening is to view it as part of the process of adapting to community needs and circumstances. In the case of Holyoke, it did not become clear until the program was implemented that work other than public safety was needed to maintain member interest and morale. Some programs, like the one in Washington, D.C., detailed here, were designed from the start to span multiple fields and there is no issue at all related to loss of focus or boundary spanning.[20]

In many ways, the very definition of "fields of activity" is somewhat problematic given the many different ways in which community needs are assessed and addressed. Beyond giving national service a common story to tell about the work that gets done, AmeriCorps' focal areas should not be seen as the final word on the nature of public work. They are more a way of organizing and telling the story of national service than anything else. What matters more than a semblance of continuity and thematic consistency across the thousands of programs funded over time is their quality and depth. For AmeriCorps to succeed, there is a critical need to find challenging and satisfying work that both realizes the potential of participants and delivers value to the community. This is the ultimate arbiter of whether or not the programs are successful.[21]

VISTA's vision of national service is notably different from that of AmeriCorps, particularly when looking back in time to the full scope and evolution of the VISTA program. With its early focus on organizing and its long-standing emphasis on helping the most disadvantaged, VISTA operates with a more activist model of public work.[22] It is a model that is committed to the idea of social justice and empowerment. The coherence of VISTA thus flows not from the nature of the public work being performed, but from the social commitment that drives the work. In many ways, this is a far more robust and coherent approach to defining public work than the topical approach of AmeriCorps. However, VISTA is also a smaller program with a more limited reach, which also accounts for the ability of the program to breathe substantive commitments into the very definition of the work that gets done.

In the end, the vision of national service as public work is an important one, since it does register most directly with the public's sense that national service is about completing projects that advance the interests of communities.[23] It is also the most politically palatable vision of service in that it is concrete and neatly translates federal dollars into local community benefits. The idea that national service is all about getting things done, however, can be taken too far and overwhelm the member-centered visions with which it competes. As we see next, the political pressure on Ameri-Corps to demonstrate results has been intense from the start. This has heightened the perceived importance of showing that these programs were "getting things done" and, at the same time, delayed a deeper appreciation of the effects of service that includes impacts in the areas of civic engagement, personal growth, and social capital.

— 8 —

The Institutional Politics of National Service

The idea of national service is based on a dual-level theory of change that operates simultaneously at the individual and community levels. To achieve its goals, national service requires the delivery of an array of national service programs that mobilize citizens in communities to work on projects that will enhance the lives of others. While this lofty goal would seem universally appealing, finding institutional arrangements capable of supporting the idea of national service has not been easy. The national service movement has been splintered across many programs and a vast array of administrative umbrellas. Agencies and programs have come and gone over the years, but the Corporation for National and Community Service (CNCS) has made the most progress to date in building a structure within which the complex goals and ambitions of service can be pursued.

Just like the broader service movement, however, the CNCS has been buffeted by the political winds surrounding it. As a consequence, much of the corporation's early institutional effort was directed at deflecting political attacks and attempts to curtail its funding. For much of its early history, this new government corporation expended a large amount of effort simply defending itself and the idea and movement it represented, rather than learning about and improving its programs. During its initial decade of funding, the CNCS sought to secure political support and legitimize itself by cataloging and conveying to its funders and authorizers a vast list of narrow output measures focused heavily on public work, the last vision of service. By showing that work was getting done, the CNCS hoped to shore up support in Congress and build broader acceptance of the idea of national service. The CNCS naturally gravitated to the public work vision of national service, which is easiest to explain, observe, and document.

This short-term political strategy of focusing on reporting work outputs has not ultimately served the CNCS well, however. In fact, the strategy had a pervasive and perverse effect, as the deeper meaning and significance of service was ultimately lost in the early rush for evidence that national service was meeting concrete needs. Service became a narrow instrumental idea about how to get things done in communities, rather than an idea linked to strong citizenship, personal growth, and social capital construction.[1] Instead of gathering evidence and fine tuning programs over time with the goal of cultivating all the different visions embodied in national service, the CNCS focused on assembling narrow program output data in a bid for legitimacy and continued funding. Why should we focus on this seemingly minor chapter in bureaucratic politics? Put bluntly, the institutional history of national service—and the politics that have shaped this history—are important because together they set the context for both what has been accomplished by national service to date and what remains to be done in the future. In many ways, the institutional politics within the CNCS are the crucible within which the idea of service was forged and they help explain many of the programmatic challenges that have been encountered since 1994.

Emergence of the Corporation

The AmeriCorps program, the most visible program of the CNCS, has long been seen as one of President Bill Clinton's signature domestic policy achievements. This status initially made it possible for the CNCS, which was charged with implementing and administering AmeriCorps, to operate for a short while after its founding under the protective cover of the Clinton presidency. This deep presidential connection is also what made it difficult to sustain support for the corporation as the political environment shifted over time on Capitol Hill and in the White House. The corporation consequently spent many of its early formative years under significant pressure from Republicans in Congress who were angered by internal audits indicating that the CNCS had severe managerial and control flaws. The toxic political environment of the time also came to be significant: Republicans in Congress developed an early and enduring visceral dislike of the program simply by virtue of its close association with the Clinton presidency.

The idea to form a new national service corps that might address important public need, help reconstruct idealism among young people, and make college more affordable for middle-class families became a goal of Arkansas governor Bill Clinton in 1988. At a conference of the Democratic Leadership Council (DLC) in Williamsburg, Virginia, Clinton first heard the idea promoted by Charles Moskos, a sociologist and military expert from Northwestern University.[2] When the Clinton presidential campaign began in 1991, domestic service was a key interest and one of his most talked about program initiatives. After the election, in a moment that many in the national service movement recollect with great pride, President-elect Clinton sat for an interview wearing a City Year sweatshirt and pronounced that when he assumed office, his four most critical objectives would be jump-starting the economy, reducing the national debt, expanding health care, and promoting national service. Five years after the DLC meeting, on 30 April 1993, President Clinton—101 days into his presidency—unveiled an elaborate and ambitious legislative proposal for national service in the form of the National and Community Service Trust Act of 1993.[3] One year after that, on 12 April 1994, the president administered an oath to the first 500 AmeriCorps members, assembled in the driveway of the White House. The oath began fatefully enough with a promise: "I will get things done for America."[4]

When Clinton delivered the legislative proposal to Congress that would become the National and Community Service Trust Act, there were more than 200 sponsors, sixteen of whom were Republicans. The bill created a unique federal agency in the form of a corporation, having a flexible personnel system, a decentralized program network, and strong ties to the business and nonprofit sectors. It set forward a plan to engage youth in useful activities that were "real work." The plan was to develop a new agency that would help remedy national trends toward balkanization and political polarization, while building job skills, instilling civic spirit, improving communities, and building bridges between classes and races.[5]

Not surprisingly, the five months between the bill's April 1993 launch and its eventual passage in September 1993 were a legislative and political scramble, involving impassioned partisanship, intense lobbying, and shrewd bargaining by and on behalf of legislators and major stakeholders that included the banking and student loan industries, colleges and universities, organized labor, civil service employees, veterans groups, and even the Internal Revenue Service (IRS).[6] Interest groups of all sizes and kinds appeared to have a stake in the modest proposal to engage young people in service and to help them pay for college in the process. When the bill authorizing the corporation was finally signed by the president and became law, few could have predicted the troubles that would lie ahead for what seemed like an idea that no one could resist.

The timing of the act was significant. Its passage came at a time when the idea of "reinventing government" was popular and when finding new ways to improve the efficiency and effectiveness of government was a priority. Under the "reinventing government" slogan, the Clinton administration claimed that the standard operating procedures and structures in the public sector needed to be reconsidered and rendered more modern, in large part by bringing some of the management savvy of the business world into the tired systems of the public sector. By creating a government-owned "corporation" rather than just another "agency," the hope was that national service would be administered with the efficiency of the private sector while avoiding the bureaucracy of the public sector.[7]

Though a new national service corporation was charged with administering a federal program funded with federal dollars, the program itself was designed to be locally based and controlled. Two-thirds of the money controlled by the CNCS would be passed through state commissions appointed by state governors. The remaining one-third would go directly from the corporation to nonpartisan, nonprofit organizations throughout the nation.[8] The new corporation was also designed to operate competitively, and would not fund grant applicants unless their work proved useful. The process of spreading funds to encourage service was also drawn up in a way so that it would be perceived as nonpartisan. This was essential, for everyone saw the possibility of favoritism and partisanship entering the program during the grant-making process.

Today, the CNCS occupies several floors of a modern office complex a few blocks from the White House, has offices and commissions in states across the country, and operates with an annual federal appropriation of more than $1 billion. Despite all these trappings and its appearance as a solid part of the federal bureaucracy, the CNCS continues to struggle for legitimacy. During its first decade of operation, the CNCS struggled mightily to find its way. Despite its status as a "corporation," it has on more than one occasion experienced severe financial management problems and has pursued a mission that has drawn criticism from many different quarters.

National Service Splits

Even before the founding of the corporation, partisan politics related to national service began to foretell how difficult it would be to manage and assess these programs. National service was applauded by liberal and new Democrats, who saw in it the enactment of President Clinton's pledge to bolster citizenship and service. Programs like AmeriCorps were thought to breed a new kind of idealism and public spiritedness that Democrats believed would strengthen democracy and political participation. Not surprisingly, as the CNCS took shape and grew, it was embraced and nurtured by several key Democrat legislators as an expression of many of their core social ideals.

Among conservative Republicans, the idea of national service became increasingly unpopular during the 1990s. Many of the newly elected Republican conservatives in the 1994 election came to ridicule the idea of paying people to volunteer, seeing the program as an attempt at social engineering that betrayed de Tocqueville's early observation that voluntary action among citizens was a critical training ground for democratic politics. Moreover, Republican skepticism of national service was stoked by the fact that AmeriCorps was one of the few programmatic achievements of the early Clinton presidency. Dismantling the program became a persistent aspiration for many conservatives, including House Speaker Newt Gingrich. In fact, the Republican takeover of Congress following the midterm elections in 1994 meant that not only would the corporation's early years be highly scrutinized, but the time horizon of programs like AmeriCorps instantly became shorter and the need for demonstrable success was suddenly acute. Over the coming years, House Republicans repeatedly refused to approve any funding for AmeriCorps in their budgets and only reluctantly funded the program after the Senate pushed them to do so.

For the senior management of the corporation, the complex and shifting politics of national service turned out to be, over and over, a major stumbling block to a thoughtful and informed rollout of AmeriCorps. Not only would the political environment push and pull the decision-making process of the corporation in many different directions, but the need to placate critics ended up truncating its mission and performance measurement systems. With national service a target of the new Republican majority, the CNCS was put on the defensive. Instead of looking to track the long-term effect of service and to seek out information on how programs might be strengthened, CNCS leadership was led to commission and disseminate a series of short-term activity reports, which failed to convince critics that vital community needs were being met and were of little help to the CNCS in its efforts to understand and improve its programs during its critical formative years.

Thus, during the manic early days of the corporation, at precisely the time it could have used sound information and data on program performance, much of the managerial attention of CNCS's leadership was focused on fighting political fires that would flare up regularly. The pressure and constraints of the institutional environment made the launch of a new national service corporation anything but smooth and easy. The price for this chaotic and conflicted beginning continued to be high for years after the start-up period, as the CNCS struggled to fully define the multiple meanings of service or carry out assessments that reflected the many different levels at which service operates. The CNCS was focused intensively on legitimizing itself, defending programs against congressional funding cuts, and generally just showing that things were, in fact, "getting done."[9]

A Government Corporation with Private-Sector Leadership

The CNCS was created as a wholly owned government corporation. When it was founded in 1993, it was the only noncommercial government corporation covered by the Government Corporation Control Act.[10] Initially, it retained the same board as its predecessor organization, the Commission on National and Community Service, established by the National and Community Service Act of 1990.[11] In September 1994, ten members of the initial Board of Directors of the corporation were confirmed by the U.S. Senate.[12] The full board met for the first time on 25 October 1994. The first board chair was Jim Joseph, an African American minister and former executive at Cummins Engine Company of Columbus, Indiana. Joseph also served as director of the Cummins Engine Foundation, and then president of the Council on Foundations, an association of more than a thousand grant-making foundations and corporate giving programs. Joseph had a reputation for progressive politics and, while at the Council on Foundations, he promulgated a set of "Principles and Practices" for foundations that included affirmative action in foundation hiring. This move to establish standards, in a world where donors had long prized their independence, set off a split in the foundation world. A new, more conservative association of grant makers, the Philanthropy Roundtable, was formed in reaction to Joseph's controversial move, and it was headed early on by Leslie Lenkowsky. Lenkowsky was a former foundation official and think tank head, and a protégé of neoconservative opinion leader Irving Kristol. Lenkowsky was appointed to the corporation's new board, and was for many years its lone conservative member. Thus, strangely enough, Joseph and Lenkowsky found themselves working together on the corporation's board.

When the corporation needed to appoint a first chief executive officer (CEO), President Clinton tapped Eli Segal. The son of a hatmaker from Flatbush in Brooklyn, New York, Segal was a former liberal political activist turned lawyer and businessman. By 1993, Segal had accumulated a string of business successes, and established himself as a major fund-raiser for the Democratic Party. He had also worked on a series of progressive Democratic campaigns, including those of Eugene McCarthy in 1968, George McGovern in 1972, and Gary Hart in 1987. Beginning in 1991, Segal had served as Clinton's campaign chief of staff. Clinton trusted Segal implicitly, and quickly made clear his intention to delegate the policy and the politics of national service to him. Admittedly, Segal was inexperienced in government, and knew almost nothing about service programs or their history.[13] Yet he was an appealing choice given his business background and reputation for making things happen.

Segal wasted little time and began to roll out the AmeriCorps program so that very quickly there would be dramatic signs of "getting things done." One of the consequences of this decision to implement at an accelerated pace was that program growth soon outstripped administrative capacity. AmeriCorps volunteers were fanning out across the country in growing numbers, but the corporation was hard-pressed to keep up with the complex task of overseeing and managing the endeavor. Things were going to get done and they were going to get done immediately. During this rollout phase, there was not a great deal of thought about the underlying purpose of national service programs, and how the corporation's many different programs related to its mission. The focus was on getting small wins, if only to be able to report something to hostile members of authorizing committees on Capitol Hill.

Segal and other early representatives of the corporation relied almost exclusively on "outputs"—unit measures of the volume of program activity—as evidence of CNCS's accomplishments. These ranged from the number of neighborhood cleanup projects completed to the number of children tutored to the number of hiking trails cleared on federal lands. There was a fatal flaw in this approach. Tracking and counting outputs is very different from measuring "outcomes"—the real, human results of an intervention or activity. Hurried and pressured from the start, the corporation grasped at what it could measure quickly and then integrate into its regular progress reports. Indeed, a cycle began in which inputs, primarily money, generated a set of outputs across multiple programs and many participants, which in turn were used as evidence of impact to secure the flow of more money into the system. Participant-level outcomes and deeper measures of mission accomplishment were more often presumed than proven. Under continuous attack and threat of defunding, the corporation initially found outcomes too nebulous, complex, and hard to track.

The inability of the CNCS to engage the evaluation challenge ultimately proved very costly. It led to a long string of descriptive studies that chronicled "achievements" (such as the number of shrubs planted in communities and the number of days spent rehabbing housing) and made it hard for the CNCS to know whether the broader visions of service were being enacted. The public work vision was thus privileged over the visions of service that focused on civic engagement, personal growth, and social capital. This early but fateful decision also meant that a multilevel and multipurpose vision of national service was sublimated for many years as the CNCS strove to demonstrate—in a highly charged partisan environment—just how much work members were carrying out in communities across the country.

Growth and Development of the Corporation

From Eli Segal's appointment as first CEO of the corporation in 1993 to the change in political regime in 2001, the CNCS grew substantially. Its budget increased from $570 million to nearly $767 million.[14] It went from having 450 employees to more than 600 employees spread across fourteen departments.[15] A new, extensive field structure consisting of forty-eight state offices and five regional service centers was developed to initiate, implement, and monitor many of the corporation's major programs throughout the country. New programs in the form of collaborative initiatives were established to create additional avenues of service for volunteers through such things as promoting literacy, teaching computer skills, providing disaster relief, and promoting observance of Martin Luther King Jr. Day as a day of service.[16] The corporation created grant programs to accommodate disabled persons in community service activities and to support the study of service through the National Service Fellows Program.[17] The CNCS developed literally thousands of partnerships and external relationships with organizations from the private and nonprofit sectors to support and leverage the work of its core programs.[18]

President Clinton had told Segal that the program had to be up, running, and popular by 1996.[19] He told the American public that he would have 100,000 service volunteers by 1997.[20] With such rapid growth came real challenges, however. First among these challenges was the politicization of the program. Republicans on Capitol Hill worried that the Clinton administration was simply using AmeriCorps—and the foot soldiers in national service—to assist liberal and Democratic-leaning organizations. By sending volunteers to work for some organizations and not others, AmeriCorps could easily be portrayed—just as conservatives previously had depicted VISTA and other programs—as a political patronage system that rewards supporters and punishes enemies.

This concern was soon rendered painfully concrete. One of the first and most pointed political conflicts at the corporation occurred when the Association of Community Organizations for Reform Now (ACORN), a large, powerful, and aggressive liberal community organizing agency, took part in a street demonstration at a speech given by Republican House Speaker Newt Gingrich. It turned out that ACORN was a grantee of the corporation, a fact brought to the attention of the political establishment by the *Washington Times* on 24 February 1995. At a CNCS board meeting on the same day, Lenkowsky quoted the article and asked the corporation staff to provide an explanation as to why a corporation grant had been awarded to ACORN. Lenkowsky used the occasion to express his general displeasure with what he perceived to be partisan remarks at the previous night's board dinner, and a general underrepresentation of conservative voices in discussions within the national and community service network.[21] When ACORN was finally audited and investigated, the organization was indeed found to have mingled funds and engaged in partisan activities outside the scope of the grant conditions connected to the receipt of public funds. This incident highlighted the fact that the conservative concern over the politicization of national service was a real issue that had to be taken seriously.

Though partisan disagreements were an early distraction, other issues soon loomed even larger. Perhaps the most conspicuous and pervasive challenge faced by the CNCS during the course of its development was its weak financial management and control system. Under the Government Corporation Control Act, the corporation is required to have an annual audit of its financial statements performed by the Office of the Inspector General (OIG). In March 1996, the OIG reported that the corporation's fiscal year 1994 financial statements could not be audited because of deficiencies in systems, lack of documentation supporting the statements, and material weaknesses in the corporation's management and control structure. The OIG made ninety-nine recommendations for corrective action necessary to produce auditable financial statements.[22]

Staying on top of the managerial minutiae related to running a government agency was simply not a priority in the corporation's early years, which is undoubtedly one of the reasons that financial management issues reached the crisis point. It was much more important to build political capital and demonstrate that national service was benefiting communities. From the start, the focus was almost exclusively on growing the corporation and generating as much service activity as possible. There was also the matter of an evolving presidential agenda, which often shaped the priorities of the implementation of AmeriCorps. Together, the precarious and shifting position of national service within an ever more hostile congressional climate made management seem secondary to the primary task of protecting the corporation's legitimacy and funding.

A review of the testimony of Eli Segal before the Subcommittee on VA, HUD and Independent Agencies of the House Committee on Appropriations in March 1995 underscores the early focus and priorities of the corporation. The subcommittee was charged with the review of appropriations requests through the VA-HUD Appropriations Bill, one of two legislative funding sources for the CNCS, and the one that covers the bulk of the corporation's budget.[23] The corporation appeared before a sympathetic audience. Congressman John Lewis of Atlanta, cochair of the subcommittee, described himself as a former member of a Peace Corps–like program in India, and a great fan of programs that are designed to attract young people to participate in service activities. Even so, Lewis expressed some skepticism about the extent to which such service programs actually benefit those for whom service is provided, and he asked Segal to tell the committee why the CNCS existed in the first place. He requested help in gaining some sense of whether corporation programs were meeting their objectives.

Segal responded to Chairman Lewis's questions with numbers. He began with data from the congressman's own home district, and reminded Lewis that ninety-two AmeriCorps members had helped restore more than 15,000 acres of the San Bernardino Forest that had been charred by fires. Segal went on to cite the findings of Aguirre International, a California consulting and evaluation firm, which analyzed the first five months of AmeriCorps operations through a selected sample of fifty-two AmeriCorps sites, representing 8 percent of the total sites. Segal presented a list of AmeriCorps accomplishments: 258 neighborhood watch and safety programs had been formed; 470 crime victims had received counseling and assistance; 8,500 schoolchildren had been assisted in getting to school safely; 238 city apartments, 296 homes of frail elderly persons, 99 rural homes, and 15 shelters had been renovated; 1,100 children had been screened for lead poisoning; 200,000 trees had been planted; 27 miles of river and stream banks had been stabilized; 88 miles of parkland trails had been built, restored, or maintained; 7,638 children had tutors; and 1,430 school kids had skilled teachers.[24]

Segal went on to report that the first phase of a three-year rollout of AmeriCorps had been completed with the placement of 20,000 volunteers in 1,200 communities. A total of 350 AmeriCorps program proposals had been selected, 6,600 individuals had participated in a Summer of Safety program, and 450,000 students had been engaged in service through Learn and Serve America.[25] Segal explained to the subcommittee that an evaluation database was being developed for AmeriCorps programs, such that the corporation would know "how many crack houses were closed in Kansas City and how many kids were immunized in Texas and how many kids' reading scores were increased in Kentucky." In a fleeting reference, the matter of measuring some of the less-tangible aspects of accomplishment in AmeriCorps programs, including the personal growth and civic engagement of those who serve and the construction of social capital in communities, Segal quoted Albert Einstein in saying: "Not everything that counts can be counted, and not everything that can be counted counts."[26] With this and other appearances before Congress during the early years of AmeriCorps, a pattern was established in which the leadership of the CNCS would report and document the units of public work that had been completed.

In October 1995, Harris Wofford, a former U.S. senator from Pennsylvania who had lost his seat in 1994, became the corporation's second CEO. Wofford had a long history of public service. He was special assistant to President Kennedy on civil rights and a key architect of the Peace Corps. By the time he took charge as CNCS's CEO, three standing board committees had been formed, including a Planning and Evaluation Committee with four sweeping goals: (1) making communities stronger through service; (2) improving individual lives through service; (3) helping solve unmet needs through service; and (4) making service a common expectation. A new Goals and Vision Statement was soon developed to establish benchmarks. It stated target numbers for collaborations, participants, and people to be served by the year 2000. It included a numeric goal for the percentage of citizens who would believe that service is an integral part of citizenship by 2000. A strategic plan for Learn and Serve was also under way, and it too contained clear goals. Among these goals, it promised that by 2000 more than 25 million K–12 students and more than 8 million college and university students annually would learn through and practice community service. Collaborations between AmeriCorps and disaster-relief organizations were also forged during this period, including the Federal Emergency Management Administration (FEMA) and the American Red Cross. A partnership was formed between the CNCS and the Points of Light Foundation with the goal of carrying out joint projects, including annual observances of Martin Luther King Jr. Day and a national day of service in spring 1996. A new corporation called the Partnership for National Service had been created as a recipient for funds from individuals or organizations not wanting to contribute directly to what they perceived as an agency of the government.[27]

In March 1997, in his capacity as CEO, Wofford testified in fiscal year 1998 budget hearings before the House Appropriations Subcommittee on VA, HUD and Independent Agencies. Representative John Lewis, still the subcommittee chair, asked Senator Wofford to explain to the subcommittee the basis for a requested increase of $146,500,000, or 36 percent more than the subcommittee's appropriations for fiscal year 1997. Once again, the response was largely driven by the numbers and projected outputs. Wofford testified that the increased budget would allow for more AmeriCorps members to serve across the nation. Wofford listed specific AmeriCorps achievements in more than a dozen states, and presented the results of a 1996 study similar to the one Segal brought before the subcommittee in 1995. The 1996 study, conducted by the same California consulting firm used before, examined the activities of one out of every ten AmeriCorps members then serving. It showed that individuals in the sample taught, tutored, or mentored almost 64,000 students; collected, organized, and distributed 974,000 pounds of food; helped 2,550 homeless people find shelter; developed and distributed 38,500 sets of information about drug abuse, HIV/AIDS, street safety, health care, and other issues; ran violence-prevention after-school programs for 50,000 youth; performed energy audits for more than 18 million square feet of buildings; and planted more than 210,000 trees. Wofford reported that the CNCS had made 26,000 payments totaling approximately $44 million in education awards for members to more than 6,000 educational institutions or lenders.[28]

Before completing his prepared statement to the subcommittee, Wofford turned to the issue of the CNCS's failed audits and the need to put the corporation's financial house in order. It had been one year since the OIG had reported that the corporation's fiscal year 1994 financial statements could not be audited, and had made ninety-nine specific recommendations for corrective action.[29] Wofford informed the subcommittee that the CNCS had appointed its first chief financial officer and that fifty-seven of the ninety-nine items flagged had either been corrected or were in the process of being corrected. Wofford stated his expectation that by 1 May 1997, all but two of the problems would be either fixed or in the process of being addressed, the more significant of the two remaining items being the installation of a new financial management system, anticipated for 1998.

Financial Management Crisis

As it turned out, it would be 2001—or four years longer than promised—before the CNCS would receive a clean opinion on the audit, with only one remaining material weakness.[30] Weak financial controls created a genuine vulnerability for the corporation, making it an easy target for its many critics, and raised the question of whether the rapid growth of AmeriCorps was outstripping agency capacity. All open audits were required by law to be reported to Congress by the OIG. For years, reauthorization was always an issue, so any evidence of weak systems, poor accountability, or costly inefficiencies played directly into the hands of political opponents who sought to reduce or eliminate CNCS appropriations. For the board, the struggle with financial statements became a major focus—second only to "getting things done." It also became a distraction, creating a mountain of technical work that siphoned energy and diverted focus from the more fundamental work of improving mission effectiveness through outcomes based on program evaluation, organizational alignment, and solid strategic planning.

Problems associated with financial management issues dominated the landscape for much of the period from 1996 to 2001. Despite its efforts to have a successful audit of fiscal year 1997 financial statements, the CNCS received only a qualified report on its Statement of Financial Position as of 30 September 1997. In issuing its audit report that year, the independent accounting firm KPMG cited the corporation's inability to provide sufficient evidence to support the reasonableness of amounts recorded for grant advances, grants payable, and the component balances of its net position. KPMG further reported material weaknesses in six financial management areas: overall control of the environment that sets the tone for the organization, the National Service Trust, cash reconciliations, grants management, financial systems, and financial management.[31]

In June 1998, Wendy Zenker was introduced as the corporation's new chief operating officer, and given the responsibility of leading its efforts to achieve clean audit reports. She was recruited from the Office of Management and Budget where she had been a member of the Senior Executive Service, managed inspectors general, and overseen government-wide reform efforts in financial management.[32] Her approach was simple. She took the original list of ninety-nine problems and proceeded to work with staff and outside consultants to reengineer the internal financial processes at the corporation until, one by one, the list of problems was reduced to zero. By March 1999, the financial management picture had improved dramatically. KPMG issued an unqualified opinion of the corporation's Statement of Financial Position on 30 September 1998, although it also issued disclaimers of opinion on the Statements of Financial Operations and Changes in Net Positions and Cash Flows for the same year, and identified eight material weaknesses. The same thing happened in March 2000 with respect to the fiscal year 1999 audit, but the number of material weaknesses had been reduced from eight to five.[33]

The board did not receive official word from its management Audit and Governance Committee until 22 May 2001 that the corporation had received its first clean opinion on the audit of its financial statements with only one material weakness remaining. The one remaining area was grants management, and a new system was in the works to integrate all CNCS grants and allow electronic record keeping and transmission of information. The sense of satisfaction and pride at putting CNCS's financial house in order disappeared five years later, however, when a new and more serious accounting problem shook the corporation and brought even more scrutiny and criticism.

Congressional Oversight and Public Scrutiny

There were criticisms other than weak financial management systems that required the corporation's constant attention. Many involved the continuing public and political scrutiny that comes with receiving large amounts of federal funds in a conspicuous and controversial program. An early episode involved the issue of the average cost per member of AmeriCorps. In 1995, Eli Segal reported to the Subcommittee on VA, HUD and Independent Agencies of the House Committee on Appropriations that the "fully loaded cost"—including the living allowance, health care where the law allows and requires it, child care where the law requires it, and the educational award—was $17,600.[34] In doing so, he compared the AmeriCorps cost to the average cost per Peace Corps volunteer that had been recently reported by the *Washington Post* to be more than $33,000.[35] The issue was on the minds of committee members after President Clinton had introduced a particular AmeriCorps member named Cindy Perry in his January 1995 State of the Union address. Perry was praised by the president as a single mother of four, making a difference through AmeriCorps.[36] Some critics took issue with the Perry example and thought that AmeriCorps should not become a job training program but rather an opportunity for young people to become active citizens who understood the responsibilities of citizenship.

Other efficiency issues surfaced from time to time, as the CNCS dealt with a broad public perception that AmeriCorps members were, or should be, essentially volunteers.[37] At a corporation meeting in 1997, board members were informed of a segment airing on the NBC nightly news about a recent General Accounting Office (GAO) report on the cost per member issue, as well as others issues that included attrition rates and proper use of AmeriCorps Trust Fund money.[38] Some at the time characterized Ameri-Corps as a successful job program, but concluded that it was not providing the educational opportunity that was intended. The GAO report did show that only 56 percent of AmeriCorps members used their education awards in the first year after service. However, the report went on to explain fully that every AmeriCorps member had seven years in which to use the award to pursue their education.[39]

Congressional reauthorization was another issue constantly lurking and requiring attention. The National and Community Service Trust Act provided initial authority for the CNCS and its programs for fiscal years

1994 through 1996, and an extension of that authority for one more year. While reauthorization was not a prerequisite for the continued appropriation of funds, it was important to the long-term stability of the corporation.[40] In the eyes of most of the top officials at the time, reauthorization was a first step toward real legitimacy, a demonstration of merit for all to see, and a sign that continued support would be forthcoming. It would further provide an opportunity for Congress and the administration to agree on the substance of activities to be carried out in the future.[41] But obtaining reauthorization was difficult, and time-consuming. In 1998, the administration developed a reauthorization bill, but neither the House nor the Senate acted on it, not even at the committee level.[42] At the end of 1999, and again in 2000, the CNCS worked with sympathetic House and Senate leaders to develop another reauthorization bill in the form of the National and Community Service Amendments Act of 2000.

Outputs, Outcomes, and Evaluation

The institutional politics of national service led to a host of other managerial challenges over the first decade of the corporation's existence. None of these challenges was as acute as the one related to program evaluation. Because the CNCS never truly settled on a well-articulated theory of change for national service that defined the intended impact beyond "getting things done," evaluation was very hard to carry out. It simply was not clear how the programs delivered by the corporation were connected to the multiple outcomes that had been posited by supporters of national service. The result was a large volume of research that was commissioned that did little to guide policy development and program design. Evaluation was first and foremost a tool for managing the political environment.

Harris Wofford's testimony before the Appropriations Subcommittee was most emblematic of the struggle to define the goals of national service: "I really warmly encourage members of this committee, and all members of Congress, to visit projects in their districts. That's the way to understand what is happening. It's hard to get a real sense of what AmeriCorps is because it's doing so many things, but it has a thrust and a focus that you can only see when you meet the members, see what they are doing, and talk to the nonprofit organizations that find this people power a tremendous new contribution to their own work."[43] This was a welcoming message, but hardly a clear statement of AmeriCorps' central value proposition or its core achievements.

Even with nebulous understanding of what exactly AmeriCorps was achieving, evaluations of CNCS's programs marched on over the years. By one estimate, more than $40 million has been spent evaluating corporation programs since 1993.[44] Records show that the corporation commissioned no less than 136 assessment and impact studies from universities and outside consulting firms over the same period.[45] In November 2000, the corporation reported that it had conducted more than 100 studies since 1994, and that every year the corporation commissions fifteen to twenty competitively awarded large-scale evaluation contracts to independent research firms.[46] The same report provides some insight into the nature of the studies that were commissioned, and what the corporation took to be significant results in at least one of the major studies. On this point, the report contains a list of key findings of a 1999 study by Aguirre International into the impacts of a random sample of programs receiving AmeriCorps State and National grants.[47] The list includes the following findings: all AmeriCorps programs studied had meaningful service accomplishments; the majority of institutions that received AmeriCorps grants reported that association with AmeriCorps improved their organization's quality or quantity of services and increased their overall professionalism; and 82 percent of community representatives interviewed reported that AmeriCorps' impact on their community had been "very good" or "outstanding."[48]

This sort of reporting and tracking raises more questions than it answers: What is a "meaningful service accomplishment," and who is it meaningful for? How does a meaningful accomplishment show that AmeriCorps is achieving impact in the areas of education, the environment, public safety, or other human needs? What is the result of having "improved organizational quality and/or quantity of services"? How are these measures connected to real social outcomes? The CNCS frequently commissioned studies of community perspectives on the activities carried out by AmeriCorps members and long inventories of programmatic outputs. In many cases, this entailed going to sites around the country and counting how many students were tutored, how many trees were planted, how many lots were cleared, or, in the alternative, how various stakeholders felt about the activities they had witnessed or in which they had participated.

Ironically, despite the huge expenditures of time and money, evaluation efforts never actually took center stage within the CNCS. In the same meeting in which it introduced its newly created Department of Evaluation and Effective Practices in 1997, CNCS's board identified the four focal points for corporation improvement: staff development, reauthorization, the Presidents' Summit on America's Future, and management and internal controls.[49] Evaluating program outcomes was not even on the list, perhaps because evaluation in the form of commissioned studies focusing on outputs and attitudes was already occurring and seemed sufficient.

The early quantification efforts were heavily driven by two factors: First, AmeriCorps promised to "get things done." Thus, measuring what was accomplished became a central focus, whether or not it explored the deeper and more complex effects of service on young people. Second, the CNCS was operating for years under heavy criticism from Republicans who more than once tried to defund and close down the program. As a consequence, the evaluation unit of the corporation, which should have been providing critical information on how well the programs were performing against the CNCS's broad, multidimensional mission, was led to adopt a defensive posture that led to a series of performance reports more intended for the authorizing environment than for its senior managers.

The 1997–2002 Strategic Plan that was presented by the Planning and Evaluation Committee in January 1997 did strongly endorse program evaluation, and not all of it in the form of output counting. The plan provided an extensive list of proposed evaluation projects for the corporation as a whole and for each of its three major programs.[50] Some were in response to requirements of the Government Performance Review Act (GPRA) and many were thus output-oriented. Others, however, were independent initiatives designed to determine program impact through outcome measurement. The description of one such project, the Longitudinal Research on National Service Participants, states that among its primary tasks would be defining what outcomes should be used to assess the impact of service on participants; determining how to operationalize those outcomes in data collection; and assessing what existing data sources could be used as baselines for longitudinal tracking.[51] Because of the need for the Office of Management and Budget to approve questionnaires, implementation of the data collection phase of the project was delayed until late 1999. This study represented a major change in direction at CNCS and it has had a lasting effect on the kinds of evaluations that have been conducted in recent years.

Abt Associates was commissioned in 2001 to track reading performance improvement by students tutored by AmeriCorps members. The study showed statistically significant gains, beyond those expected for a typical child at that grade level.[52] Another study is described as assessing the role that the CNCS has played, if any, in the increasing institutionalization of service learning in schools. The intent was to inform the corporation of its success so it could design its programs to maximize the integration of service learning into academic structures.[53] These efforts and others that moved beyond tracking units of public work delivered to communities represented positive progress.

Still, institutional and cultural patterns were hard to break. The sheer number of output enumeration projects was staggering. The CNCS developed an early propensity for counting things instead of evaluating them, which dated back to its years of struggling for legitimacy. With the funding of the longitudinal study of AmeriCorps and the retrospective study of VISTA, the CNCS finally moved to a broader and more outcome-oriented approach to evaluation. For the corporation, effective program evaluation remains essential to the central task of achieving an alignment of mission and programs within the highly complex political environment in which it must operate.

Expansion and Funding Crisis

In an effort to give meaning to the campaign mantra of "compassionate conservatism," the Bush administration planned two high-profile domestic policy initiatives. The first was the launch of an initiative out of the White House aimed at articulating a new vision of the role of faith-based organizations in social service provision. The second was the reconstruction of the idea of national service. This latter task required the reorientation of the CNCS. Under Republican control for the first time after the 2000 election, the corporation's new leadership was given the job of turning around what had become seen as a troubled and ineffective agency. To do so, the CNCS's new CEO, Leslie Lenkowsky, attempted to gain control of the corporation's financial and management processes that had been in considerable disarray, and to build an argument for national service that could resolve some of the long-standing partisanship surrounding the idea of government-supported volunteerism.

The events of September 11 affected all aspects of government, including national service. The Bush administration's interest in faith and community responses to public problems was pushed almost completely off the radar screen. Homeland security and international affairs took center stage as the country sought to understand what had happened and how to prevent future attacks. The tragedy raised major questions about the purpose of national service and the kind of work that volunteers should carry out in communities around the country. As the corporation wrestled with these issues, the past loomed large. Not only was the CNCS adrift for much of its brief history, but the new Republican administration did not have much time before September 11 to develop and enact a new vision of national service. Still, President Bush announced in his State of the Union address his plan to increase the number of AmeriCorps slots from 50,000 to 75,000 and to channel these young people to work that would benefit the nation, particularly during periods of crisis and challenge. This ambitious goal was thwarted, however, when a complex financial problem at the CNCS took precedence.

As AmeriCorps expanded, concerns arose about the financial management assumptions the CNCS had relied upon in setting its budget and planning its work. Congressional auditors became concerned that the growing enrollments could not be supported by the trust fund out of which the education awards for AmeriCorps members were to be paid. After finishing their service, volunteers had up to seven years to use their education award of $4,725 to help defray the cost of college tuition and related costs. The CNCS had come to rely on a model that predicted how many volunteers would, in fact, use these education awards and thus how much money needed to be in the trust fund to pay these obligations. However, the auditors took issue with the model and objected that more funds needed to be set aside to meet potential obligations in the future. The problem was important because it once again raised questions throughout government about the management of the corporation. It was even more important because the financial crisis threatened to cut short the president's plan to expand and grow national service programs. New enrollment in AmeriCorps was suspended until the crisis was resolved, creating confusion and frustration in the field. The financial crisis gave birth to a national movement, the Save AmeriCorps Coalition, made up of leaders from the largest nonprofits that hosted AmeriCorps members and who stood to lose the most by any sudden curtailment of the size of the program in light of the possible shortfall in the trust fund. Interestingly, this crisis actually had a positive effect on the broader service movement, in that it mobilized service stakeholders and united them in the face of what could have been very large and enduring cuts in the program.[54]

As the financial crunch eased, the CNCS was put under new leadership. In late 2003, David Eisner, a former AOL Time Warner executive with experience in technology and media, was brought in to lead the CNCS. His tenure has been marked by a steady improvement in the financial management of the corporation and by a stabilization of the political support for national service. A revised strategic plan for the corporation was released in early 2006, emphasizing increased attention to accountability issues and identifying four focal areas for the corporation's initiatives: (1) mobilizing more volunteers; (2) ensuring a brighter future for all of America's children and youth with special attention to our neediest young people; (3) engaging students in their community through service learning; and (4, harnessing baby boomers' experience through engaging them in service and volunteerism.

The tragedy of September 11 and the national disasters associated with hurricanes sweeping through the Gulf of Mexico brought out the desire to help in many citizens. To date, more than 1 million Americans have volunteered to rebuild Louisiana, Mississippi, and Alabama following Katrina. More continued to arrive for years after the first wave of support, in relief efforts organized through AmeriCorps, faith-based, and other community organizations. Most AmeriCorps members are now routinely trained in basic first aid by their local Red Cross affiliate. Today, the United States continues to be vulnerable to terrorist attacks and natural disasters. While Americans are to be commended for their desire to provide disaster relief, there is still no fully articulated plan for managing their engagement. For example, the Gulf rebuilding efforts involved harnessing the skills and resources of teams of volunteers from around the country. While well intentioned, the volunteers did not always have requisite technical skills and they ended up needing constant supervision. A considerable amount of time had to be devoted to their orientation and basic organization. Frequently, there were not enough tools or well-defined work projects to engage all the members of the teams. In sum, almost everyone involved in these efforts came to agree that much work remains to be done to improve the capacity of AmeriCorps to serve and help coordinate other volunteers in times of crisis.

National service continues to evolve. By mid-2007, AmeriCorps had enrolled 500,000 members. This is a very large number by any measure and a testament to the power of the idea of service. In the end, however, the evolution of the CNCS, the organization charged with stewarding this idea, is the story of a government agency that began its early work under political pressure and then operated over a long period of time in a defensive posture. The Peace Corps was able to flourish for years because it basked in the glow of John F. Kennedy's legacy. AmeriCorps had Bill Clinton as its face, which proved to be a major political liability as the president's political problems mounted. Unclear about what the real effects of national service might be and how to measure them, the CNCS ended up focusing heavily on producing data that tracked levels of programmatic activity, rather than the effectiveness of programs and the individual, or the organizational and community-level, outcomes produced by service. Propelled forward by the urgent need to show that "things were getting done," the corporation never was able during its formative years to define a clear theory of change that rendered explicit how programmatic activity would produce outcomes—at both the individual and community level—constituting meaningful progress toward fulfilling CNCS's mission.

In the middle of its second decade, the evolution of the corporation finally appeared to take a favorable turn. In July 2007, Congress finally reauthorized the corporation, reflecting increased bipartisan support for the agency. The next chapter in the evolution of national service will be written by the Obama administration. To date, however, the transformation of the CNCS from an idea about the importance of service to a functioning tool of government action remains incomplete. Slated for substantial expansion by the Obama administration, the idea of national service has gained greater political acceptance and legitimacy. As the new leadership of the corporation attempts to meld the traditional goals of national service with the desire to contribute to homeland defense in the aftermath of September 11 and in light of the Obama administration's domestic priorities, the CNCS will surely continue to evolve and seek to find a rationale for national service—and a set of outcome measures—that will allow everyone to better assess whether the CNCS is achieving its mission.

Looking back at the institutional history of national service, there are clear accomplishments and many missed opportunities. The early tendency to view evaluation as a tool of political management rather than as a tool of operations management was particularly problematic given that the corporation was struggling to articulate the multidimensional value of service. The CNCS could have benefited from data that tested some of the core assumptions about national service's impact on young people much earlier on. Perhaps concerned about what might be discovered or what might not even be measurable, the evaluations of the corporation shied away for more than a decade from the most difficult but important questions related to the value of national service programs. The data in this study from both the longitudinal study of AmeriCorps and the retrospective study of VISTA highlight some of the programmatic challenges that now exist and should now be confronted, especially as AmeriCorps is poised for expansion. While we wish that the policy recommendations we offer in Chapter 9 could have been formulated a decade or more earlier, the data was simply not present during the early years of the corporation to render grounded conclusions about which elements of national service work and which parts need reform and rethinking. Still, we believe our research-based recommendations sketch a new and more productive direction for national service that will increase the public benefits of these important programs.

— 9 —

New Directions for National Service

To this day, national service remains a contested concept because there is no consensus on what its single, overriding purpose truly is. Multiple, overlapping ideas coexist about why we have national service and what kinds of benefits it produces.[1] One reason why it is so difficult to assess the effectiveness and impact of service is precisely because no fundamental agreement exists about what service aims to accomplish. In Chapter 1, we posited that service is supported by four very different visions. The first two visions—service as a promoter of civic engagement and as a supporter of personal growth—define service in terms of the benefits it generates at the participant or individual level. The third vision—service as a builder of social capital—has both individual and community dimensions, since social capital resides in individuals yet creates shared resources that can enrich many people and entire neighborhoods. The fourth and final vision—service as a contributor of public work—focuses on the concrete community-level benefits that flow from national service programs. These visions are not mutually exclusive, and they can even be mutually reinforcing, but they do raise questions about emphasis and focus.[2]

The data presented here sketch a picture of national service that is not flat and consistent but rather multidimensional and changing, reflecting the many different intentions, impacts, and ideals embodied in the subject. Much of the evidence we have examined, based on a longitudinal study of AmeriCorps and a retrospective study of Volunteers in Service to America (VISTA), yields results that are nuanced and at times unexpected. Positive effects are intertwined with negative effects, right alongside findings of no effects at all. Short-term and long-term effects at times coincide and at times conflict. Still, some might contend that the ultimate value of national service—in aggregate—is greater than what these mixed results tell us. By way of conclusion, we estimate in a different way what the value of service might be on a national level, and propose a number of programmatic reforms aimed at assisting the idea of national service to reach its full potential in practice.

The Value of National Service

Volunteering is a vital part of our economy and a critical part of the fabric of many communities.[3] In a 2006 issues brief, the Corporation for National and Community Service (CNCS) estimated that there were more than 61 million volunteers who served more than 8 billion hours. What if these volunteers were fully paid for their services? Or, put differently: What would organizations have to pay for the work done by volunteers if they had to employ regular workers? To give us a sense of the value of volunteer work, we must calculate the opportunity cost of volunteering.[4] The Independent Sector, the trade association representing the nonprofit field, uses the average hourly wage in the United States of $18.77 per hour when valuing volunteer labor. To calculate the real dollar value of volunteer labor, another recent study estimated the average hourly rate for volunteering by surveying nonprofit managers and asking them what they would pay for the work done by volunteers.[5] In this empirical study, the value of an hour of volunteering was found to be just over $20. Using the $20 figure, the value of all work done by volunteers in 2006 would have been more than $160 billion. Clearly, volunteering has a huge impact on our economy and is a major economic force.[6]

Of course, in the context of national service, there are costs associated with volunteering. After all, the CNCS is funding various programs, local organizations are locating and organizing volunteers, and volunteers are most likely spending their own money to volunteer (e.g., paying for their transportation). Just looking at the dollar value can thus inflate the benefits of volunteering. Across a large number of nonprofits and a wide variety of settings, it would be a major research challenge to accurately measure the average administrative and personal costs of using volunteers to meet community needs. To date, this kind of organizational- and individual-level cost accounting has not been done systematically. In the case of national service, the task of estimating costs is a bit more manageable given that the monetary costs of recruiting, placing, and paying members are more easily traced to public budgets. In thinking about the value of national service, we thus propose to look at the public costs and public benefit of volunteering, not simply the potential dollar value of the toil and hard work that volunteers deliver year in and year out. A critical first step in understanding the cost-benefit of national service is to decompose the underlying costs and benefits.

To break down the costs of volunteering, we focus again on three CNCS programs—AmeriCorps State and National, National Civilian Community Corps (NCCC), and Volunteers in Service to America (VISTA). As indicated in Chapter 3, the cost of running programs such as AmeriCorps State and National, NCCC, and VISTA appear high. For State and National, the CNCS provided $430.52 million to fund this program across the country. Many state and national programs also get additional funding from other sources to cover costs associated with running their programs. The CNCS spent $25.29 million in 2005 to fund the NCCC and $94.24 million to fund VISTA. In sum, it cost the CNCS $550 million to fund these programs. These funds were distributed as grants to local programs, and as educational awards and stipends to volunteers.[7] While we cannot readily assess the administrative and support costs to nonprofit organizations of hosting volunteers nor the state-level costs associated with supporting AmeriCorps, and these are very real costs indeed, we can at least make a rough estimate of what the costs and benefits look like from the perspective of the federal government.

If we look at the value of these three programs, the numbers appear encouraging. For VISTA and the NCCC, volunteers serve on a full-time basis, which translates into 1,700 hours per person. For State and National programs, there is a combination of full-time, part-time, and reduced part-time status. According to the Fiscal Year 2007 Congressional Budget Justification from the CNCS (2006c), there are approximately 45 percent who serve full-time, 16 percent part-time (which ranges from 900 to 1,699 hours), and 39 percent reduced part-time (which ranges from 300 to 899 hours) for State and National programs. Using the more conservative Independent Sector rate for the hourly value of volunteering, the net benefit for each program is high, and the benefit–cost ratios are positive. For State and National, the ratio is 3.52; for the NCCC, it is 1.45; and for VISTA, the ratio is 2.27.

Table 9.1 displays the summary of these results. While definitive claims cannot be made on the basis of these rough benefit–cost results, the estimates do suggest that the benefits of national service programs likely outweigh the costs. This positive conclusion is due in part to the low wages that are paid corps members and to the value that one can reasonably attach to the actual hourly value of the work that is completed. The benefit–cost ratio for the residential NCCC program is the most accurate because the cost that the CNCS spends includes lodging, transportation, and other incidentals for volunteers. The benefit is also more accurate because all NCCC volunteers serve full-time for ten months (or 1,700 hours). While VISTA is also a full-time program, it is not residential. So while we are able to accurately capture the benefits of volunteering (hours of volunteer service), additional costs such as lodging, transportation, and other incidentals that volunteers must cover are not included.

The results for State and National are admittedly a crude estimate because there is great variability in the number of hours served by members and because many real costs are not captured fully. While the CNCS spent $430 million to fund State and National programs, it is not a residential program, so additional costs incurred by volunteers are not taken into account. Also, some local programs have the ability to request additional funds from their state or local government, or through donations from individuals and foundations. These costs have not been included as well. In our analysis, for part-time and reduced part-time hours volunteered, we used the average hours (1,299 and 599 hours, respectively) to calculate benefit. Still, whatever methodology is used to assess the costs and benefits of national service, the ratios are very likely to be positive in the end.[8]

Supporting the overall validity of the rough conclusion presented here that the benefits of national service outweigh its costs are the results of a meta-analysis conducted by Perry and Thomson (2004). In their cost-benefit meta-analysis, they collected fourteen studies of volunteer programs from the 1960s through the 1990s. These programs include AmeriCorps State and National, VISTA, conservation and youth corps programs, Foster Grandparents, and other civic service programs. Table 9.2 displays a summary of Perry and Thomson's cost-benefit meta-analysis. Across fourteen studies included in their analysis, seventy-three programs were evaluated, with sixty-five being distinctly separate programs. Several studies researched the same volunteer programs, but in different years. The most extensive cost-benefit analysis was conducted by Aguirre International as part of an impact analysis of AmeriCorps State and National programs. They looked at forty-four State and National programs between 1994 and 1995. Across

Table 9.1

Cost-Benefit Summary (2005 program year)

	State and National	NCCC	VISTA
Enrollment	66,830	1,152	6,707
Hours of Participation	45% full-time (1,700 hours per person) 16% part-time (900–1,699 hours per person) 39% reduced part-time (300–899 hours per person)[a,b]	Full-time (1,700 hours per person)	Full-time (1,700 hours per person)
Cost (Funding 2005)	$430.52 million	$25.29 million	$94.24 million
Net Benefit	$1.08 billion	$11.47 million	$119.77 million
Benefit-Cost Ratio	3.52	1.45	2.27

[a]Percentage based on 2005 figures. From CNCS Fiscal Year 2007 Congressional Budget Justification Report; see p. 189.

[b]To estimate the hours for part-time and reduced part-time, the average was taken from the range. For part-time, average hours served is 1,299 hours (range 900–1,699). For reduced part-time, average hours served is 599 hours (range 300–899).

the forty-four programs, the benefits were valued at $53 million and the costs at $36.7 million, or a benefit–cost ratio of 1.44. Looking across all the studies, the overall average benefit–cost ratio was 1.61. It is particularly interesting that the benefit–cost ratios had not changed since the 1960s, when some of these studies were first conducted.

Overall, these prior studies have consistently shown that volunteer programs are cost-effective. Schools and communities benefit greatly from the services of volunteers—from tutoring to cleanups and conservation projects and, more recently, to homeland security activities.[9] While we have noted earlier the problems associated with capturing all the costs associated with using volunteers to meet public needs, there is a final consideration to bear in mind. The benefits of national service likely extend way beyond the narrow monetized value of the work product. Other benefits to consider, though hard to estimate in monetary terms, are the long-term

Table 9.2
Summary Results of Previous Studies

Author and Study	Program Type	N	Years	Benefit-cost Ratio
Aguirre International, *Making a Difference*	AmeriCorps State and National Programs	44	1994–1995	1.44
Booz, Allen, Public Administration Services, Cost-Benefit Study of the Foster Grandparent Program	Foster Grandparent Program	1	1965–1971	1.14
California Conservation Corps, 1976–1979	California Conservation Corps	1	1976–1979	1.20
Carlson and Strang, *Volunteers in Service to America*	AmeriCorps VISTA	1	1994	1.40
Control Systems Research, Program for Local Service	Program for Local Service	1	1972	1.90
Frees et al., Final Report: National Service Demonstration Programs	National Service Demonstration Projects	1	1993–1994	1.30
Jastrzab et al., *Impacts of Service*	Conservation and Youth Corps Programs	8	1993–1994	1.04
Neumann et al., *The Benefits and Costs of National Service*	AmeriCorps for Math and Literacy, Project First, East Bay Conservation Corps	3	1994–1995	2.51–2.58 2.02–2.15 1.59–1.68
Public Interest Economics—West, Economic Impact of California Conservation Corps Projects	California Conservation Corps	1	1979	1.20

Study		Year	Benefit-Cost Ratio
Shumer, YouthWorks AmeriCorps Evaluation: A Cost-Benefit Analysis	3	1994–1995	1.23–1.65 2.94 3.90
Shumer and Cady, YouthWorks AmeriCorps Evaluation: Second Year Report, 1995–1996	3	1995–1996	1.34–1.93 2.15 1.94
Shumer and Rentel, YouthWorks AmeriCorps Evaluation: Third Year Report, 1996–1997	3	1996–1997	2.26 1.65 2.45
Wang, Owens, and Kim, Cost and Benefit Study of Two AmeriCorps Projects in the State of Washington	2	1994–1995	2.40 (2% discount rate) 1.80 (5% discount rate)
Wolf, Leiderman, and Voith, California Conservation Corps	1	1984–1985	0.96
Total	73		1.61[a]

Education Enhancement, Juvenile Crime, Construction Training of At-Risk Youth

Education Enhancement, Juvenile Crime, Construction Training of At-Risk Youth

Education Enhancement, Juvenile Crime, Construction Training of At-Risk Youth

Washington State AmeriCorps Programs

California Conservation Corps

Source: Adapted from Perry and Thomson (2004).

[a] This is an average benefit-cost ratio. Ranges were converted into an average ratio so that each study had a single benefit-cost ratio. Then, the average was taken across 14 benefit-cost ratios.

benefits to the participants and clients. For example, many AmeriCorps programs offer tutoring services in school and in after-school community programs. These volunteer tutors offer a safe environment for students to learn, make positive connections, and develop their long-term potential. While hard to quantify, there are significant long-range benefits to our society in terms of building the human capital of both the children being served and the members doing the work. Though it may be hard to monetize the increased lifetime productivity associated with many national service interventions in terms of greater earning potential and reduced costs of incarceration, these benefits are still very real.[10]

In the end, even if one finds the evidence compelling that national service is a bargain and that its benefits outweigh its costs, this does not in any way imply that the program is fulfilling all elements of its complex mission or that the implementation of national service programs could not be improved. We turn now to ideas for improving the performance of national service, which are aimed at ensuring not just that benefits of national service continue to outstrip its costs but also that these programs reach their full potential.[11]

The Future of National Service

In this book, we have done little to fundamentally resolve the ongoing competition between the four main visions of service: civic engagement, personal growth, social capital, and public work. We have not attempted to marshal evidence that service is "really" about one of the visions to the exclusion of the others. Nor have we sought to demonstrate that one of these visions is of greater value than the others. We have, however, developed multiple forms of empirical evidence to suggest which of these four visions is actually being fulfilled through AmeriCorps and VISTA. By way of conclusion, we propose to sum up the evidence and develop some concrete proposals for how national service could, in fact, more fully achieve all four of the visions we have outlined. Whatever one concludes the fundamental end or rationale for national service might be, there is room to improve the implementation of these programs in order to give them a real chance to achieve their full potential.[12] Thus, while we do not take a stand about the right vision for service because we believe all four visions are credible, we do offer some ideas on how national service might be recast and fine-tuned so that it has a better chance of achieving its ends, whether they are focused on one, two, three, or all four of the visions of national service.

Many of the recommendations we describe here for the improvement of national service focus on targeting these programs on the young people who will benefit most from service and on bringing greater simplicity to the structure of these efforts. We see many opportunities to sharpen national service and to streamline the administration of these programs.[13] By making a few selective changes—anchored in the empirical findings of our study—we see the possibility of moving national service to higher levels of performance in the years ahead.[14] Since researching and writing this book, important policy changes have taken place that will significantly shape the national service landscape. Both President Obama and the First Lady are advocates for engaging all of our citizens in service. Congress passed, and the president signed, the Edward M. Kennedy Serve America Act in 2009, which greatly expands and makes key changes in the national service agenda. We believe the new legislation includes a number of positive ideas for improving AmeriCorps. However, the changes do not go quite far enough in ensuring all of the necessary improvements required for a successful scaling-up of AmeriCorps are in place. By way of conclusion, we provide recommendations in five major areas where AmeriCorps' program design and implementation can and should be improved.

Recruiting Young People

One of the most pressing challenges facing AmeriCorps is ensuring that the program reaches people who are most likely to benefit from the experience. In terms of simple demographics, AmeriCorps is attracting a disproportionate number of women. It is not clear why the program is more appealing to women than to men, but it is apparent that recruiting for national service should target young men and attempt to bring greater gender balance to these programs.[15] One reason why gender balance is important is that service is intended to be a way of introducing young people to the workplace and to the challenge of working with people from different walks of life. If AmeriCorps does not achieve greater gender balance, it will not be a very accurate representation of the broader work environment.

Recruitment needs to change in at least one other way. When it comes to promoting civic engagement, we found that the program did have a significant effect on the engagement of members. However, we also noted that the program was serving young people who were already highly engaged in civic life. AmeriCorps members were on the whole, and at the extreme, already very engaged with their communities. Indeed, when comparing the treatment and comparison groups at baseline, we found that there was a substantial difference in terms of the level of civic engagement. Those in the program were more engaged in civic life than those who ultimately did not to enroll in AmeriCorps.

Rather than boosting the civic enthusiasm of people who are already engaged, we believe that the CNCS should launch a full-fledged outreach effort at marketing the program to disenfranchised and excluded populations. Our ancillary analyses showed that members without prior volunteer experience achieved larger gains across many measures than members who entered the program with prior volunteer experience. This means that service opportunities should be advertised in ways that target young people who are outside the civic mainstream and who have no real connection to their community. It also may require a fresh approach to framing service that makes it appealing to those who may have never even thought about serving. There is no clear brand associated with the various service programs. The sheer number of different programs—from AmeriCorps to VISTA to the NCCC—makes it hard to explain what national service is and what it implies. The AmeriCorps "brand" is also further diluted by competing marketing from the local programs that operate AmeriCorps and promote their own mission and image. Cleaning up the AmeriCorps brand and targeting populations outside civic life would be a good first step.

While the CNCS could help in the process of increasing awareness of service opportunities, there are other ways to ensure that national service programs are directed at the most needy populations. One alternate way of opening up AmeriCorps to new and needier populations would be to reward local nonprofit organizations that recruit and retain disenfranchised people. Nonprofit organizations that currently host members are given tremendous autonomy in selecting the members who will fill the ranks of their organizations. This is critical to ensuring that local organizations view members as assets that they have selected, rather than cost centers that have been imposed from outside. Without tampering with this autonomy, the CNCS could still introduce modest incentives in the form of additional training and support grants to nonprofit organizations that reach out to the most disenfranchised members of the local community.

Another way to interest a larger number of currently disengaged young people in national service would be to focus on the system of rewards and incentives within the program. The educational award and even the living stipend could be adjusted in order to attract the poor and alienated. If national service is really to promote civic engagement, it must take seriously the task of differentially motivating and rewarding the young people who enter the program. For members coming from affluent families who are already imbued with the ethos of service and for whom AmeriCorps represents a natural culmination of their commitment to find ways to connect to public problems, the current system of living stipend or educational reward is not a central consideration in their calculus about whether to serve. However, for those who enter the program with few or no resources, the financial elements of service are a very important consideration in deciding to join. Increasing the educational award would attract more members from families with modest means for whom the financing of a college education is an enormous and daunting challenge.

The educational allowance is only perceived as an important benefit to a narrow subgroup of participants, namely those with college plans. One route to increasing diversity in recruitment would be to make the educational awards more flexible or transferable. This is especially important for the ever-growing baby boomer generation, which should be an important target group for national service. AmeriCorps does not appeal to many boomers right now, nor do the other senior programs. One possible way to draw in this talented and socially engaged generation would be to make the educational award transferable to the children and grandchildren of members who serve. This would allow older participants to do service and help their extended families reach their educational goals.

Revamping, redirecting, and fully funding outreach efforts related to national service would represent a small fraction of the CNCS's annual budget. This single step would, however, help ensure that the program actually reaches the population of young people who could most benefit from the service experience. The new national service legislation makes some progress toward broadening AmeriCorps' reach in terms of increasing the involvement of disenfranchised and underrepresented populations from service. The act encourages targeting of disadvantaged populations, consistent with our recommendation to expand recruitment in groups most likely to benefit from opportunities to participate in service. However, it does not address the real challenge of specifically targeting individuals who are civically disengaged and who have little experience with volunteer service. The act takes an important step in increasing the amount of the educational award over time. This will be an important incentive for lower-income members who can use the award to cover a large proportion of the costs of their postsecondary education. The new law will also encourage boomers to serve by allowing members who are fifty-five and older to transfer the award to their children or grandchildren. While these changes make some steps to broaden AmeriCorps' recruitment "tent" by targeting a broader base of potential enrollees, AmeriCorps still needs to expand its horizons and focus on enrolling the entire population of prospective members, particularly those who would likely not find an opportunity to serve outside of the program and whom our research indicates are very likely to benefit from the national service experience.

Sharpening Program Focus

One of the more appealing aspects of national service is that there are so many different ways that members can give of themselves to communities. Members are doing many different forms of public work. While AmeriCorps has defined five key areas of public work, in reality there are many programs that span these areas or that simply do not fit into any clear category. In addition, the potential work of VISTA volunteers is extremely broadly defined. Though VISTA members concentrate their service in high-poverty communities, they have over time listened very closely to the issues that residents say they want to work on. In practice, this makes service responsive, but also very diffuse. VISTA can and does accomplish many small and distinctive tasks for communities. It remains unclear, however, whether this adds up within the community to a coherent agenda or whether a common approach is being built across all VISTA projects that rests on proven best practices.

The diffusion of effort across a large number of service tasks has at least a couple of substantial drawbacks. First, it is very difficult to ever understand the underlying model of national service if the program is constantly experimenting by putting volunteers in unique tasks. Without greater concentration in the range of tasks that are carried out by members, it is difficult to imagine how progress can be made over time with regard to program implementation. Getting programs to perform at a high level requires year-to-year adjustment and refinements, something that is only possible when there is a high level of focus and consistency, particularly in the roll-out of new programs. Interestingly, there is anecdotal evidence that some level of program concentration is, in fact, desirable. City Year, one of the largest recipients of AmeriCorps funding and which operates in more than a dozen cities around the country, has narrowed its range of service opportunities to focus on education. In Chicago, for example, all City Year members work in schools, and this has allowed the program to do a large-scale evaluation and hone the program significantly from year to year. This is a major departure from City Year's original model, where local affiliates had more opportunity to adapt the range of services projects based on local interest.

It might appear that by highlighting the downside of diffusing effort across a range of projects we are tilting slightly toward the public work vision of service at the cost of the personal growth vision. But this is not the case. While we argue for an approach that will increase the efficacy of the program in terms of the public benefits that will be generated, there are also likely to be benefits for members in terms of improved training and work skills associated with a honing of the programmatic scope of national service programs.

Another benefit of narrowing the scope of work completed through national service is that it would make possible the refinement of a national training model that would get young people off to a good start. At present, training for AmeriCorps, VISTA, the NCCC, and other programs is highly decentralized and geared to local conditions. While this approach empowers local agencies to prepare members, it does not necessarily lead to the most thorough and well-conceived training programs. In fact, the very idea of preservice training is something that the national service movement has wrestled with for decades. We heard many accounts of unorthodox training during the early days of VISTA and we also listened to accounts of recent minimal or ineffectual training for some AmeriCorps members. With a honing of the kind of work that members do, a better and more useful training program could be developed at the national level and disseminated locally for customization. While one would not want to strip local nonprofit organizations of the responsibility of preparing members for their assignments, having some kind of national training modules would be helpful to guide the member orientation and preparation that goes on in communities around the country. Improving the quality of training does, however, depend at least in part on rendering more manageable the range of tasks that members are being trained to assume.

The new legislation charting the future of AmeriCorps does attempt to narrow the range of AmeriCorps service targets somewhat. The act creates five new AmeriCorps State and National programs, each defined by a priority service area: Education Corps, Healthy Future Corps, Clean Energy Corps, Veterans' Corps, and Opportunity Corps. This could be an important first step in honing AmeriCorps programming. However, by creating a new set of AmeriCorps program areas, it may further confuse the public's understanding of what AmeriCorps is all about in the short run. At the same time, each of the programmatic areas remains diffuse—for example, Clean Energy members could distribute low-energy light bulbs to seniors, train for "green jobs," run summer youth programs in national parks, or pick up trash on beaches and other public areas. Moreover, programs can choose to focus on any one or all of the five priority areas or simply elect to operate a national service program that does not fit in with any of the priority areas. Even if several programs operate within a single priority area, they may be doing very different kinds of service, making it nearly impossible to compare impacts across programs. This will make it difficult to address President Obama's mandate for national service "to enhance what works and avoid using resources on ineffective programs" and ensure that "volunteering is tied into a united and measured effort across the nation."[16] In sum, relabeling broad categories is no real substitute for working toward greater actual program focus in the kinds of work that members carry out around the country.

Improving Placements and Training

Even if the range of work done through service were narrowed and refined and even if training were improved, there would still need to be a fair amount of variation in the actual tasks defined for members. Members enter national service with the ability to take on everything from very basic tasks to highly skilled work. This leads to another way that the actual implementation of national service programs could be improved. AmeriCorps in particular requires much more careful matching of people to tasks. The education levels of AmeriCorps members range from high school dropouts all the way to holders of advanced degrees. Finding the right placement for each member is essential to both maximizing the skill development of members and producing the greatest possible public benefit. In any one school where service takes place, helping a teacher get her classroom set up requires a very different skill level than successfully tutoring math to a struggling high school student. Effectively placing members requires a heightened sensitivity to the range of skills that members bring into service. Placing highly skilled people in demanding service projects and lower-skilled young people in easier placements not only makes sense for the members but also for the community. Unfortunately, we encountered a fair amount of anecdotal evidence throughout this research project that good matches are not always accomplished. Within one AmeriCorps program, we heard of a high school graduate doing one-on-one school-based tutoring, and a college graduate engaged in a cleanup project focused on a garbage-strewn empty lot. This sort of talent allocation is far from optimal.

Failure to find appropriate placements that recognize the wide range of skills that members bring to their work will be very costly in the long run. It will lead to lower program completion rates and to disaffected young people giving up on the ideal of making a difference. To be sure, there is an egalitarian ethos within national service that wants to work with all members and treat them the same. However, the demonstrable fact remains that members are heterogeneous, come from very different backgrounds, and possess divergent skill sets. National service should strive to serve the single mother who wants to get some community work experience while getting a GED, and also be ready to tap the talents of elite college graduates who are ready to volunteer. Our main concern is that the tasks assigned to members reflect their skill sets and their interests. Failure to sensibly align members with tasks and responsibilities will not only underutilize talent but also weaken recruitment in the long term. Thus, after focusing the programs of national service in terms of subject matter, an appropriate matching of talent to task is a requisite to effective service programs. The Kennedy Serve America Act adds a new requirement that members serving as tutors have a high school diploma, but remains largely silent about improving the match between members' skill levels and their service experience and ways to improve member training.

The weak findings we discovered in several areas of personal growth indicate that more thought and effort needs to be put into the time members spend outside their work sites. AmeriCorps needs a more refined and grounded curriculum to supplement the community work that is the centerpiece of the program. This could entail offering more guidance to nonprofits that host members on how to cultivate their talents, build leadership skills, and prepare them more effectively for life after service. With an entire year to work with young people, national service should be more than just a set of tasks that get accomplished. It should include a rigorous and well-considered introduction to work and civic life, grounded in well-defined readings, discussions, and exercises. Without more attention and thought to placement and training, national service programs will lose an extraordinary opportunity to shape the skills and attitudes of young people in a very positive way.

Deepening Member Experience

The availability of part-time (and limited part-time) positions as an option for those not able or willing to take on a full-time position requires reconsideration. One reason why these part-time positions arose is simply to accommodate as many people as possible and to open national service up to new populations that otherwise would not be able to participate. Part-time participants cost less than full-time members on a per-participant basis. Though part-time members were not part of our study, we believe there is little chance that spending less time in service will generate improved gains by members. In fact, given the less than completely positive results we found in our study of full-time members, particularly in the areas of education and employment, we think more program time and training is called for, not less. As part of the broader effort to simplify the programs of national service and focus on what has proven to work, we believe that targeting resources on full-time placements would be in the best interests of members and the communities in which they work. One way to drive more members to full-time participation would be to increase the educational award, and to prorate it more conservatively for those who opt for part-time service.

At present, there is a tremendous diffusion of national service placements across a very large number of nonprofit organizations. By spreading the wealth of service, the CNCS has succeeded in supporting pluralism and decentralization, two critical and valuable components of service. However, there is a price to be paid for the wide dispersion of national service placements: It is hard to channel members into larger efforts, which aim at more ambitious social objectives. Another price to be paid is in the form of a loss of economies of scale that would be possible if there were a greater concentration of resources.[17] One way that the CNCS has traditionally sought to balance the value of supporting local initiatives and larger-scale change is through the national direct grants programs. By channeling larger allotments of slots to organizations like the American Red Cross, Teach for America, and other national nonprofit organizations, the CNCS has sought to have it both ways. While the current balance is a wise compromise between complete fragmentation of effort and total concentration of resources, we think the balance could be shifted slightly more in favor of national endeavors. Again, by developing more relationships with organizations that can deploy large numbers of members, the CNCS would be able to reduce some of the problems of sustainability that arise when small allocations are given to fragile nonprofit organizations. A bit more consolidation in placements across nonprofit organizations would also go a long way toward driving down some of the administrative expenses associated with operating these programs.

Any concentration of effort on full-time placements and more national direct grant recipients would demand that more rigorous performance measurement systems be put in place.[18] The CNCS must be able to justify the awarding of larger blocks of placements to a select group of high-performing organizations and this requires a systematic and defensible system for assessing and ranking the performance of its national recipients. The new legislation discourages the recent trend toward increased part-time service by members serving in AmeriCorps and requires that the corporation ensure that at least 50 percent of members serve full-time. We believe this change will enhance the quality of both the member experience and community services.

Streamlining Administrative Structure

One of the most clear-cut recommendations that flows from our study of national service relates to residential programs. We were surprised to find that far from building group cohesion and tolerance of difference, the NCCC residential program actually made members significantly more intolerant in the short run, though not in the long run. While we speculate in Chapter 6 about the many possible reasons for this finding, the recommendation that flows from this finding is fairly simple. We see a need to substantially revamp the NCCC program in light of the evidence that it does not perform any better and, in some areas such as tolerance, it actually creates short-term problems that are not present in the nonresidential version of national service. What, then, is the distinct competency and highest value use of a residential national service program?

The most successful response to Hurricane Katrina and other disasters was provided by the NCCC. The first volunteers to reach New Orleans after Katrina ripped into the Gulf of Mexico were not from the Red Cross, but from the NCCC. To this day, the NCCC plays a critical role in the gulf's recovery. The NCCC provided an immediately available and deployable contingent of trained volunteers to help mitigate the effects of the disaster. Unlike the hordes of volunteers who trekked to the gulf to serve for a few days or weeks, the NCCC members were there for protracted periods of time, and they did not require time-consuming training and orientation. The NCCC played an important role in providing largely labor-intensive services—debris removal, reconstruction, distribution of food and clothing, and general cleanup. The commitment and desire of short-term volunteers to help is noteworthy and was surely appreciated by gulf residents; however, many of these volunteers were often underskilled, undersupervised, and lacked sufficient tools and materials to make efficient contributions. Although short-term volunteers may reap benefits in terms of their own satisfaction with helping and gain in their knowledge about poverty and our nation's infrastructure, residents recovering from disasters need intensive and lasting assistance. This is something that the NCCC could provide in the future. By developing the capacity of the NCCC to serve as a quick-response unit in times of disaster and by retooling the training and support that members receive, the CNCS could accomplish something important: It could improve a documented problem in its program portfolio. In the absence of such a retooling, questions will linger about why this residential option lives on and what justifies the administrative costs associated with this small and distinct program.

Beyond this first step in program redesign, the CNCS should ask itself why AmeriCorps and VISTA remain distinct programs. VISTA does have a long history and it once had a distinctive programmatic identity. Over time, however, the activist and organizing element of VISTA has receded, and the program has become focused on the target population served, namely poor communities. The Alinsky-driven content of the program in the 1960s and 1970s has been displaced by a generalized preference for serving those most disadvantaged. While this does represent an important focus, it does not justify maintaining a special program name and administrative apparatus. The broader array of initiatives in the corporation's "family" of programs is confusing and overlapping. College students mentor children as part of both AmeriCorps and the separate Learn and Serve program. Senior volunteers serve in all three major programs, not just those defined as Senior Corps. Adding to the confusion are the additional programs announced in recent years, such as the Citizen Corps and USA Freedom Corps. Amid all this confusion, there is the need for a much clearer and coherent brand or identity that will draw in and motivate large numbers of new people who want to serve, rather than confuse them with an array of overlapping and ill-defined subprograms.

In addition to narrowing and strengthening the national service brand, the entire state-level system of commissions also requires reconsideration. Critics have long pointed out the inefficiencies of having in many cases both state-level commissions administering AmeriCorps and state-level corporation offices operating VISTA and Senior Corps. This arrangement also makes accessing programs and funds for community groups needlessly complex. With both holdover government bodies from the early days of a predecessor service program (ACTION) and more recently created administrative bodies operating alongside one another, the national service movement is saddled with a cumbersome administrative structure. To make matters worse, Learn and Serve operates autonomously through state Departments of Education. Because communication between the states and the CNCS is critical to effective program administration, pruning the older administrative structure and bringing consistency across states could only help. The national service movement is currently spread across too broad an array of duplicative programs and managed by a set of overlapping agencies. All of this needs radical simplification and streamlining.

Most of the recommendations we have advanced involve modest changes in program design and implementation.[19] Drastic changes in the structure of national service have been proposed, however, including voucherizing the entire program. This approach would put a service voucher in the hands of members and allow them to go out and find a nonprofit organization where they would choose to work. The voucher would provide the host nonprofit with funding to support the member's stipend and other related expenses. While this approach has the merit of depoliticizing the selection of sites (particularly the national direct grantees) by allowing members to decide where service is to be delivered, it is ultimately impractical because it does not allow for necessary organizational screening for competence and capacity to execute. Moreover, a voucher system would not encourage year-to-year stability in site selection that is required to build learning about how best to deploy members and improve the quality of national service. We believe that the data we have collected and analyzed suggest very strongly that more—not less—work needs to be done to improve the quality of service experiences. Still, a small experiment to test the voucher idea will be implemented and this will allow for a fuller understanding of what happens when AmeriCorps allows members to choose the organizations where they work.

Another idea that has been floated is to radically expand the size of AmeriCorps by allowing members to serve for up to four years with the possibility thereafter of having money to pay for four years of college. While this sounds like a promising and ambitious agenda, the timing may not yet be right to take on this level of program expansion. There are many reforms and improvements that need to be implemented in the existing AmeriCorps program before any massive expansion can sensibly be broached. Thus, while there is great potential to extend the service experience to many more young people over time, we believe that the first order of business is the more mundane and less-glamorous work of program reform and refinement.

We believe it is critical to solidify the national service infrastructure to ensure a stable foundation for the rapid scale-up called for by the Kennedy Act—an increase in AmeriCorps members from the current level of 75,000 to 250,000 by 2017. The legislation of 2009 has addressed several of our structural recommendations, in particular those concerning the NCCC. The act requires NCCC campuses to be cost-effective and a feasibility study to be conducted before a campus is located on a military base. It also makes the significant change of allowing the NCCC to operate nonresidential programs. The law recognizes the important role the NCCC can play in disaster relief and encourages the corporation to target disadvantaged youth as prospective corps members. However, the new legislation does nothing to reduce the number of similar service programs. In fact, it increases the number of AmeriCorps State and National programs, and the result is that the array of AmeriCorps programs remains overlapping and confusing. National service needs to be simplified in the years ahead, not rendered more complex.

Looking Ahead

We have arrived at a turning point for national service. Once relegated to the laundry list of "feel good" and symbolic initiatives, national service is emerging as an idea with real potential to improve and revitalize American civic culture. As research shows an ever-increasing distrust of government, national service stands out as a promising way to recharge the country's civic energy, develop the potential of a large number of young people, increase trust and cooperation in communities, and actually accomplish important community tasks at a reasonable cost. It is an idea that has a lot of potential, only a small part of which has been realized to date.

A new vision for national service must not be based only on a superficial reshuffling of existing service institutions and programs. Rather, it requires renewed thinking about the role of national service and the infrastructure needed to support it, building on the lessons learned over time. We have outlined here a fivefold set of reforms that would address many of the performance shortcomings revealed in the data and help chart a new direction for national service. The five areas of reform we outline—(1) recruiting more disenfranchised young people who would truly benefit from the experience, (2) focusing programs on a narrower range of work domains, (3) reengineering the placement and training components, (4) deepening the volunteer experience by focusing more on full-time service, and (5) streamlining the administrative apparatus supporting national service—are all overlapping and mutually reinforcing. They constitute a reform agenda that is not only doable but readily achievable.

Can progress be made on any or all of these fronts? With support coming now from both sides of the political spectrum, the conditions are much more conducive to fixing and remodeling national service than has been the case since the earliest days of AmeriCorps. The idea of service is no longer under assault, the needs of communities—particularly those struck by disaster—are demonstrably great, and the country is more attuned since 9/11 to the need to build a national sense of purpose and a strong sense of the responsibilities of citizenship. We have reported here the successes and failures of national service. We have also outlined how the national service movement could best be reformed. All that is needed now is a commitment to act on the data and to improve national service so that it can make the greatest possible contribution to our country and to our communities.

Appendices

Appendix A
Information about the Four Rounds of Participant Surveys

Tool	Timing[a]	Focus
Baseline Survey (September 1999–March 2000)	*Members:* Within days of enrolling *Comparison Group:* 3–4 months after inquiring about AmeriCorps (roughly when they might have enrolled)	• Prior service experience • Other background characteristics • Attitudinal information related to outcomes
Postprogram Survey (September 2000–May 2001)	*State and National Members:* 1–2 months after completing service (approximately 1 year after baseline survey) *NCCC Members:* During final weeks of service (approximately 10 months after baseline survey) *Comparison Group:* 12–15 months after baseline survey	• Attitudinal information related to outcomes • Information on AmeriCorps program experience (members only)

235

Appendix A
(continued)

Tool	Timing[a]	Focus
Supplemental State and National Member Survey (September 2002–June 2003)	*Members:* 3 years after baseline survey (approximately 2 years after most members completed their service) *Comparison Group:* 3 years after baseline survey	• Additional background information to address selection bias • Social networking behavior • Additional information on program experience (members only) • Limited data on postprogram activities
Follow-Up Survey (March–September 2007)	*Members:* 8 years after baseline survey (approximately 7 years after most members completed their initial year of service) *Comparison Group:* 8 years after baseline survey	• Attitudinal and behavioral information related to outcomes • Limited data on postprogram activities • Information about Segal AmeriCorps Education award usage (members only)

[a] A note on survey timing: The duration of AmeriCorps programs was generally between 10 and 12 months. Cases were released for the postprogram and the postprogram supplemental interviews at 12 and 36 months, respectively, after baseline interview. Most respondents were interviewed within a few weeks of survey release. In some instances, it took longer (up to 5 months) to locate and interview respondents.

Appendix B
Development of Composite Measures

Neighborhood Obligations

Do you feel that each of the following is not an important obligation, a somewhat important obligation, or a very important obligation that a citizen owes to the country (Not important = 1, Very important = 3)?

1. Reporting a crime you may have witnessed
2. Participating in neighborhood organizations
3. Helping keep the neighborhood safe
4. Helping keep the neighborhood clean and beautiful
5. Helping those who are less fortunate

Community Problem Identification

How much do you feel you know about problems facing the community such as (Nothing = 1, Great deal = 5):

1. The environment
2. Public health issues
3. Literacy
4. Crime
5. Lack of civic involvement

Active in Community Affairs

How often do you do each of the following (Never = 1, Always = 5):

1. Participate in events such as community meetings, celebrations, or activities in my community
2. Join organizations that support issues that are important to me
3. Write or e-mail newspapers or organizations to voice my views

Grassroots Efficacy

Think about how hard it would be for you to accomplish each of the following activities (I would not be able to get this done = 1, I would be able to get this done = 3):

1. Organizing an event to benefit a charity or religious organization
2. Starting an after-school program for children whose parents work
3. Organizing an annual cleanup program for the local park

Personal Effectiveness of Community Service

Thinking about all of your voluntary community service or volunteer activities over the past 12 months, please indicate how much you agree with the following statements (Strongly disagree = 1, Strongly agree = 5):

1. I felt I made a contribution to the community.
2. I felt like part of a community.
3. I felt I could make a difference in the life of at least one person.

Personal Growth through Community Service

Thinking about all of your voluntary community service or volunteer activities over the past 12 months, please indicate how much you agree with the following statements (Strongly disagree = 1, Strongly agree = 5):

1. I reexamined my beliefs and attitudes about myself.
2. I was exposed to new ideas and ways of seeing the world.
3. I learned about the real world.
4. I did things I never thought I could do.
5. I changed some of my beliefs and attitudes.

Basic Work Skills

For each skill area, indicate how much experience you have and how important it is to you (Little or none = 1, A lot = 3, Not important = 1, Very important = 3):

1. Solving unexpected problems or finding new and better ways to do things
2. Knowing how to gather and analyze information from different sources such as people/organizations
3. Listening and responding to other people's suggestions or concerns
4. Stopping or decreasing conflicts between people
5. Leading a team by taking charge, explaining, and motivating coworkers
6. Negotiating, compromising, and getting along with coworkers, supervisors
7. Learning new ways of thinking or acting from other people
8. Adapting your plans or ways of doing things in response to changing circumstances
9. Managing your time when you're under pressure
10. Dealing with uncomfortable or difficult working conditions

Connection to Community

Please indicate how strongly you agree with each of the following statements (Strongly disagree = 1, Strongly agree = 5):

1. I have a strong attachment to my community.
2. I often discuss and think about how larger political issues affect my community.
3. I am aware of what can be done to meet the important needs of my community.
4. I have the ability to make a difference in my community.
5. I try to find the time or a way to make a positive difference in my community.

Appendix B
(continued)

Appreciation of Cultural and Ethnic Diversity

Please indicate how much you agree with each of the following statements
(Strongly disagree = 1, Strongly agree = 5):

1. If people from different backgrounds took the time to understand each other, there wouldn't be so many social problems.
2. Some of my friends are of different backgrounds from me: racial, cultural, ethnic, or language.
3. Racism affects everyone.
4. I feel comfortable belonging to groups where people are different from me.

On a scale of 1 to 5, where 1 = not very interested and 5 = very interested, how would you describe your interest in forming friendships with people who come from a different race or ethnicity from you?

Please indicate how much you agree with each of the following statements
(Strongly disagree = 1, Strongly agree = 5):

1. Diverse viewpoints bring creativity and energy to a work group.
2. Multicultural teams can be stimulating and fun.
3. People are more motivated and productive when they feel they are accepted for who they are.
4. Diversity improves the work of organizations.
5. Diversity brings many perspectives to problem solving.
6. I am comfortable interacting with people from a different racial or ethnic background.

Constructive Group Interactions

How often have you been in a group situation with others where the following things have occurred (Never = 1, Always = 5)?

1. We discuss issues and problems and share ideas.
2. We involve everyone and avoid favoritism.
3. We can disagree and be different from one another without fear.
4. We take time to work out any conflicts.

Constructive Personal Behavior in Groups

Please answer how often you do the following (Never = 1, Always = 5):

1. I try to understand other team members' ideas and opinions before arguing or stating my own.
2. I try to present my ideas without criticizing the ideas of others.
3. I encourage different points of view without worrying about agreement.

Appendix B
(continued)

4. I try to consider all points of view or possible options before forming an opinion or making a decision.
5. I encourage the participation of other team members and support their right to be heard.
6. I help find solutions when unexpected problems arise.

Appendix C
Demographic Comparison among VISTA Cohorts

| | VISTA Cohort 1 | | | | VISTA Cohort 2 | | | | VISTA Cohort 3 | | | |
| | Treatment Group | | Comparison Group | | Treatment Group | | Comparison Group | | Treatment Group | | Comparison Group | |
Characteristic	Mean	S.D.	Mean	S.D.	Mean	S.D.	Mean	S.D.	Mean	S.D.	Mean	S.D.
Demographic Characteristics												
Female	.50	.50	.62	.48	.64	.47	.65	.47	.81	.38	.75	.43
Age (in years)	23.00	3.23	22.20	3.46	26.30	7.22	26.10	6.73	35.40	11.80	36.30	14.20
White	.91	.28	.89	.31	.85	.34	.82	.37	.74	.43	.62	.48
African American	.04	.21	.02	.14	.06	.24	.09	.29	.16	.37	.23	.42
Hispanic	.02	.15	.04	.19	.05	.21	.04	.20	.07	.26	.09	.28
Other Races	.02	.14	.02	.15	.03	.18	.03	.17	.04	.20	.07	.25
High School Diploma or Less	.11	.31	.24	.42	.12	.35	.11	.32	.20	.40	.35	.48
Some College (or two-year associate's degree)	.40	.49	.39	.49	.29	.45	.25	.43	.35	.47	.26	.44
College Graduate	.48	.50	.35	.48	.57	.49	.62	.48	.44	.49	.36	.48
Volunteered in Their Youth	.62	.48	.66	.47	.72	.44	.75	.43	.68	.46	.62	.48

S.D. = standard deviation

Notes

1. Visions of National Service

1. While we focus on the United States in this book, national service has been implemented in many different forms in countries around the world today. For a sense of how the national service issue manifests in other nations, see McBride, Sherraden, et al. (2004) and McBride and Sherraden (2004).
2. Smith (2000: 19) provides a discussion of the role of volunteer groups and voluntary altruism in society. Voluntary altruism is "the presence for an entity (person or group, using an average for groups) of a special form of altruism that includes (being) genuinely based on some significant mix of humane caring for, social support of, and sharing of oneself and one's resources with other entities including co-members as three primary goals of the provider-entity deemed helpful to the helpee, not simply by philanthropic, charitable, public benefit, public purpose, public welfare serving, or non-member serving in the traditional narrow senses."
3. For clear statements of the progressive perspective on national service, see Galston (2005) and Magee and Marshall (2003).
4. Moskos (1988) contains the most eloquent and comprehensive collection of arguments for national service.
5. See, for example, Bandow (2002 and 1996) and Chapman (2002 and 1990), where many different arguments against national service are offered, including that stipended service undermines true selfless caring, and that the national service threatens the autonomy of nonprofits by subjecting them to special oversight conditions and reporting requirements. Bandow (1990: 5) observes colorfully that "Advocates of Uncle Sam as sugar daddy do not seem to realize that federal subsidies might squelch individual volunteer spirit and corrupt service groups, changing their focus from helping people to collecting government funds."

6. Beem (1999: 17) discusses Tocqueville's focus on associational life: "The American proclivity to join associations was part of our culture, our identity as a nation. What's more, compared to other nations, Americans' level of voluntary activity, especially church groups and the like, remains extremely high. But Tocqueville also believed this proclivity was largely responsible for the success of American democracy."

7. Bandow (1999) makes the point that the stipended service undermines the impulse to give freely of one's time.

8. Gorham (1992: 31) analyzes the debate and dilemmas surrounding national service and notes that "the architects of national service contend that the fundamental philosophical dilemma surrounding the program is whether or not individuals opt to join the service voluntarily. They maintain that any practical proposal must address the issue of compulsory service versus voluntary service. Compulsory service generates problems that voluntary service bypasses—for example, how to accommodate large numbers of enrollees, and what to do with those who refuse to comply. The institutional structure of the programs must differ in order to account for the nature and extent of the program. The actual tasks in which the participants will engage will be the same, however regardless of the voluntariness of the program."

9. Evers (1990a: xxii–xxxix) provides a discussion of the meaning of the term "national service" and reasons for the debate over its definition. He claims that proponents of national service "stress military manpower, unmet social needs, the future of young blacks from poor families, equity, social integration, welfare benefits without corresponding duties, building character, citizenship, and national purpose." However, he notes that critics emphasize "the costs, the nature of service, the nature of politics, moral instruction by the government, and the nature of a free society."

10. For a discussion of which kinds of service are genuinely valuable, see Dionne and Drogosz (2003: 2), where they explain that "Many who honor military service are skeptical of voluntarism that might look like, in Armey's terms 'social activism' . . . [while] supporters of work among the poor are often dubious of military service."

11. See Bass (2004), which explores the relationship between national service and civic education through an examination of the Civilian Conservation Corps and VISTA. Bass presents multiple paradigms of citizenship, including constitutional citizenship, critical citizenship, and citizenship as patriotism, service, and work.

12. Some programs are more permissive, for instance, VISTA members are able to engage with government institutions and have an opportunity to learn how they work.

13. Buckley (1990) discusses citizenship, civic obligations, and the reshaping of national ethos. He offers a plan for universal voluntary national service for

men and women eighteen years and older, includes suggestions on how a program might be structured and administered, and analyzes the benefits, material and spiritual, that would come to those who serve.

14. On the importance of engagement and participation in order to sustain democratic institutions, see Barber (1998).

15. See Bass (2004) for a discussion of this issue.

16. Nonprofits must get more value from volunteers than it costs to recruit and supervise them. On the complexity of managing part-time volunteers, see Brudney (2005) and Brudney and Hager (2004).

17. What leadership is and how it is learned are subjects of some contention. See Ancona (2005), which describes leadership as distributed, personal, and developmental.

18. There is an abundant literature on social capital spurred on by the work of Robert Putnam. See, for example, Putnam (2000, 1995, and 1993), which include some of his important formulations of the issues related to social capital.

19. For an early and original discussion of social capital, see Coleman (1990: 305): "The function identified by the concept 'social capital' is the value of those aspects of social structure to actors, as resources that can be used by the actors to realize their interests. By identifying this function of certain aspects of social structure, the concept of social capital aids in both accounting for different outcomes at the level of individual actors and making the micro-to-macro transition without elaborating the social-structural details through which this occurs."

20. Seligman (1997: 174) argues that the "devaluation of trust seems to be emerging with a revaluation of collective, often primordial group identities as defining the locus of self, if not of new terms of collective membership and participation. How such identities will reshape politics of the next century is an open question, as is the continued existence of trust in either private or public realms if this reorientation of society's principles of generalized exchange does indeed come to pass."

21. In assessing the causes of this civic retreat, Putnam sorted through dozens of possible factors—daily time pressures, economic hard times, residential mobility, suburbanization, the movement of women into the paid labor force, divorce, political disillusionment after Vietnam, the growth of the welfare state, the civil rights revolution—and eventually pointed to television and the information technology revolution as the two culprits perhaps most likely to be critical factors in declining levels of social capital. By driving people into private experiences outside the public square, television and the Internet have led to increased isolation and separation.

22. See Eberly (1998). National service programs are not the only avenues for linking people together. Several institutions exist for the purpose of

strengthening the nation's communities and civic networks, such as the National Commission on Civic Renewal, the Communitarian Network, and the Points of Light Foundation.

23. On the challenge of bridging the gap between individuals and the political sphere, see Weir and Ganz (1999). For a more sobering perspective, see Elshtain (1998: 28): "Civil society creates spaces for the enactment of human projects, yes, but it also reminds us that this is a world of ties that bind. You cannot have all the good things of democratic life and culture without accountability and duty."

24. Ehrenberg (1999: 163) discusses Tocqueville's legacy: "Tocqueville's culturally driven notion of American civil society attached a profoundly individualistic people to the general welfare in conditions of widespread social equality. Free institutions, the rule of law, and freedom of association were essential if equality, democracy, and solidarity were to be reconciled."

25. O'Connell (1983: 57) reprints a key excerpt from Alexis de Tocqueville where he takes up the American penchant for civil and political associations and discusses how their existence is related to political stability: "If men are to remain civilized or to become so, the art of associating together must grow and improve in the same ratio in which the equality of conditions increased."

26. Wuthnow (1991: 13) discusses the problem of individualism as an "American Paradox" and explains: "Self-interest is a cultural pillar undergirding our way of life. In economic terms this means looking out for ourselves: getting the most for our money, making wise investments, driving the hardest bargains we can. But throughout our nation's history self-interest . . . has generally encompassed a wide range of bodily pleasures and material comforts."

27. For additional research on social capital and its decline, see Paxton (1999). She found that social capital (as a measure of a combination of trust and associational activity) showed a decline between 1975 and 1994.

28. The most detailed arguments for the idea of national service as public work are found in Boyte (2005, 2003) and Boyte and Kari (1996).

29. A study by Thomson and Perry (1998: 407) examined the community-building effects of the AmeriCorps program in five areas. Their findings revealed that school employees "reported their students' attendance had improved at all six schools, in which Corps members worked, and teachers perceived better attitudes and eagerness to learn among students. Furthermore, Corps member enthusiasm at one AmeriCorps site resulted in board members becoming more active in promoting the programs of the organization." Although some effects of AmeriCorps were positive, other areas of organizational capacity building were unaffected. Areas such as internal evaluation systems, strategic planning, and fundraising skills did not show improvement.

30. It is not immediately obvious how AmeriCorps programs are supposed to achieve these results. It is easier to see a capacity building function with

VISTA because members have an explicit mandate to think about the sustainability of their efforts. However, there are only 6,000 VISTA members compared to 50,000 members in the State, National, and National Civilian Community Corps (NCCC) branches of AmeriCorps.

31. See Eisner (2005: 58), who reports on the leveraging effect of AmeriCorps: "Over the past four years, CNCS [Corporation for National and Community Service] grantees have raised nearly $1.5 billion in matching funds, or about $360 million a year, to support their national service programs. That nonfederal revenue stream adds a critical element of sustainability to their programs."

32. For a further discussion on the role of entrepreneurship in renewing U.S. communities, see Henton, Melville, and Walesh (1997: 225). They assert that "economic communities in the twenty-first century are going to require a strong tradition of civic entrepreneurship. For aspiring regions, identifying and recruiting civic entrepreneurs into economic community building is essential. Civic entrepreneurs will be the key to new global networks of economic communities. They will build relationships among regions in the global economy, forging a new era of regional internationalism. They will be the leading voices in redefining the relationship between regions and national governments, forging a new era of economic federalism. And they will connect to one another and begin to pass on their experiences to a younger generation of civic entrepreneurs."

33. For more information on City Year, see Goldsmith (1993), which provides a detailed insider perspective on the lives of corps members.

34. Gorham (1992) discusses how the ambiguity in the goals of national service complicates substantially the evaluation of these programs.

35. We use these two unique data sets to shed light on the plausibility of the competing claims and visions of national service that now exist. To ensure that the AmeriCorps project was methodologically strong, the research team drew on the expert knowledge of Christopher Winship in the best uses of propensity scores. On the VISTA project, Doug McAdam served as a consultant to Abt Associates and shared his experience designing and executing a similar retrospective study.

2. The Evolution of National Service

The financial support of the Center for Public Leadership at Harvard's Kennedy School of Government is gratefully acknowledged, as is the work of Brendan Miller in helping to research and develop this chapter.

1. The link between military and civic service is discussed in Bandow (1990: 1), where he uses the People's Republic of China as an example of "the latest

country to impose a service requirement on the young . . . [China] announced in August 1989 a twofold plan: students must spend up to a year in military camps before entering the university, and once they graduate they must work one to two years in factories or villages before furthering their studies."

2. See Moskos (1988: 13), which discusses voluntary and mandatory service in the United States by saying, "Our country has no greater exemplars of national service than those young people who have performed as citizen soldiers, as conscientious objectors, or as volunteers in conservation and human services."

3. There is some terminological confusion today with how we generally think about volunteers in the context of civilian national service. In civilian service, volunteers (e.g., AmeriCorps members) are contrasted with the professional staff of nonprofit organizations. In contrast, under a universal system of short-term military service, the long-term volunteers are also the professionals.

4. See www.nationalserviceact.org/14.html, accessed 7/7/09.

5. For more information on changes in U.S. political life following the American Revolution, see *The Good Citizen* by Schudson (1998: 91): "The Federalists stood for social hierarchy in their combat with the Jeffersonians, their battles raging in all spheres of life: in the family, in religion, in conflict over economic development and change, in contention over language, culture, and education, and in constitutional struggles in the states."

6. The full quote from Federalist Paper No. 57 is: "The electors are to be the great body of the people of the United States. They are to be the same who exercise the right in every State of electing the corresponding branch of the legislature of the State. Who are to be the objects of popular choice? Every citizen whose merit may recommend him to the esteem and confidence of his country. No qualification of wealth, of birth, of religious faith, or of civil profession is permitted to fetter the judgment or disappoint the inclination of the people. If we consider the situation of the men on whom the free suffrages of their fellow-citizens may confer the representative trust, we shall find it involving every security which can be devised or desired for their fidelity to their constituents. In the first place, as they will have been distinguished by the preference of their fellow-citizens, we are to presume that in general they will be somewhat distinguished also by those qualities which entitle them to it, and which promise a sincere and scrupulous regard to the nature of their engagements. In the second place, they will enter into the public service under circumstances which cannot fail to produce a temporary affection at least to their constituents. There is in every breast a sensibility to marks of honor, of favor, of esteem, and of confidence, which, apart from all considerations of interest, is some pledge for grateful and benevolent returns."

7. Warren (2001: 42) notes that "two features of association are prominent in Tocqueville's analysis. First, there exists a relative social equality of individuals given by the fact that inequalities are sphere specific and do not map onto generalized ascriptive status. Second attachments are much more likely to be chosen by individuals, a fact in part explained by the availability of land, increasing as it did the opportunities of exit from relations of dependency—at least for white males."

8. Becker and Dhingra (2001: 329) document the relationship between religious involvement and volunteering. Their study finds that "social networks, rather than beliefs, dominate as the mechanism leading to volunteering, and it is the social networks formed within congregations that make congregation members more likely to volunteer."

9. Hall (2005: 5) provides a discussion on voluntary associations in early America: "Citizens were usually compelled by law to labor on behalf of the public. Service of this kind was a common way of paying taxes in a primitive colonial economy in which barter usually took the place of money. Militia duty and service in public office were often required by law, and those who failed to 'volunteer' to serve were often punished by fines."

10. For more information on the history of volunteer firefighting, see http://www .firefightersrealstories.com/volunteer.html.

11. See http://www.ushistory.org/franklin/philadelphia/fire.htm.

12. Paul Hirst (1994: 44) gives insight into the importance of voluntary associations in a democracy. If "human actors are given the greatest possible freedom to associate one with another in voluntary bodies to perform the main tasks in society, then the affairs of that society will be better governed than if they are left either to the isolated activities of individuals or to the administrative organs of a centralized state."

13. Hall (2005: 7) provides a discussion on the role of voluntary associations in the New Republic: "Many states actively discouraged private charity. Favoring public over private institutions, Virginia established the first state university in 1818. This would become a common pattern in many southern and western states. In contrast, New England states actively encouraged private initiatives of all sorts. Voluntary associations—formal and informal; religious and secular—flourished. As a result, the New England states became national centers for education, culture, and science as the wealth from the region's industrializing economy poured into the coffers at colleges, hospitals, libraries, and museums."

14. Janowitz (1983: 30–31) explains that the citizen soldier "is both a political and a military concept, a mixture of genuine utility and effective myth. There has been endless debate about the effectiveness of the citizen soldier in contrast to the performance of the 'regular' soldier. Military historians have come to the

conclusion that local militia and state volunteer units played an important role in supporting the Continental army in the ultimate defeat of British forces. The citizen soldier is a political ideal with important goals because it served (a) to reinforce civilian control, (b) to balance local political interests against the power of the central establishment, and (c) to mobilize a wide range of relevant talents and skills from civilian society for use in the military."

15. Moskos (1988: 26) offers a discussion of the history of conscientious objectors: "From the earliest times, the American colonies allowed certain exemptions to militia obligations for members of pacifist religious groups, the so-called peace churches—Mennonites and Brethren coming out of rural German Anabaptist tradition and Quakers of English stock who were mainly well-educated city and town dwellers. No colony, it seems, ever forced religious objectors to bear arms if they were willing to pay for exemption."

16. Moskos (1988: 17–18) provides a discussion of the nature of volunteers during the Civil War: "Under Civil War conscription, each congressional district had a draft ('enrollment') board responsible for meeting quotas set by national draft calls. If the quota could not be met by volunteers, then additional men were selected by lot to meet the quota. The Civil War draft was actually designed to use the threat of conscription to spur voluntary enlistments."

17. See James (1962).

18. See Galston (2005: 108), who comments: "It is one thing to invoke civic arguments in favor of universal service, quite another to make them real. As we reconsider the all-volunteer recruitment model for armed service, we should also return to Clinton's vision of national service as a package of responsibilities and privileges available to every young American."

19. From a speech given by Franklin D. Roosevelt at the Democratic National Convention, Chicago, Illinois, 1932.

20. Franklin D. Roosevelt's message to Congress on Unemployment Relief, Washington, DC, March 21, 1933.

21. See Moskos (1988) for a more complete history of the CCC and its work.

22. See Shapiro (1994: 39).

23. For the history of the GI Bill and Congress's motivation for creating it, see Moskos (1988) at http://veterans.house.gov/benefits/gi60th/birth.html.

24. This is a long-standing impulse in American political culture, dating back at least to the 1840s and the doctrine of Manifest Destiny. It could be argued that it goes back much further, tapping into the missionary zeal of the first Pilgrims.

25. Shapiro (1994) addresses the idea of voluntary international service by individual citizens through the Peace Corps.

26. In a letter to the president of the Senate and the Speaker of the House transmitting a bill to strengthen the Peace Corps, Kennedy (1963) states: "Peace

Corps Volunteers are ... building those human relations which must exist for a happy and peaceful understanding between people. They are bringing home important skills and experience which will greatly enhance our knowledge of the world and strengthen our role in international affairs. More than one-third of the 700 Volunteers returning this year have indicated a desire to work in international programs. Their ability and usefulness is attested to by the action of thirty-five universities in the United States which have established two hundred scholarships for returning Volunteers."

27. Hoffman (1998: 183).
28. Fischer (1998: 20) notes: "Shaffer wanted the volunteers to live the challenging life of their forbears and in so doing regain a sense of rugged American individuality."
29. Hoffman (1998: 190).
30. In recent years, AmeriCorps has had nearly ten times the number of Peace Corps members.
31. Hoffman (1998: 123) gives an overview of the history and purpose of the Peace Corps: "Peace Corps staff struggled over what their message would be. Like the volunteers, they had to frame the experience to make it understandable, but the frames did not always fit and could even be at odds with the deeper intent of the program."
32. See Franklin (1983) for an account of this period.
33. See Pass (1976: 194). Schwartz (1988: 20) comments: "The Nixon administration was quietly preparing plans to eliminate VISTA altogether. Nixon proposed zero funding for VISTA in 1971 (in an attempt) to kill the program. The federal program ACTION was created to serve as an umbrella organization for all existing volunteer agencies."
34. See Schwartz (1988: 25).
35. Schwartz (1988: 447) remarks: "Many volunteers were already headed in that direction, so the program's impact and the support Volunteers gave each other naturally felt good. With VISTA providing that last bit of thrust, many Volunteers either deliberately or unknowingly moved into service careers. These former Volunteers have identified their VISTA service as the single most influential event in determining their career directions. Their exposure to a range of knowledge—the social, racial, bureaucratic, and personal curriculum of their VISTA education—has created an internal momentum this group seems compelled to continue."
36. There has been a good deal of research on the effects of service learning on young people. For a sampling, see Billig (2000), Eyler and Giles (1999), Boyte and Farr (1997), and McCarthy and Tucker (1999).
37. Chapman (1990: 143) takes up this issue of autonomy and concludes: "Points of Light would build on the traditional American commitment to an independent

service sector and rejoice in its recent growth. The opposition of Points of Light to federal funding for programs reflected the hostility that conservatives and liberals alike feel for federal strings that go with federal money. It would not stigmatize volunteers with stipends and vouchers."

38. See Shapiro (1994: 137).

39. Waldman (2005) provides a detailed account of Clinton's National Service Bill as it comes before Congress and then meets opposition and must cope with various special interests. It covers one of Clinton's earliest legislative proposals from a vague idea to its passage in Congress. This is both a detailed account of the development of a policy idea into law and a laying bare of the political struggle that the idea of national service unleashed.

40. See Husock (2004a, 2004b, 2004c) on the budget crisis and the move to block proposed cuts to AmeriCorps.

41. Volunteerism and public service have long played an integral role in a variety of federal programs and initiatives that range from 4-H in the Department of Agriculture to the National Parks Service to SCORE in the U.S. Small Business Administration and the Department of Veterans Affairs. Volunteering with state and local government entities have an even richer and more familiar history in the form of volunteer fire companies, the Neighborhood Watch Program, jury duty, and the service of members of Congress and senators. See also Rehnborg (2005) for more on this topic.

42. The National and Community Service Trust Act of 1993 created the Corporation for National Service (later the Corporation for National and Community Service) and AmeriCorps. The primary components of Service Learning and the National Senior Service Corps already existed in 1993, but became part of the new corporation when it was formed. For example, Service Learning includes Learn and Serve America, which was authorized under the National and Community Service Act of 1990 as Serve America. Within the National Senior Service Corps, the Retired and Senior Volunteer Program (RSVP), the Foster Grandparent Program, and the Senior Companion Program were all developed in the 1960s and 1970s. See Corporation for National and Community Service (1995b: 2), where the Minutes of the Board of Directors Meeting state: "Volunteer activities have been accelerated and continued due to the impact of the three national service products: Learn and Serve America, AmeriCorps, and Senior Corps."

43. For more information on Learn and Serve America (spearheaded by the CNCS), see Corporation for National and Community Service (2004b: 1), which concludes: "A national study of Learn and Serve America programs suggests that effective service-learning programs improve grades, increase attendance in school, and develop students' personal and social responsibility. A growing body of research recognizes service-learning as an effective

strategy to help students by promoting learning through active participation in service experiences; providing structured time for students to reflect by thinking, discussing and writing about their service experience; providing an opportunity for students to use skills and knowledge in real-life situations; extending learning beyond the classroom and into the community; and by fostering a sense of caring for others."

44. See Corporation for National and Community Service (2004a: 2). "Ameri-Corps is administered by the Corporation for National and Community Service, which also oversees Senior Corps and Learn and Serve America. The programs of the Corporation provide opportunities for Americans of all ages and backgrounds to serve their communities and country. Together with the USA Freedom Corps, the Corporation is working to build a culture of citizenship, service, and responsibility in America."

45. For a full description of current program types and their impact, see Corporation for National and Community Service (2004c).

46. See Magee and Marshall (2005: 6) for more on the operation of the National Civilian Community Corps (NCCC).

47. See Corporation for National and Community Service (1999: 5) for Minutes of the Board of Directors Meeting of September 9: "General Chambers recounted that 5,000 NCCC Corps members and team leaders have graduated from the NCCC program, operating 500 teams, completing more than 2,000 projects, and serving more than 8.5 million hours."

48. See Corporation for National and Community Service (2004d). The purpose of state and national programs is to engage AmeriCorps members in direct service and capacity building to address unmet community needs. Local programs design service activities for a team of members serving full-time or part-time for one year or during the summer. Activities include tutoring and mentoring youth, assisting crime victims, building homes, and restoring parks, among others. AmeriCorps members also mobilize community volunteers and strengthen the capacity of the organizations where they serve.

49. See Corporation for National and Community Service (2004c). Full-time members who complete their service earn an AmeriCorps Education Award of $4,725 to pay for college, graduate school, or to pay back qualified student loans.

50. Corporation for National and Community Service (1997a: 9–10).

51. For more information on the Senior Corps, see Corporation for National and Community Service (2006b).

52. See Obama and Biden (2009) on the need to increase the size of AmeriCorps and improve the benefits the program conveys to young people.

53. Bellah, Madsen, et al. (1985: 212) provide a chapter on citizenship in their book *Habits of the Heart*. Citizenship requires several components: "Vigorous citizenship depends on the coexistence of well-established groups and institutions,

including everything from families to political parties, on the one hand, and new organizations, movements, and coalitions responsive to particular historical situations on the other."

54. See Etzioni (2000: 133), where he explains that "the difference between a good and a civil society regarding the core institution of voluntary association . . . these play different roles within these two societies. In civil societies, voluntary associations serve as mediating institutions between the citizen and the state, and help cultivate citizen skills. In the good society, voluntary associations also serve to introduce members to particularistic values, and to reinforce individuals' normative commitments. Thus, while from the perspective of a civic society a voluntary association is a voluntary association, from the view of a good society, no two voluntary associations are equivalent. The regard to which voluntary associations are held ranges from those that are celebrated (because they foster the social virtues the good society seeks to cultivate), to those that are neutral, to those that—while voluntary—sustain values divergent from or even contradictory to those the society seeks to foster."

55. See Chapman (2002) on the flaws inherent in the idea of national service.

3. The Shape of National Service Today

1. The challenge of doing research that spans both the micro (individual) level and the macro (community) level is discussed in Alexander, Giesen, et al. (1987).

2. See also Boudon (1987) and Gerstein (1987) on the complex interaction of micro and macro levels in sociology.

3. Oi (1990: 84) remarks that "the period after high school is a turbulent one. An interruption in a structured environment (for example, national service) may prove to be beneficial for at least two reasons. First, an individual has time to establish priorities about what he/she wants to do for the rest of his/her life. Second, s/he will be a more mature person after a tour of national service duty and thus get more out of college."

4. See Markus, Howard, and King (1993) and Billig (2000).

5. See Youniss and Yates (1997: 36), where the idea of social-historical identity is drawn from Erikson's position on identity to understand "how service makes a long-term impact on youth participants. When youth are given opportunities to use their skills to redress social problems, they can experience themselves as having agency and as being responsible for society's well-being. When they participate as a cohort and when participation is encouraged by respected adults, youth begin to reflect on the political and moral ideologies used to understand society. It is this process of reflection, which takes place publicly with peers and adults, as well as privately, that allows youth to construct

identities that are integrated with ideological stances and political-moral outlooks."

6. See Conrad and Hedin (1991) and Tschirhart (1998).

7. Rosenblum (1998: 51) contains a chapter entitled "The Morality of Association," in which she develops the idea of membership leading to a capacity for commitment: "A plurality of associations presenting an array of ideals and demands on individuals, some more complex and comprehensive than others, is crucial. So is access to associations by individuals. The idea is that as we assume a succession of more demanding roles in more complex schemes of rights and duties, we enlarge our experience of cooperation and our moral horizons, and our capacity for commitment to liberal principles of justice increases."

8. For an extensive discussion of how community service stimulates political and moral development in adolescents, see Youniss and Yates (1997: 2), which asserts that moral maturity is "the willingness to grasp the moral aspect in everyday events and take action on its behalf. [Community service] promotes action-based engagement with conditions of personal need and social inequality."

9. Erikson (1968: 133) finds that "identity is as unfathomable as it is all-pervasive. It confronts a process that is located both in the core of the individual and in the core of the communal culture. As the culture changes, new kinds of identity questions arise." Furthermore, Youniss and Yates (1997) found that given the right circumstances, young people are fully capable of judging themselves as having maintained or deviated from an ideology that emphasizes the individual's responsibility to confront and help correct society's problems.

10. Wilson (2000) cites sociodemographic correlates of volunteering in addition to the various benefits that it provides. For instance, those who volunteer tend to be more politically active, have better physical health, and have a low risk of mortality. Not only does volunteering result in more integration in one's community, but volunteers experience elevated self-esteem, self-confidence, and overall life satisfaction.

11. For more information on evaluating the impact of nonprofit and voluntary action, see Weisbrod (2001: 280), where he observes: "Supporters of nonprofits claim benefits that include efficiency and output quality, particularly in dimensions that are difficult for consumers to observe, access by consumers regardless of ability to pay, provision of collective goods that complement those of government, encouragement of altruistic values such as the opportunity to volunteer, alternatives to government in the social welfare area and preserving national identity."

12. See Aguirre International (1999a).

13. See Putnam (1993, 1995, 2000).

14. See Dionne and Drogosz (2003).

15. See Corporation for National and Community Service (1996).

16. Evers (1990a: xxxvi) worries about attempts to channel the volunteer impulse, even if it is in the name of efficiency: "Why should a governmental national service program certify or disallow work in a church, hospital, or community agency? In a society with liberal political institutions, a person should be able to serve others as a volunteer without authorization from or accountability to a government agency. Indeed . . . any requirement that volunteer groups and service projects must meet government standards of acceptability would destroy their independent character."

17. See Aguirre International (1999a, 1999b).

18. Gerstein (1987 :86) maintains that "the concepts of micro and macro, however, have not been systematically analyzed in sociology. They are taken to refer to two levels of analysis: individual mental processes, personal preferences, or primary interaction versus very large-scale social organization such as transnational corporate capitalism, modern occupational prestige hierarchies, the formation of nation-states, or technological rationality. The issue of linkage is how to create theoretical concepts that translate or map variables at the individual level into variables characterizing social systems and vice versa."

19. Coleman (1990) makes the point that sociologists rarely are able to explain how individual-level phenomena translate into community-level phenomena. The challenge lies in the fact that the macro level cannot be understood as the simple aggregation of everything at the micro level. A deeper theory of this interlevel transition is ultimately needed.

20. See Corporation for National and Community Service (2006c), where the relative size and scope of the programs are detailed.

21. Each of the three AmeriCorps programs operates with slightly different foci and organizational arrangements: AmeriCorps State and National generally serves in teams with hundreds of local community-based organizations and national organizations—including groups such as Habitat for Humanity, the American Red Cross, and Boys and Girls Clubs—to expand the number or types of service that these agencies can offer. AmeriCorps National Civilian Community Corps (NCCC) is a residential program administered directly by the corporation and enrolls younger adults; NCCC members serve in teams to meet community needs in cooperation with nonprofit organizations and state and local agencies located throughout their assigned geographic regions. AmeriCorps VISTA also works with nonprofit and government agencies, typically individually or in small teams to build the capacity of their host agencies. VISTA members are precluded from providing direct services to clients and focus instead on strengthening neighborhoods, locating and mobilizing resources, and enabling communities to reach their potential.

22. For additional information about AmeriCorps programs and structure, see Corporation for National and Community Service (2004c).

23. The third AmeriCorps program, VISTA, was not included in the longitudinal study; VISTA was the subject of the retrospective study of its members.

24. See Corporation for National and Community Service (2004d, 2004e). The final baseline sample of AmeriCorps members and comparison group members consists of 4,153 observations. These individuals completed a baseline survey in the period commencing in September 1999 and concluding in March 2000. Of these respondents, 3,300 completed a postprogram interview and 2,975 completed a postprogram supplemental survey. Despite the decrease in number of respondents, the sample is sufficiently robust to support rigorous analysis.

25. See Abt Associates (2008b). The administration of the postprogram survey started in September 2000 and was completed by May 2001, while the data collection effort associated with the postprogram supplemental survey started in September 2002 and concluded in June 2003. The decrease in respondents reflects a challenge inherent in longitudinal studies—maintaining a robust sample over time.

26. For producing weights using population-based estimates, each program in the sample as well as each member in that program received a sampling weight. The final sampling weight combined the base sampling weight, which reflects the probability of selection and an adjustment for nonresponding members. The base sampling weight for a program selected in the sample reflects the probability of selection of a program in the stratum. In this case, it is simply the ratio of the number of programs in the population divided by the number selected in the sample. The weights are used to compute the estimates of population parameters relating to member characteristics described in this analysis.

27. Each measure was constructed as the mean of the scaled values for selected items from the survey instrument; items were selected for inclusion in each composite measure based on their use in preexisting surveys, the theoretical implications of the study's logic model, and consultation with outside experts.

28. The composite measures were tested for internal consistency by calculating the Chronbach alpha coefficient. All scales showed a Chronbach alpha greater than 0.65, demonstrating adequate levels of internal consistency. We refined the composite measures used in our exploration of baseline survey data. We chose principal components analysis (PCA) for this task, because it allowed us both to verify the strength and coherence of the baseline constructs and to further explore more complicated relationships among the variables of which they are composed. PCA generates a linear combination (principal component)

of a set of related variables, retaining as much information from the original variables as possible. The PCA procedure first standardizes the observed variables so that each variable contains one unit of variance. The information in this variance is then redistributed among a number of composites. The composites formed by the process are a weighted linear combination of the standardized variables. The criterion for optimality is maximum variance (maximum information), so that the optimal component is the one that contains the maximum proportion of the original units of variance. This component is called the first principal component. The variances of the components are shown as eigenvalues; typically, only those components with more than one unit of variance (i.e., eigenvalue > 1) are retained. The eigenvectors for each principal component contain the weight of each variable in that component.

We conducted PCA on the baseline variables from each hypothesized composite measure. In addition, we graphed the eigenvector of the first principal component against that of the second principal component, which allowed us to see which variables belonged together on the basis of their bivariate relationship. When significant subgroups of variables were identified, we used PCA on each group of variables to form more than one composite measure. While the results of the PCA on the baseline data were consistent with the original composite measures, they led us to a more fine-grained representation of the original composites. Specifically, in some cases, results showed that the composite measures were better represented by several discrete subconstructs. The subconstructs based on the PCA more accurately capture the information in the data. In order to verify this approach from a person-oriented perspective (i.e., whether groups of people respond differently to certain questions), we also performed cluster analysis on each of the composite measures. The results of the cluster analysis confirmed the patterns observed in the PCA. We then reconfirmed all analyses by conducting a PCA of the postprogram data; results were consistent with the patterns found in the baseline data. Missing values were replaced by the mean, median, or mode of the nonmissing observations' values for that variable. We retained indicators to test whether nonresponse to a particular item was related to participation. In cases where it was, we incorporated the fact of nonresponse in the model. Again, imputations were performed separately according to State and National or NCCC status.

For each group of variables, the PCA procedure standardized each of the variables at baseline (mean = 0, standard deviation = 1) and then found the linear combination with maximum variance—the first principal component. Each individual's value on the first principal component was his or her baseline score. The follow-up data on the same variables were transformed correspondingly (standardized relative to the baseline mean and standard deviation, and combined using the loadings of the first principal component from baseline) to calculate the follow-up score on the composite.

29. Whether or not study participants made progress in their educational pursuits after AmeriCorps service is represented as a binary variable measured as: 0 = did not make educational progress, 1 = did make educational progress.

30. Whether or not study participants pursued public service employment after AmeriCorps service is represented as a binary variable measured as: 0 = did not pursue pubic service employment, 1 = did pursue public service employment.

31. See Giordono, Jastrzab, et al. (2003). The quasi-experimental design that has been chosen for this study can be highly sensitive to selection bias based on such characteristics as basic demographics, background history, and motivation to participate. Planning for the impact analysis began during the preparation of the baseline report, when it became evident that there were some potentially important differences between the treatment and comparison groups at baseline. In a random assignment study, we would expect there to be no systematic differences between the treatment and comparison groups in the expected values for preprogram demographic characteristics and outcomes. In addition, it became apparent that the baseline survey instrument did not capture sufficient background history and other motivational factors that are hypothesized to be correlated with both selection into and out of treatment as well as postprogram outcomes. Finally, concerns were raised about the appropriateness of statistical models traditionally used in random assignment settings to accurately estimate the impact of participation in AmeriCorps because they did not adequately address problems of selection bias. We expect that the use of Propensity Score Analysis (PSA) reduced the selection bias associated with the use of the comparison group because it makes full use of the measured variables to distinguish between participants and nonparticipants. We believe that the surveys have produced a rich set of variables about respondents' attitudes and backgrounds that allowed for the development of a robust predictor of participation. In addition, we measured the goodness-of-fit of the model by examining the correlation between predicted and actual probabilities. Nonetheless, it is important to note that if any unmeasured variables significantly affect both the likelihood of participation and outcomes of interest, then PSA does not protect against selection bias from that source.

32. The study used self-reported data to explore the effects of participation on the three broad areas of interest. The overall treatment effect was estimated by taking an average of the estimated treatment effects weighted by the number of treated observations within each stratum. We computed standard errors for the overall treatment effect using the bootstrapping method described by Becker and Ichino (2002) in order to take account of possible measurement error in the propensity scores.

33. For a further explanation of propensity score matching, see Becker and Ichino (2002).

34. These data were collected in fall/spring 2002 as part of the postprogram supplemental survey.

35. We weighed the decision to use propensity scores for conducting this analysis rather than other approaches (such as instrumental variable approaches like Heckman's). It is our opinion that propensity score matching is the most appropriate method for the analysis. A major concern for this analysis is selection bias. Instrumental variables (IV) techniques can in principle cure selection bias. They require that the researcher find a variable (the instrument) that causally affects participation but does not affect the outcome. Variations in outcome associated with variations in this variable then represent effects of participation. Yet, this requirement poses an extremely strict condition. Variables that do not causally affect outcomes, but are correlated with outcomes, are not legitimate instruments. IV assumes that the entire relationship between the instrument and the outcome is due to program participation. But two variables can be correlated if they are effects of the same cause, even if neither causes the other. It is impossible to be certain that the noncorrelation condition is met. Heckman's insight was that the expected value of the residual in the outcomes equation is not zero, but differs between participants and nonparticipants. He therefore proposed including the "inverse Mills ratio" as an additional regressor, equal to the estimated expected value of the residual, based on an auxiliary participation equation. This approach optionally uses an instrument, plus an assumption that the distribution of residuals is known (e.g., bivariate normal). Consequently, the results are very sensitive to distributional assumption—plus any issues with instruments. It would seem practically definitional that the area in which we would have the least confidence in our assumptions is the distribution of the residuals, so it would be reckless to base our estimates entirely on these assumptions ("identification by functional form"). Adding an instrument as an additional prop, for the reasons given above, does not greatly bolster our confidence. For more on Heckman, see Blundell (2001).

36. We included terms for these strata in our regression models to estimate treatment effects on change score (a.k.a. gain score) outcomes within each stratum as shown in the following equation:

$$X_i = \beta_0 + \sum_{j=1}^{s-1} \hat{\beta}_{1j} Q_{ji} T_i + \sum_{j=1}^{s-1} \hat{\beta}_{2j} Qji + u_i$$

where X_i is the outcome for individual i, Q_{ji} is an indicator that individual i is in stratum j, T_i is an indicator of whether individual i is in the treatment group, s is the number of propensity strata, $[\hat{\beta}]$ is the set of parameter estimates, and u_i is the residual. See Jastrzab, Giordono, et al. (2004a, 2004b). The equation has been written out as an individual-level relationship and was estimated that way for convenience. The right-hand side variables are all invariant within treatment group / propensity stratum. Hence, the parameter estimates are numerically identical to those that would be obtained based on a calculation of mean outcomes within each treatment group / propensity stratum.

37. The postprogram supplemental survey was designed to collect a great deal of information about background and motivational characteristics that might affect both selection into treatment and the outcomes of interest; this information was used in the Propensity Score Analysis (PSA).

38. See Giordono, Jastrzab, et al. (2003). Several methods of adjustment using propensity scores were considered, including matching, stratification, weighting, and regression adjustment. Stratification was chosen because it provides for the inclusion of the largest number of cases and does not impose a functional form (e.g., linear) on the relationship between propensity to participate and treatment effect.

39. See Rosenbaum and Rubin (1984).

40. In general, we did not exclude variables from the logistic model merely because of lack of significance. All pretest variables were included regardless of whether they predicted participation. We accepted collinearity among the predictors because the model was not intended to predict anything outside the sample space.

41. Baseline survey variables entered the second model in two ways. First, the linear combination produced by applying the first model to their values was included as a single measure. Second, the race and ethnicity indicators were entered separately because they appeared in interactions with some of the postprogram supplemental survey (PPSS) measures.

42. We divided the sample into strata within which participants and members of the comparison group had equal mean propensity scores (based on level 0.01 t-tests). Within each of these strata we then tested for significant differences between participants and nonparticipants on any variable. We continued adjusting the model until all such differences were removed (except for a few that involved one or two people).

43. We looked at how much the standard errors are increased by including these "near-certain participants" in the analysis (including respondents with propensity scores between .91 and 1.0) instead of limiting the sample to respondents with propensity scores of less or equal to .90. The details depend on which outcome measure is considered, but a majority of the measures of treatment effect become at least 62 percent less precise when applied to the full NCCC group, and 92 percent less precise when applied to the whole State and National group, as compared with the error for estimates confined to those with propensity scores below 90 percent. Normally, we are reluctant to drop cases from analysis samples because of the adverse effects on statistical

power. Therefore, we conducted additional analysis to show how much the standard errors are increased by including half of these "near-certain participants" in the analysis (including all respondents with propensity scores between 0 and .95) instead of limiting the sample to respondents with propensity scores of less or equal to .90. Again, the details depend on which outcome measure is considered, but a majority of the measures of treatment effect become around 2.4 percent less precise when applied to the full NCCC group, and 2.1 percent less precise when applied to the whole State and National group, as compared with the error for estimates confined to those with propensity scores below 90 percent. In this situation, dropping a subset of cases not only substantially improves statistical power, but makes use of as many participants as possible for the analysis.

44. Ordinary least squares (OLS) regression was used for these outcomes: civic engagement and personal growth (including educational progress and employment), as well as tolerance, teamwork, and life skills. OLS regression analysis is typically utilized to assess whether or not an outcome is associated with one or more independent variables. Multiple OLS regression can control for secondary factors that may influence the outcome variable but are not considered the primary explanatory variables of interest. OLS regression predicts the value of the response variable at specific values of the explanatory variables. Logistic regression was used for these outcomes: volunteering participation, voting participation, educational progress, and public service employment since they are dichotomous outcomes, where 1 = yes, 0 = no. For example, if former AmeriCorps participants volunteer, 1 = do volunteer, 0 = do not volunteer. Therefore, we conducted logistic regression for these outcomes. Binomial (or binary) logistic regression is used when the dependent is a dichotomy. Logistic regression can be used to predict a dependent variable on the basis of continuous and/or categorical independents and to determine the percent of variance in the dependent variable explained by the independents, to rank the relative importance of independents, and to understand the impact of covariate control variables. Logistic regression applies maximum likelihood estimation after transforming the dependent into a logit variable (the natural log of the odds of the dependent occurring or not). In this way, logistic regression estimates the probability of a certain event occurring. Note that logistic regression calculates changes in the log odds of the dependent, not changes in the dependent itself as OLS regression does.

45. See Abt Associates (2008a).

46. For an in-depth exploration of Freedom Summer, see McAdam (1988: 4): "The 1964 Mississippi Freedom Summer Campaign, or known at the time as the Summer Project. (More than) 1,000 people, the vast majority of them white, Northern college students, journeyed south to work in one of the forty-

four local projects that comprised the overall campaign. Their days were taken up with a variety of tasks, principally registering black voters and teaching in so-called Freedom Schools."

47. See Jastrzab, Giordono, et al. (2004b).

48. According to the Independent Sector (2001), 44 percent of adults in the United States volunteer. Therefore, those who join AmeriCorps may have a high propensity to volunteer in comparison to the average U.S. citizen. Oesterle, Johnson, and Mortimer (2004) document that on average, volunteering in adolescence continues through the transition into adulthood. Findings show that attending school during the transition to adulthood positively influences volunteering.

49. An article by Wilson and Musick (1997) shows that engaging in volunteer work requires both individual and social resources. Human capital (in the form of education) and social capital (occupational status, family income, and family assets) positively influence hours of volunteering.

50. Waldman (1995: 80) comments on the link between faith and service: "Under the Bush administration, faith-based programs have become a bigger part of AmeriCorps, and the Corps has become a bigger part of President Bush's faith-based initiative."

51. Moskos and Butler (1996: 152) cite some facts about early VISTA recruitment: "In 1969, Congress authorized the recruitment of low-income individuals to do VISTA work in their home communities, and enrollment rose through the 1970s to a peak of 5,000 in 1980. During the Carter years, VISTA became embroiled in controversy when given the responsibility of 'empowering the poor,' which soon led to volunteer-organized tenant strikes and welfare rights advocacy." There was a change in the demographics of those who joined VISTA. Originally, the recruitment targeted white affluent youth, yet new members were primarily poor and over the age of thirty-five.

52. Schwartz (1988: 5) observes: "Volunteers were trained according to program guidelines of helping people help themselves. In Arkansas, that often meant overcoming barriers of racism, mistrust of outsiders or anything that smacked of government, and the economic or political inertia of local power groups."

53. An article by Malekoff (2002: 75–76) narrates his experiences as a former VISTA volunteer. After he formed and worked with a group of Mexican American adolescents, he "began to feel less like a stranger. When I sensed that people had become comfortable with me, I thought it made sense to get a few of the kids together. I thought that forming a club might serve to address some of their needs, such as preventing alcohol abuse and strengthening cultural identity." Malekoff goes on to explain how the VISTA experience can be emotionally charged and driven by complex relationships.

4. Civic Engagement

1. Citizenship is the recognition and appreciation of a set of legal rights and obligations, the fulfillment of democratic responsibilities, and a commitment to country and fellow citizens. It can be cultivated when individuals are empowered and made to believe that their engagement and participation can make a difference. Participation in national service can be an outlet for civic engagement and a significant learning experience for what it means to be a citizen.

2. See Bellah, Madsen, et al. (1985); Youniss and Yates (1997); Barber (1998); Furco, Muller, and Ammon (1998); Galston (2001); and Zaff and Michelsen (2002).

3. Aguirre International (1999a, 1999b), submitted to the Corporation for National and Community Service on civic involvement.

4. See Youniss and Yates (1997) for a discussion of the way high school experiences with service have lasting effects on young people. In a survey of the alumni of three high school classes, researchers found that of the sixty-eight alumni who had not done community service while in high school, 29 percent had volunteered after high school graduation, while 68 percent of the alumni who had volunteered during high school also volunteered after graduation.

5. Both the AmeriCorps member and VISTA participant surveys included a treatment group (those who actually participated in the program) and a comparison group (individuals who had no, or very limited, exposure to the program).

6. For a complete list of survey questions used to construct the gain scores, see Appendix B.

7. On the many reasons that people have for volunteering and joining volunteer associations, see Bekkers (2005).

8. Wilson and Musick (1997) find that the level of attachment volunteers have to their work is determined by the level of resources they bring to it, the rewards they derive from it, and the context in which the work is carried out. Remaining in the volunteer labor force in greater numbers are the more highly educated, those who report higher rates of formal and informal social interaction, and those who have children in the household. Those who increase their working hours are more likely to cease volunteering.

9. Volunteering may be a habit, but it is triggered by a request. See Independent Sector (2001), which finds that the primary reason reported for volunteering is that the individual was asked to serve.

10. Research on the implications of volunteerism suggests it has spillover effects. Wilson and Musick (1997) find that formal volunteering is positively related to human capital, number of children in household, informal social interaction, and religiosity. Informal helping, such as assisting a neighbor, is influenced by gender, age, and health. When Wilson and Musick look at reciprocal

effects, they find that formal volunteering has a positive effect on helping, but helping does not affect formal volunteering.

11. By way of comparison, Independent Sector (2001), a national study of adult volunteering, found that 44 percent of U.S. adults volunteer.

12. Youniss, McLellan, and Yates (1997: 624–625) address how civic engagement and volunteering during adolescence can influence civic participation in adulthood. In addition, it is critical for engendering civic identity that includes agency and social responsibility: "Service allows youth to see society as a construction of human actors with political and moral goals rather than as a distinct, preformed object. Instead of viewing themselves as too young to have power, youth observe that their actions have effect both in helping individuals who are homeless and in comprehending the forces that pertain to poverty and its consequences." In addition, Wilson and Musick (1999) found that the likelihood of volunteering (over time) is greater for those with more education, increased formal and informal social interactions, and those who have children in the household (specifically for women).

13. Wilson and Musick (1997) formulate a theory of formal and informal volunteer work. They assert that volunteer work requires human, social, and cultural capital. In a study that incorporates race and volunteering, Mattis, Jagers, et al. (2000) found that among African American men, church involvement was associated with a greater likelihood both to volunteer and to be a member of a community-based organization. Men who were more involved in church life dedicated more time to volunteer work.

14. According to Independent Sector (2001), only 44 percent of adult Americans volunteer, and religion is a critical force in the phenomenon. On the link between faith and volunteerism, see Janoski and Wilson (1995) and Becker and Dhingra (2001). Ozorak's (2003) study of religious involvement's influence on volunteering among college students shows that the best predictor of intention to repeat volunteer service is intrinsic motivation to volunteer, which is associated with religious commitment.

15. National service increases the enthusiasm of volunteers for social change and attracts young people who are interested in making a difference. People we interviewed recounted stories of national service that allowed them to cultivate a deep commitment to their fellow citizens and to the country as a whole. The experience of service in a community of like-minded others with a shared purpose creates relationships that might otherwise be absent.

16. Some of the drivers of volunteering go back early into a person's childhood. Youniss, McLellan, and Yates (1997) take the position that there is a developmental process in the formation of citizenship. They reviewed prior studies that reported a link between a youth's participation in organized activities and his or her civic behaviors in adulthood, fifteen or more years later. Data

regularly showed that individuals who had participated as students in high school government or community service projects (meant in a broad sense) were more likely to vote and to join community organizations than adults who were nonparticipants during high school. These results support the authors' view that participation during the youth era can be seminal in the construction of civic identity that includes a sense of agency and social responsibility in sustaining the community's well-being.

17. See Markovitz, Schneider, et al. (2007).

18. See Markovitz, Schneider, et al. (2007).

19. Briggs (2008) argues that civic capacity is critical to effective democratic polities. Briggs suggests that without a citizenry that is able to frame problems and imagine solutions, government will struggle to find ways to contribute effectively to the public good.

20. For a discussion of how national service motivates former volunteers toward political action, sometimes in the form of opposition and protest, see Coles (1993: 63): "Young men and women (VISTA) volunteers become outraged by what they see and hear, and the result is estrangement or bitterness and defiance; the government—local or state or federal, or all three—becomes the enemy."

21. Hart, Donnelly, et al. (2007) use the National Educational Longitudinal Study and find that community service during high school is positively related to both volunteering and voting in early adulthood. Furthermore, an article by Zaff, Moore, et al. (2003) finds that adolescents' involvement in extracurricular activities predicts future volunteering and voting in national and regional elections.

22. Verba, Schlozman, et al. (1993).

23. See Verba, Schlozman, et al. (1993: 453): "African-Americans are slightly, and Latinos are substantially, less (politically) active than Anglo-Whites. However, the resources that facilitate participation—some of which, for example, education, are related to social class and others of which, for example, religious preference and activity are associated with race or ethnicity—are distributed very unevenly across the three groups, with Latinos at a particular disadvantage. A well-established line of analysis—one on which we build— places differences in political involvement among racial or ethnic groups in the context of their distinctive socioeconomic positions: groups that are disadvantaged with respect to education or income are correspondingly less active politically. According to this argument, even though social class and ethnic or racial group membership are intimately related to one another, what drives the relationship to political participation is class."

24. See Simon (2002) on the personal political formation of young people in AmeriCorps.

5. Personal Growth

1. See Aguirre International (1999a, 1999b).
2. For a complete list of survey questions used to construct the gain scores, see Appendix B.
3. Simon and Wang (2002: 533) found that among the 1998–1999 cohort of former AmeriCorps members, the top three values they felt are important were happiness, family security, and freedom. In addition, the authors claim that "long-term impact of AmeriCorps service on this cohort of participants may be relatively limited unless these individuals become less cynical about public institutions and their ability to influence policy outcomes via the democratic process."
4. Bush and Yablonski (1996) question whether government should be in the business of promoting the personal development of young people: "Some of the difficulty can be traced to an overreliance on government and a willingness to step back from our own character-building responsibilities. But this is only part of problem—and, hence, only part of the solution. The trouble goes deeper than a simple surrender to government. Unfortunately, these character-building institutions have lost the language of virtue. Our complex and diverse society now functions not under a universal set of moral principles but rather under competing personal and group value systems. Values—embodied in personal beliefs, opinions, and preferences—have replaced virtues as our moral beacons, and there are many different value systems present in our culture. Our character-building institutions have bought into the idea that we have to recognize any and all value systems. Instead of providing us guidance, they now provide us with the tools to justify a wide variety of deviant behaviors. In other words, they do not teach our children right from wrong, but rather how to make informed choices. As one prison chaplain recently observed, our young children need direction, not choices."
5. Rhoads (1997: 163–164) describes the intrinsic reward gained from students' service learning: "As part of a commitment to community building, community service is concerned not only with temporary solutions, but because individuals care for those they serve, a desire also exists to alter conditions permanently for those in need."
6. As reported by former AmeriCorps members.
7. On the link between service and educational attainment, see Youniss and Yates (1997), which takes a close look at the educational and attitudinal impacts of community service on a class of 1993–1994 high school juniors in a mostly African American urban school in Washington, D.C. The authors contend that by integrating a community service experience into the learning process, thereby creating a "complementarity of instructional and reflective

components in a service curricula," schools can advance learning far beyond what occurs in just reading about or hearing lectures on the subject.

8. Marshall and Magee (2005: 22) note the contingent nature of the awards over time: "AmeriCorps members must earn their education awards before they can put them to use. Doing so requires completing the program, which 74 percent of AmeriCorps members did during the Corps' first decade."

9. An article by John (2005) shows that the social capital gained from volunteering positively influences educational progress, specifically in the area of students' self-confidence, which affects motivation and academic success. An additional study by Eccles and Barber (1999) found that among adolescents, prosocial activities such as volunteering contribute to educational success and low rates of involvement in risky behaviors.

10. Information on post-AmeriCorps employment status was taken from the postprogram supplemental survey, administered to members and nonmembers from September 2002 to June 2003.

11. Schwartz (1988: 426) comments on the fact that members have to be at a point in their lives at which they can listen and give something to others: "The successful (VISTA) volunteer has been identified as a good listener. A person overwhelmed with his own problems will not possess the qualities that allow him to be a good listener."

12. Wolf (1983) notes that the number of federal, state, and local employees grew from 1955 to 1980 due to government's expanding role in the nation's business. During this time, public sector jobs gained more prestige, too. The employees of the baby boom generation are significantly better educated than the cohorts of workers before them. Rather than an expansion of opportunities, there's been a decrease in the employment possibilities in the public service sector. Organizations must adjust to the career plateau brought about by increasing workforce competition for decreasing position opportunities. The baby boom generation has influenced the demographic composition of the U.S. labor force. Even within the public service sector, jobs are scarce; in addition, raises and promotions are becoming fewer and farther between. Also, McEntee (2006) holds that public service workers and the unions that represent them have taken on the role of defending attacks at every level of government. The future of the U.S. public service sector will rest on the ability of the American Federation of State, County and Municipal Employees (AFL-CIO/AFSCME) unions to address several areas of privatization, including civil service reform and pension reform.

13. It is important to recall that the NCCC sample size was smaller. Although 40 percent of NCCC members were employed in public service in comparison with 32 percent of their comparison group, participation in the NCCC program did not result in a statistically significant effect on postprogram employment in public service.

14. Research from Rompf and Royse (1994) found that volunteering is positively related to students choosing social work as a career. Social work students have experienced specific life events that exert a compelling influence on their career choices.

15. After the VISTA term of service, respondents were asked, "Before taxes, what was your total household income, from all sources in the last year, that is, 2004? Total income includes interest or dividends, rent, Social Security, other pensions, alimony or child support, unemployment compensation, public aid (welfare), armed forces or veteran's allotment." Despite their employment in public sector or government jobs, a higher percentage of VISTA members had household income in the highest income bracket, compared with near VISTA members. Twenty-nine percent of near members and 36 percent of members reported a household income of $90,000 or higher. Twenty percent of near members and 20 percent of members reported their household income to be between $60,000 and $89,999. Only 5 percent of near VISTA members and 3 percent of VISTA members reported their household income to be $1,000 to $9,999.

16. Wilson and Musick (2003) shows that volunteering in young adulthood is unrelated to whether or not women work for pay in later life. However, volunteering in young adulthood has a positive influence on occupational status among those who do work in later life.

6. Social Capital

1. See Coleman's (1988) foundational article, "Social Capital in the Creation of Human Capital."

2. See Putnam (2000).

3. As noted earlier, the researchers did not attempt to define "community" for survey respondents.

4. Youniss, McLellan, and Yates (1997: 625) remark: "Participation in the remediation of social problems stimulates the civic aspect of identity just when youth are beginning to articulate the extent of their agency, their social responsibility to others, their part in the political process, and their commitment to moral principles."

5. See Schwartz (1988: 432–433): "Volunteers were able to gain fulfillment from their group identity. Working in conjunction with others of the same spirit gave their roles a higher meaning. It reinforced their concept of what was right. That group identity could not appease the guilt and secret unhappiness that Woods said her group shared. She has lost contact with all but one other volunteer because of those feelings, emotions similar to what a war veteran might feel."

6. While many bemoan the decline of trust, Guterbock and Fries (1997) found in their survey that while individuals were almost evenly divided about whether or not people can be trusted, participants in their national telephone survey reported being far more involved with each other—both as individuals and as members of communities and organizations—than might be expected under such circumstances.

7. Simon and Wang (2002: 529) found that about half of the 1998–1999 cohorts of AmeriCorps members felt "that government is being run by a few big interests, and over half felt that government wastes a lot of money they pay in taxes. Approximately 22 percent of respondents reported that they do not feel exploited by local government, but they do not feel that political leaders are generally concerned about them." See also Simon and Wang (1999a and 1999b) on how service shapes personal growth and social capital of participants.

8. Garr (1995: 237) argues that "webs of grassroots organizations are moving toward covering the gaps in services in their regions by recognizing that a team effort can often accomplish what an individual can't."

9. Social capital has received a great deal of attention. See Bourdieu (2001), however, on the many other forms of capital.

10. See Putnam (2000).

11. For more on social identity theory, see Ashforth and Mael (1989) and Turner, Hogg, et al. (1987).

12. See Cox, Lobel, and McLeod (1991) on ways that identity groups define themselves.

13. The idea that tight-knit in-groups may have troublesome dynamics is explored in Waldzus, Mummendey, et al. (2002).

14. According to Mummendey and Wenzel (1999), social identity theory suggests that people tend to view positively those groups with which they identify. Group members tend to perceive their in-group, relative to an out-group, as more prototypical of the superordinate category encompassing both groups. Conversely, they tend to regard the out-group as deviating from the norms of the superordinate category.

15. See Brewer (1999) and Brewer and Pierce (2005) on the complex dynamics that small groups can take on and how this can shape tolerance.

16. A measure was constructed to determine how close the people in the respondents' networks were to each other. The respondents were each asked, "How close are person 1 and person 2?" Options were: total strangers (1), know each other (2), or especially close (3). Then, we took the sum of the values of those relationships and divided it by the number of people in the respondent's network. This question was asked of all the relationships within the respondent's network (min. = .5, max. = 6).

17. See Granovetter (1973), who argues that the analysis of processes in interpersonal networks provides the best way to make the bridge between the micro-macro levels. He goes on to note that it is through these networks that small-scale interactions between individuals and groups get translated into large-scale patterns, which then reverberate back to the small groups.

18. See Coleman (1990: 318), who cryptically observes that in the creation, maintenance, and destruction of social capital, "closure is important if trust is to reach the level that is warranted by the trustworthiness of the potential trustees."

19. See Little (1999) for more information on what volunteers need from the leaders of nonprofit organizations. For volunteers to be successful, they have a number of basic needs, one of which is adequate training and orientation. Others mentioned by Little are a safe, comfortable working environment, follow-up to see that the task is completed, appreciation, recognition, and rewards that match the reasons for volunteering.

7. Public Work

1. The first line in the AmeriCorps pledge begins: "I will get things done for America." See http://www.americorps.gov/about/pledge/index.asp, accessed 11/15/2009.

2. As a proponent of the public work vision, Boyte (2002) argues that social capital is not the ultimate end of service and that it has its limits as a master concept.

3. One long-standing worry about national service programs—no matter how neutral the projects might appear—is that they will be politicized. Some believe that national service has the potential to become highly political by selecting certain types of public work and by partnering with select nonprofit and community groups. Simon (2002) collected data from national service participants in four western states and showed that the programs were neutral and that they were accomplishing their objective of building commitment to civic engagement.

4. All public work is not created equal. There has been a fair amount of fieldwork on what kind of public work is most likely to capture the attention of young people and build their commitment. Metz, McLellan, and Youniss (2003), for example, examine which types of voluntary service might facilitate the civic development of adolescents. They found that the connection between community service and civic development may well be dependent on the specific nature of volunteer activity that young people perform.

5. A 1994–1996 report by Aguirre International surveyed 310 AmeriCorps programs, representing the service of 11,099 members. Over the course of one

year, these members taught more than 350,000 Head Start students in elementary and high schools. Furthermore, they developed curricula, assembled library collections, or provided instructional materials for more than 700,000 students. For more information on educational accomplishments of AmeriCorps, see Aguirre 1996a and 1996b.

6. See Schwartz (1988: 397) for a different portrait of a VISTA program that worked with previously incarcerated individuals. In 1980, in Washington County, Arkansas, Schwartz describes how volunteers "from the Mari Spehar Health Education Project initiated the first health counseling program for women at the Washington County jail and later expanded its women's services to the community at large."

7. Aguirre International (1996a) found that AmeriCorps members organized more than 800 neighborhood watches, conducted more than 3,000 conflict mediation and resolution programs, and started more than 250 community policing programs.

8. For a discussion of the changing demands of the workplace and the characteristics of effective community leaders, see Crislip and Larson (1994). They argue that as American society becomes increasingly diverse, the traditional community problem-solving methods will need to be rethought. Working together successfully today requires a profound shift in our conception of how change is created, and an equally profound shift in our conception of leadership. The book describes how to design, initiate, and sustain a constructive, collaborative process, and the character traits needed in the people who will be essential parts of this new workplace.

9. Aguirre International (1996b) also found that AmeriCorps members planted more than 22,000 trees in urban areas and rural towns and more than 80,000 in parklands. Furthermore, AmeriCorps members restored or conserved more than 3,000 miles of rivers, beaches, and fish habitats and more than 90,000 acres of public lands and fowl habitat.

10. Bradley and Gilkey (2002) use a post hoc matching research design to compare children who participated in HIPPY who had no preschool experience to children who had other preschool experiences in the third and sixth grades. The program showed modest positive impact on school suspensions, grades, classroom behavior, and achievement test scores at both grade levels.

11. In a qualitative analysis of a VISTA program in Texarkana, Arkansas, Schwartz (1988: 155) found that the most substantial contribution volunteers made was "making the community more sensitive to human values." The educational, health, and other governmental services constitute a lasting legacy of VISTA. The effects of service are enduring because of the VISTA volunteers' influence on local leaders.

12. Requiring a willingness to live in barracks and work on spikes means that older candidates for national service are more likely to pursue the traditional

AmeriCorps option rather than the NCCC. The NCCC may be missing out on talent, since Van Willigen (2000) discovered that older volunteers experience greater increases in life satisfaction over time as a result of their volunteering efforts than younger volunteers do (especially among those with high rates of volunteering).

13. The residential nature of the NCCC tends to attract younger, more adventuresome members than the other national service programs. This can be challenging, since Tschirhart (1998) found that younger coworkers have different autonomy needs than older workers. In addition, varied perceptions of the same work task handled by different age groups can lead to differences in satisfaction. Tschirhart's findings mean that the NCCC should be sensitive to the age of its participants when it structures and implements public work projects.

14. See Skelton, Boyte, and Leonard (2002) for a discussion of the way service can both accomplish public work and shape the development of young people.

15. While VISTA tends to have broad goals, Tschirhart, Mesch, et al. (2001: 422) found that there was a link between clarity of goals and satisfaction of members: "The relationship of initial goals to subsequent service outcomes, satisfaction, and intention to volunteer was empirically investigated. Among a sample of 362 AmeriCorps members, the goals that stipended volunteers brought to their service were found to influence outcomes related to these goals one year later. Self-esteem was an important moderator of the relationship between goals and outcomes." This suggests that tightening up the design of VISTA projects might help increase member satisfaction, assuming that members are committed to these clarified goals.

16. It is hard to overstate the need in nonprofit organizations for capacity building and work that contributes to sustainability. VISTA aims to do more than simply provide temporary help. The public work it does has to create lasting capacity within the community. On the challenge of building sustainable organizations, see Lowell, Silverman, and Taliento (2001).

17. On the historical proclivity of organized philanthropy to focus on elite cultural and educational institutions, see Bremner (1988).

18. See Perry and Thomson (2004: 81). Past research on how AmeriCorps impacts communities finds that civic service programs strengthen communities by developing "consortia or alliances of existing organizations, typically consisting of a coalition of community organizations."

19. The question of appropriate balance between directive leadership and empowerment in VISTA is explored in Schwartz (1988: 38): "In poverty communities, the concept of leadership has to grow from within. It must crystallize in words, action, and character, and it must manifest itself as an integral part of that group. VISTA leadership had to inspire communities and individuals to take their own first steps."

20. The idea of members doing public work is criticized by Walters (1996): "AmeriCorps reveals the administration's fundamental misreading of the components of healthy citizenship. The program provides government subsidies for voluntary activity at the federal, state, and local levels. By so doing, it conflates volunteering—which nearly 90 million Americans regularly do—with a federal-government jobs program run by a centralized bureaucracy. It is, in essence, a Great Society-style program trying to pass as a plan to reinvigorate citizenship and heal communities." Defenders of the idea of public work, like Boyte (2005), counter that supporting strong citizenship through public work is essential to democracy itself.

21. To accomplish more public work, perhaps during times of crisis or war, national service could become compulsory. However, Stukas, Snyder, and Clary (1999: 59) have shown that this may be problematic: "To investigate the consequences of such 'mandatory volunteerism' programs, we followed students who were required to volunteer in order to graduate from college. Results demonstrated that stronger perceptions of external control eliminated an otherwise positive relation between prior volunteer experience and future intentions to volunteer. A second study experimentally compared mandates and choices to serve and included a premeasured assessment of whether students felt external control was necessary to get them to volunteer. After being required or choosing to serve, students reported their future intentions. Students who initially felt it unlikely that they would freely volunteer had significantly lower intentions after being required to serve than after being given a choice. Those who initially felt more likely to freely volunteer were relatively unaffected by a mandate to serve as compared with a choice."

22. Schwartz (1988: 388) found that in 1985, approximately sixty-five volunteers "were assigned to 20 active projects across the state. From a strict policy analysis, the balance of decreasing volunteer support and increasing project independence and growth is altogether fitting. This can be interpreted to mean the state [of Arkansas] is decreasing its need for VISTA workers."

23. On the capacity of service to create connections, see Goldsmith (2005: 92): "Service connects people to neighborhood groups, building them up and extending their reach. When a shelter in a church basement gets stronger through more volunteers, it builds up its influence and produces badly needed social capital."

8. The Institutional Politics of National Service

1. In some ways, the research in this book on the multiple dimensions of service marks a major change in emphasis and orientation that we hope will give more depth to the discussion of the performance of national service programs.

2. Reflecting on Moskos's influence, Waldman (1995: 3) comments: "The Northwestern University military expert thought he saw a way to bolster the military, keep seniors out of nursing homes, broaden access to college, and revitalize the Democratic Party—all in one visionary step." Moskos's vision of national service "would mean either military service—which could ease impending manpower shortages—or two years of tough, full-time civilian work helping to alleviate real social problems."

3. On the specific historic details, see Waldman (1995: 130): "On Friday morning, April 30, despite the pandemonium, everything seemed finally to have come together. They had a good site for the event, a large auditorium at the University of New Orleans."

4. Waldman (1995: 241) notes: "The AmeriCorps oath is 'I will get things done for America—to make our people safer, smarter, and healthier. I will bring America together—to strengthen our communities. Faced with conflict, I will seek common ground. Faced with adversity, I will persevere. I will carry this commitment with me this year and beyond. I am an AmeriCorps member, and I am going to get things done."

5. Waldman (1995: 24) points out that in June 1991, President Clinton said: "If we can do (service) across lines of race and income and neighborhood and work, we will be able to make a major stride toward reestablishing a sense of community, without which this country cannot begin to solve its long-term problems."

6. On this point, see Waldman (1995), especially chapter 4.

7. Waldman (1995: 248–249) states: "Clinton's national service plan is a big idea—in fact, a noble one. It is one of the rare attempts to encourage Americans of different social classes to strive toward some larger national purpose. It stresses commonality instead of differences. And while Clinton muddied the message of sacrifice by emphasizing the college benefit, AmeriCorps is still one of the rare federal endeavors that asks Americans to contribute something other than taxes toward their nation. The program even has a political logic to it that can make it sustainable and real, as it gives the middle class a stake in helping the poor."

8. Waldman (1995: 111) explains that *Reinventing Government,* a book written by David Osborne, a consultant to Vice President Gore's task force on reforming the federal government, had been consulted early by the management team on the issue of state versus national control of the distribution of funds.

9. Lenkowsky and Perry (2000) make a similar point.

10. See Corporation for National and Community Service (2001a: 12).

11. See Corporation for National and Community Service (1993).

12. The full board had eleven members.

13. See Waldman (1995: 36). Eli Segal was handpicked by President Clinton, who "wanted someone to whom he could give complete control, someone he could trust unequivocally with not only the policy decisions but the politics."

14. See Corporation for National and Community Service (2000b: I–8).

15. See Corporation Organizational Charts for 1995 and 2000 (Corporation for National and Community Service [2000b], III–1).

16. See Corporation for National and Community Service (2000b: 59–60).

17. See Corporation for National and Community Service (2000b: 59–60).

18. See Corporation for National and Community Service (2000b).

19. See Waldman (1995: 36): "Although the president-elect [Clinton] became known early on in his administration for grasping policy detail, on the non-economic issues he often delegated authority to key subordinates. National service would be up to Eli."

20. He almost made it. It was in 1998, after cumulative congressional appropriations exceeding $3 billion, that the corporation celebrated having 100,000 service volunteers. Corporation for National and Community Service (2000b: VI–22).

21. See Corporation for National and Community Service (1995a).

22. See Corporation for National and Community Service (1997c)

23. The National and Community Service Trust Act authorizes funding for Ameri-Corps State and National; National Civilian Community Corps; Learn and Serve America; National Service Trust; Innovation, Demonstration, Assistance, and Evaluation Activities, and the OIG. Appropriations for these programs come through the VA-HUD Appropriations Bill. The Domestic Volunteer Service Act authorizes funding for AmeriCorps Volunteers in Service to America (VISTA) and National Service Corps. Appropriations for these programs come through the Labor-Education-HHS Appropriations Bill.

24. For an example of this kind of early output–focused assessment, see Aguirre International (1996a, 1996b).

25. See Testimony of Eli Segal before the Subcommittee on VA, HUD and Independent Agencies of the House Committee on Appropriations, 24 March 1995. Opening remarks of Mr. Segal (pages unnumbered).

26. See Testimony of Eli Segal before the Subcommittee on VA, HUD and Independent Agencies of the House Committee on Appropriations, 24 March 1995, p. 566.

27. See Corporation for National and Community Service (1995b).

28. See Testimony of Harris Wofford regarding fiscal year 1998 appropriation for the Corporation for National and Community Service before the Subcommittee on VA, HUD and Independent Agencies of the House Committee on Appropriations, 11 March 1997, pp. 138–139.

29. In Report 96–38, a two-volume report to the OIG, Williams, Adley and Company, LLP and Arthur Anderson, LLP had made ninety-nine recommenda-

tions for corrective action necessary to produce auditable financial statements for the CNCS.

30. See Corporation for National and Community Service (2001a).

31. See Corporation for National and Community Service (1998). The National Service Trust is the repository for education awards earned by AmeriCorps members. In addition to deposited sums, the trust consists of interest on and proceeds from the sale or redemption of any obligations held by the trust.

32. See Corporation for National and Community Service (2000b: I-13).

33. See Corporation for National and Community Service (2000b: III–2).

34. See Segal Testimony, 24 March 1995, p. 569.

35. See Segal Testimony, 24 March 1995, p. 571.

36. Following President Clinton's address, Congressman Thomas Petri of Wisconsin wrote a letter to his congressional colleagues. The letter began: "you call this volunteerism?" It contained a hypothetical calculation of the total benefit package that a person in Perry's situation was eligible to receive through AmeriCorps VISTA on an annualized basis. In determining the amount to be nearly $34,000, Representative Petri exclaimed in dismay: "This is what President Clinton calls a volunteer? Oh puh-leez! The taxpayers have been hoodwinked again!" A copy of the letter is found in the transcript of the Segal Testimony, 24 March 1995, p. 581.

37. See Segal Testimony, 24 March 1995, p. 572.

38. See Corporation for National and Community Service (1997b: 4): "Mr. Toscano also informed the Board of a segment airing on the NBC nightly news about the General Accounting Office's (GAO) report on State Commissions, attrition rates, usage of the Trust Fund, and cost per member issues. He acknowledged that it is not likely to be a positive story. Mr. Rogers stated that the story will not raise any unknown questions, in that it will focus on Issues the Corporation is aware of and continues to deal with."

39. See Corporation for National and Community Service (1997b). "Mr. Toscano added that the news coverage will most likely portray AmeriCorps as the successful job program, instead of as an educational opportunity as described by President Clinton. Specifically, the GAO shows that only fifty-six percent of AmeriCorps Members use their education award in the first year; however, they don't mention the seven year provision."

40. See Corporation for National and Community Service (1998: 6): "In response to a question from Eli Segal on the consequences of reauthorization not passing this year, John Gomperts explained that the Corporation's appropriations were not in jeopardy, given the President's strong support. He stressed the importance of reauthorization for the national service movement, and the powerful message of reaffirmation that would be expressed if this Congress passed a reauthorization bill. This would culminate in the growing support

found among governors, mayors, grantee organizations, and others in the national service family."

41. See Corporation for National and Community Service (2000b: VI–4).
42. See Corporation for National and Community Service (2000b: VI–4).
43. See Wofford Testimony, 11 March 1997, p. 133.
44. Confidential interview with CNCS official, January 2005.
45. A list of evaluations, studies, and reports on CNCS programs from 1973 to 2001 was provided by the corporation to Peter Frumkin.
46. See Corporation for National and Community Service (2000b: II–68).
47. See Aguirre International (1999a and 1999b).
48. See Corporation for National and Community Service (2000b: II–68).
49. See Corporation for National and Community Service (1997b: 1): "Mr. Rogers continued by listing four major issues identified as focal points for Corporation improvement: staff development, reauthorization, President's Summit on America's Future, and management and internal controls."
50. See Corporation for National and Community Service (1996: 38).
51. This study became the AmeriCorps longitudinal study and generated the findings presented in Chapters 4, 5, and 6 of this book.
52. See Corporation for National and Community Service (2000b: 68).
53. See Corporation for National and Community Service (1996: 39).
54. See Beadle (2003) for an example of how the threat to AmeriCorps mobilized its defenders.

9. New Directions for National Service

1. One of the best collections of widely divergent visions of national service is Evers (1990b), which includes both supporters and critics of the idea of service. Based on the Hoover Institution Conference on National Service, the volume brings together and frames for researchers many of the issues that we have addressed is this book.
2. Boyte and Kari (1996, 1999) have argued that three distinctive conceptions of civic identity have long competed against one another: (1) a government-centered civics view, in which a citizen is imbued with rights and modest responsibilities; (2) a communitarian view that interprets citizenship as an altruistic service reflecting the values of civic responsibility; and (3) a commonwealth view of citizenship as public work. They note that "the public work perspective was once central to land-grant and state colleges and universities. In recent decades, it has sharply eroded. Its renewal is essential."
3. The very definition of what constitutes a volunteer is contested. Cnaan, Handy, and Wadsworth (1996) attempt to delineate the boundaries of the term volunteer, by reviewing eleven widely used definitions of the term. They suggest

that there is a continuum for each of four different dimensions of volunteering and each helps to distinguish between pure and broadly defined volunteers.

4. See Handy and Srinivasan (2004) for an attempt to place a value on volunteerism. One of the challenges of quantifying the value of service stems from the enormous range of tasks carried out by volunteers in terms of complexity and value.

5. See Hager and Brudney (2004). Also, the Independent Sector (http://www .independentsector.org/programs/research/volunteer_time.html, accessed 11/29/2009) estimates that "the value of volunteer time is based on the average hourly earnings of all production and nonsupervisory workers on private nonfarm payrolls (as determined by the Bureau of Labor Statistics). Independent Sector takes this figure and increases it by 12 percent to estimate for fringe benefits."

6. Rehnborg (2005) explores how traditional volunteering is different from government-sponsored service and makes the case that the two activities should not be confused.

7. While local programs may incur other costs, it is much harder to pinpoint such additional costs, and the majority of the local AmeriCorps programs rely heavily on CNCS grant monies for funding. Therefore, using CNCS funding to measure the cost of volunteering should be accurate.

8. We owe a special thanks to Ryoko Yamaguchi for her work on these estimates.

9. Perry and Katula (2001) offer more meta-analysis and discuss how service-related research has diffused to a wide array of disciplines and policy fields. However, they note that a common interest across disciplines has not translated into a more coherent understanding of service.

10. On the complexity of managing national service when the intended impact is contested and interpreted very differently by different groups, see Lenkowsky and Perry (2000): "Partly because of the century-old debate over it and partly as a result of the Clinton administration's efforts to build political support for it, the idea of national service has rightly been dubbed the Swiss Army knife of American public policy. Its advocates have, at various times, portrayed it as an instrument for solving critical social problems, helping college students finance their educations, building harmony among racial and ethnic groups, fostering community planning, invigorating retirees, and instilling a sense of civic spirit—or 'gratitude,' as William F. Buckley, Jr. (1990) once put it—among the young." The authors also note that although that public work vision of service is the easiest to communicate to the public, it has its limits: "Notwithstanding its own effort to focus on getting things done, consensus on the CNS's [Corporation for National Service] principal mission remains elusive. (Moreover, congressional oversight is split between two sets of committees, one rooted in the ethos of the ACTION programs, the other attuned to the goals of the national service movement.) And even getting things done calls

for further explication—Which things? At what cost?—if it is to usefully guide results-oriented management."

11. Looking at early data from the longitudinal study of AmeriCorps, Magee and Marshall (2005) note: "It is hard to say if AmeriCorps is living up to its promise. The AmeriCorps Experiment has sometimes exceeded expectations, yet fallen short in others, and in some areas; we still cannot make a definitive judgment." With the long-term data now in, the successes and weaknesses of the program must be confronted by both the critics and supporters of national service.

12. Lenkowsky and Perry (2000) make the point that the ability of the CNCS to adjust and refine programs was long delayed by the tense political environment in which AmeriCorps operated: "The Corporation for National Service is a new agency that has had anything but a peaceful childhood. Its senior leadership has had to devote its primary attention not to implementing the principles of reinventing government, but to building political support for the agency and its key programs. For the most part, its principal partners—gubernatorially appointed state commissions—are also new and still establishing working relationships with local nonprofit organizations and other potential grantees, including state governments. Its main initiatives are more developmental than mature. Compounding this uncertainty is the ambiguity of purpose with which the agency was born."

13. On the fact that research to date has at times pointed in contradictory directions, see Perry and Imperial (2001), which finds that service-related research has diffused to a wide array of disciplines and policy fields, but that this has not translated into a more coherent understanding of service. The authors recognize the importance of good data, not just in assessing service but also in improving it going forward.

14. Ideas about improving national service abound. For a slate of good ideas from conservatives on how to shape national service effectively, see Bridgeland, Goldsmith, and Lenkowsky (2002).

15. On the broader challenge of attracting volunteers to service, see Clubine and Rehnborg (2004).

16. The Obama administration's goals for national service are discussed on the White House Web site: www.whitehouse.gov/issues/Service (accessed 11/29/2009).

17. It is difficult to preserve both the close connection to community that small nonprofits possess with the economies of scale that larger organizations offer. One solution has been the establishment of franchise or federation structures linking many smaller nonprofits into something larger. See O'Flanagan and Taliento (2004), who argue that the federation structure remains a viable model for nonprofit organizations if managements transform themselves and affiliates collaborate more closely.

18. By having deeper and more meaningful service experiences, AmeriCorps could build a stronger and more active alumni base. See Chou, Jordan, and Kilpatrick (2004).

19. Kahne and Westheimer (2002) show that program design and goals affect participants' attitudes toward civic participation and their sense of efficacy.

Bibliography

Abt Associates Inc. (2008a). *Improving Lives and Communities: Perspectives on 40 Years of VISTA Service.* Washington, DC: Corporation for National and Community Service.

Abt Associates Inc. (2008b). *Still Serving: Measuring the Eight-Year Impact of AmeriCorps on Alumni.* Washington, DC: Corporation for National and Community Service.

Abt Associates Inc. (2004). *Serving Country and Community: A Longitudinal Study of Service in AmeriCorps, Early Findings.* Washington, DC: Corporation for National and Community Service.

Aguirre International. (2001). *Foster Grandparents Accomplishment Report.* Washington, DC: Aguirre International, October 1999–September 2000.

Aguirre International. (1999a). *An Evaluation of AmeriCorps.* Washington, DC: Aguirre International.

Aguirre International. (1999b). *AmeriCorps State/National Direct Five Year Evaluation Report.* San Mateo, CA: Aguirre International.

Aguirre International. (1996a). *Making a Difference: Impact of AmeriCorps State and National Direct on Members and Communities 1994–1995 and 1995–1996.* San Mateo, CA: Aguirre International.

Aguirre International. (1996b). *AmeriCorps State/National 1995–1996 Accomplishment Summary: A Summary of Accomplishments from 381 AmeriCorps State/National Programs.* San Mateo, CA: Aguirre International.

Aguirre International. (1994). *AmeriCorps Evaluation Plan.* San Mateo, CA: Aguirre International.

Alexander, J. C., B. Giesen, et al., eds. (1987). *The Micro-Macro Link.* Berkeley: University of California Press.

Ancona, D. (2005). *Leadership in an Age of Uncertainty.* Cambridge, MA: MIT Center for eBusiness, MIT Sloan School of Management.

Ashforth, B. E., and F. Mael. (1989). Social Identity Theory and the Organization. *Academy of Management Review* 14(1): 20–39.

Bandow, D. (2002). Big Brother, National Nanny. *National Review Online*.

Bandow, D. (1999). Taking the Voluntary Out of Voluntarism. Retrieved 11/28/2009 from http://www.cato.org/dailys/03-25-99.html.

Bandow, D. (1996, October 3). AmeriCorps Not Necessary, Even Harmful. *Scripps Howard News Service*.

Bandow, D. (1990). National Service Initiatives. In *National Service: Pro and Con,* edited by W. M. Evers. Stanford, CA: Hoover Press.

Barber, B. (1998). *Strong Democracy: Participatory Politics for a New Age*. Berkeley: University of California Press.

Bass, M. (2004). *Civic Education through National Service: Lessons from American History*. Washington, DC: CIRCLE.

Batchelder, T. H., and S. Root. (1994). Effects of an Undergraduate Program to Integrate Academic Learning and Service—Cognitive, Prosocial Cognitive, and Identity Outcomes. *Journal of Adolescence* 17(4): 341–355.

Bates, S. (1996). *National Service: Getting Things Done?* Chicago: Robert R. McCormick Tribune Foundation.

Beadle, A. D. (2003, September 1). Inside the Fight to Save AmeriCorps. *Youth Today*.

Becker, P. E., and P. H. Dhingra. (2001). Religious Involvement and Volunteering: Implications for Civil Society. *Sociology of Religion* 62(3): 315–335.

Becker, S. O., and A. Ichino. (2002). Estimation of Average Treatment Effects Based on Propensity Scores. *Stata Journal* 2(4): 358–377.

Beem, C. (1999). *The Necessity of Politics: Reclaiming American Public Life*. Chicago: University of Chicago Press.

Bekkers, R. (2005). Participation in Voluntary Associations: Relations with Resources, Personality, and Political Values. *Political Psychology* 26(3): 439–454.

Bellah, R., R. Madsen, et al. (1985). *Habits of the Heart: Individualism and Commitment in American Life*. New York: Harper and Row.

Benitez, L., E. Eizenberg, et al. (2004). Participatory Evaluation: How It Can Enhance Effectiveness and Credibility of Nonprofit Work. *Nonprofit Quarterly* 11(1): 54–60.

Billig, S. H. (2000). Research on K–12 School-Based Service-Learning: The Evidence Builds. *Phi Delta Kappan* 81: 658–664.

Blundell, R. (2001). James Heckman's Contributions to Economics and Econometrics. *Scandinavian Journal of Economics* 103(2): 191–203.

Bohrnstedt, G. W., and D. Knoke. (1994). *Statistics for Social Data Analysis*. Itasca, IL: F. E. Peacock Publishers.

Boudon, R. (1987). The Individualistic Tradition in Sociology. In *The Micro-Macro Link,* edited by J. C. Alexander, B. Giesen, et al., pp. 45–70. Berkeley and Los Angeles: University of California Press.

Bourdieu, P. (2001). The Forms of Capital. In *The Sociology of Economic Life*, edited by M. S. Granovetter and R. Swedberg, pp. 96–111. Cambridge, MA: Westview.

Bowman, W. (2004). Confidence in Charitable Institutions and Volunteering. *Nonprofit and Voluntary Sector Quarterly* 33(2): 247–270.

Boyte, H. C. (2005). Reframing Democracy: Governance, Civic Agency, and Politics. *Public Administration Review* 65(5): 536–546.

Boyte, H. C. (2003). Civic Populism. *Perspectives* 1(4): 737–742.

Boyte, H. C. (2002, Winter). On Silences and Civic Muscle, or Why Social Capital Is a Useful but Insufficient Concept. *Campus Compact Reader,* 1–22.

Boyte, H. C., and J. Farr. (1997). The Work of Citizenship and the Problem of Service-Learning. Working paper, Center for Democracy and Citizenship, Humphrey Institute, University of Minnesota.

Boyte, H. C., and N. Kari. (1999). Renewing the Democratic Spirit in American Colleges and Universities: Higher Education as Public Work. In *Civic Responsibility and Higher Education,* edited by T. Ehrlich, pp. 37–60. Westport, CT: Greenwood.

Boyte, H. C., and N. Kari. (1996). *Building America: The Democratic Promise of Public Work.* Philadelphia, PA: Temple University Press.

Bradley, R. H., and B. Gilkey. (2002). The Impact of the Home Instructional Program for Preschool Youngsters (HIPPY) on School Performance in 3rd and 6th Grades. *Early Education and Development* 13(3): 301–311.

Bremner, R. H. (1988). *American Philanthropy.* Chicago: University of Chicago Press.

Brewer, M. B. (1999). The Psychology of Prejudice: Ingroup Love or Outgroup Hate? *Journal of Social Issues* 55(3): 429–444.

Brewer, M. B., and K. P. Pierce. (2005). Social Identity Complexity and Outgroup Tolerance. *Personality and Social Psychology Bulletin* 31(3): 428–437.

Bridgeland, J. M., S. Goldsmith, and L. Lenkowsky. (2002). New Directions: Service and the Bush Administration's Civic Agenda. *Brookings Review* 20(4): 18–21.

Briggs, X. D. (2008). *Democracy as Problem Solving.* Cambridge, MA: MIT Press.

Brown, M. (1995). *Putting Idealism to Work: A City Year User's Guide.* Boston: City Year Inc.

Brudney, J. L. (2005). Designing and Managing Volunteer Programs. In *The Jossey-Bass Handbook on Nonprofit Leadership and Management,* edited by R. D. Herman & Associates, pp. 310–244. San Francisco: Jossey-Bass.

Brudney, J. L., and M. A. Hager. (2004). *Volunteer Management Practices and Retention of Volunteers.* Washington, DC: Urban Institute.

Buckley, W. F., Jr. (1990). *Gratitude: Reflections on What We Owe to Our Country.* New York: Random House.

Bush, J., and B. Yablonski. (1996, January). Virtuous Reality: Character Building in the Information Age. *Policy Review*. Available at http://www.hoover.org/publications/policyreview/3585251.html.

Butterfoss, F. D., A. Wandersman, and R. M. Goodman. (2001). Citizen Participation and Health: Toward a Psychology of Improving Health through Individual, Organizational, and Community Involvement. In *Handbook of Health Psychology*, edited by A. Baum, T. Revenson, and J. Singer. Hillsdale, NJ: Lawrence Erlbaum Associates.

Campbell, A. L. (2003). *How Policies Make Citizens: Senior Citizen Activism and the American Welfare State*. Princeton, NJ: Princeton University Press.

Carlson, E., and W. Strang. (1996). *Volunteers in Service to America: An Analysis of the Benefits and Costs for Selected AmeriCorps and VISTA Projects*. Washington, DC: Westat, Inc.

Cassidy, D. J., S. A. Hicks, et al. (1998). The North Carolina Child Care Corps: The Role of National Service in Child Care. *Early Childhood Research Quarterly* 13(4): 589–602.

Chapman, B. (2002). A Bad Idea Whose Time Is Past: The Case against Universal Service. *Brookings Review* 20(4): 10–13.

Chapman, B. (1990). Politics and National Service: A Virus Attacks the Volunteer Sector. In *National Service: Pro and Con*, edited by W. M. Evers, pp. 133–144. Stanford, CA: Hoover Institution Press.

Checkoway, B. (1997). Institutional Impacts of AmeriCorps on the University of Michigan. *Journal of Public Service and Outreach* 2(1): 70–79.

Checkoway, B. (1994). AmeriCorps Is Coming. *Education Week* 31.

Checkoway, B., K. Richards-Schuster, et al. (2003). Young People as Competent Citizens. *Community Development Journal* 38(4): 298–309.

Chou, A. A., C. Jordan, and A. R. Kilpatrick. (2004, February). Nonprofit's Untapped Resource. *McKinsey Quarterly*, no. 1: 21–23.

Clubine, B., and S. J. Rehnborg. (2004). *Volunteer Recruitment: Tips from the Field*. Retrieved 12/14/2009 from http://www.serviceleader.org/new/managers/2004/03/000213.php.

Cnaan, R. A., F. Handy, and M. Wadsworth. (1996). Defining Who Is a Volunteer: Conceptual and Empirical Considerations. *Nonprofit and Voluntary Sector Quarterly* 25(3): 364–383.

Coleman, J. S. (1990). *Foundations of Social Theory*. Cambridge, MA: Harvard University Press.

Coleman, J. S. (1988). Social Capital in the Creation of Human Capital. *American Journal of Sociology* 94 (S1): S95–S120.

Coles, R. (1993). *The Call of Service: A Witness to Idealism*. New York: Houghton Mifflin.

Conrad, D., and D. Hedin. (1991). School-Based Community Service: What We Know from Research and Theory. *Phi Delta Kappan* 72(10): 743–749.

Corbin, J., and A. Strauss. (1990). *Basics of Qualitative Research: Grounded Theory Procedures and Techniques.* Newbury Park, CA: Sage Publications.

Corporation for National and Community Service. (2008). *Still Serving: Measuring Eight-Year Impact of AmeriCorps on Alumni.* Washington, DC: Corporation for National and Community Service.

Corporation for National and Community Service. (2007). *Issue Brief: Volunteer Hours and Dollar Values by State 2006.* Washington, DC: Corporation for National and Community Service.

Corporation for National and Community Service. (2006a). *Corporation Budget Chart Fiscal 2001–2006.* Washington, DC: Corporation for National and Community Service.

Corporation for National and Community Service. (2006b). *Fact Sheet: Senior Corps.* Washington, DC: Corporation for National and Community Service.

Corporation for National and Community Service. (2006c). *Fiscal Year 2007 Congressional Budget Justification.* Washington, DC: Corporation for National and Community Service.

Corporation for National and Community Service. (2004a). *Issue Brief: AmeriCorps Longitudinal Study: Impacts of Service in Members.* Washington, DC: Corporation for National and Community Service.

Corporation for National and Community Service. (2004b). *Issue Brief: Learn and Serve America Performance Report Program Year 2005–2006.* Washington, DC: Corporation for National and Community Service.

Corporation for National and Community Service. (2004c). *Performance and Accountability Report Fiscal Year 2004.* Washington, DC: Corporation for National and Community Service.

Corporation for National and Community Service. (2004d). *Serving Country and Community: A Longitudinal Study of Service in AmeriCorps, Baseline Data.* Washington, DC: Corporation for National and Community Service.

Corporation for National and Community Service. (2004e). *Serving Country and Community: A Longitudinal Study of Service in AmeriCorps, Final Post-Program Data.* Washington, DC: Corporation for National and Community Service.

Corporation for National and Community Service. (2003). *Performance and Accountability Report Fiscal Year 2002.* Washington, DC: Corporation for National and Community Service.

Corporation for National and Community Service. (2001a). Minutes of the Board of Directors Meeting, Washington, DC, 22 May, 1–10.

Corporation for National and Community Service. (2001b). *Performance and Accountability Report.* Washington, DC: Corporation for National and Community Service.

Corporation for National and Community Service. (2000a). *A Brief History of AmeriCorps.* Washington, DC: Corporation for National and Community Service.

Corporation for National and Community Service. (2000b). *Transition Briefing Book.* Washington, DC: Corporation for National and Community Service.

Corporation for National and Community Service. (1999). Minutes of the Board of Directors Meeting, Washington, DC, 9 September, 1–11.

Corporation for National and Community Service. (1998). Office of Inspector General, Report 99–02, 14 September 1998. Washington, DC: Corporation for National and Community Service.

Corporation for National and Community Service. (1997a). Minutes of the Board of Directors Meeting, Washington, DC, 29 June, 1–14.

Corporation for National and Community Service. (1997b). Minutes of the Board of Directors Meeting, Washington, DC, 13 March, 1–12.

Corporation for National and Community Service. (1997c). Office of Inspector General, Report 97–29, 14 July. Washington, DC: Corporation for National and Community Service.

Corporation for National and Community Service. (1996). Strategic Plan (Fiscal Years 1997 to 2002). Washington, DC.

Corporation for National and Community Service. (1995a). Minutes of the Board of Directors Meeting, Washington, DC, 24 February, 1–10.

Corporation for National and Community Service. (1995b). Minutes of the Board of Directors Meeting, Washington, DC, 23 October, 1–12.

Corporation for National and Community Service. (1993). Minutes of the Board of Directors Meeting, Washington, DC, 28–29 April, 1–9.

Cox, T. H., S. A. Lobel, and P. L. McLeod. (1991). Effects of Ethnic Group Cultural Differences on Cooperative and Competitive Behavior on a Group Task. *Academy of Management Journal* 34(4): 827–847.

Creswell, J. W. (2003). *Research Design: Qualitative, Quantitative, and Mixed Methods Approaches.* Thousand Oaks, CA: Sage Publications.

Crislip, D. D., and C. E. Larson. (1994). *Collaborative Leadership: How Citizens and Civic Leaders Can Make a Difference.* San Francisco: Jossey-Bass.

Davis, L. E., M. J. Strube, et al. (1995). Too Many Blacks, Too Many Whites: Is There a Racial Balance? *Basic and Applied Psychology* 17(1–2): 119–135.

Democratic Leadership Council. (1988). *Citizenship and National Service: A Blue Print for Civic Enterprise.* Washington, DC: Democratic Leadership Council.

DiLorenzo, T. (1990, March). National Service: A Solution in Search of a Problem. *The Freeman* 40: 3.

Dionne, E. J., Jr., and K. M. Drogosz. (2003). United We Serve? The Promise of National Service. In *United We Serve: National Service and the Future of*

Citizenship, edited by E. J. Dionne Jr., K. M. Drogosz, and R. E. Litan, pp. 1–10. Washington, DC: Brookings Institution Press.

Dionne, E. J., Jr., K. M. Drogosz, and R. E. Litan, eds. (2003). *United We Serve: National Service and the Future of Citizenship.* Washington, DC: Brookings Institution Press.

Dobbs, M., and W. D. Crano. (2001). Outgroup Accountability in the Minimal Group Paradigm: Implications for Aversive Discrimination and Social Identity Theory. *Personality and Social Psychology Bulletin* 27(3): 355–364.

Eberly, D. E. (1998). *America's Promise: Civil Society and the Renewal of American Culture.* Lanham, MD: Rowman & Littlefield.

Eberly, D. J. (1991, June). *National Youth Service: A Democratic Institution for the 21st Century.* Washington, DC: National Service Secretariat.

Eberly, D. J. (1988). *National Service: A Promise to Keep.* Rochester, NY: John Alden Books.

Eccles, J. S., and B. L. Barber. (1999, January). Student Council, Volunteering, Basketball, or Marching Band: What Kind of Extracurricular Involvement Matters? *Journal of Adolescent Research* 14(1): 10–43.

Ehrenberg, J. (1999). *Civil Society: The Critical History of an Idea.* New York: New York University Press.

Eisner, D. (2005). A Frontline View. In *The AmeriCorps Experiment and the Future of National Service,* edited by W. Marshall and M. P. Magee. Washington, DC: Progressive Policy Institute.

Elshtain, J. B. (1998). Not a Cure-All: Civil Society Creates Citizens, It Does Not Solve Problems. In *Community Works: The Revival of Civil Society in America,* edited by E. J. Dionne Jr., pp. 24–29. Washington, DC: Brookings Institution Press.

Emerson, J., and P. Carttar. (2003). *Money Matters: The Structure, Operations and Challenges of Nonprofit Funding.* Boston: Bridgespan Group.

Epstein, S. G. (1989). The Merits of National Youth Service. *Christian Science Monitor,* p. 20.

Erikson, E. H. (1968). *Identity: Youth and Crisis.* New York: W. W. Norton.

Etzioni, A. (2000). Communitarianism and the Moral Dimension. In *The Essential Civil Society Reader: The Classic Essays,* edited by D. E. Eberly, pp. 123–140. Lanham, MD: Rowman & Littlefield.

Evers, W. M. (1990a). Introduction: Social Problems and Political Ideals in the Debate over National Service. In *National Service: Pro and Con,* edited by W. M. Evers. Stanford, CA: Hoover Institution Press.

Evers, W. M., ed. (1990b). *National Service: Pro and Con.* Stanford, CA: Hoover Institution Press.

Eyler, J., and D. E. Giles Jr. (1999). *Where's the Learning in Service Learning?* San Francisco: Jossey-Bass.

Ferrara, R. (1995). *A Bibliography of the Scholarly and Technical Literature on AmeriCorps VISTA.* Washington, DC: Corporation for National Service.

Fischer, F. (1998). *Making Them Like Us: Peace Corps Volunteers in the 1960s.* Washington, DC: Smithsonian Press.

Fiske, E. B. (2001). *Learning in Deed: The Power of Service-Learning for American Schools.* Battle Creek, MI: W. K. Kellogg Foundation.

Flanagan, C. A., J. M. Bowes, et al. (1998). Ties That Bind: Correlates of Adolescents' Civic Commitments in Seven Countries. *Journal of Social Issues* 54(3): 457–475.

Flanagan, C. A., B. Jonsson, et al. (2006). Adolescents and the Social Contract: Developmental Roots of Citizenship in Seven Countries. In *Roots of Civic Identity: International Perspectives on Community Service and Activism in Youth,* edited by M. Yates and J. Youniss, pp. 135–155. Boston: Cambridge University Press.

Flanagan, C. A., and L. R. Sherrod. (1998). Youth Political Development: An Introduction. *Journal of Social Issues* 54(3): 447–456.

Flynn, F. J., J. A. Chatman, and S. E Spataro. (2001). Getting to Know You: The Influence of Personality on Impressions and Performance of Demographically Different People in Organizations. *Administrative Science Quarterly* 46: 414–442.

Franklin, J. H. (1983). Achieving Civil Rights. In *America's Voluntary Spirit: A Book of Readings,* edited by B. O'Connell, pp. 213–226. New York: Foundation Center.

Frumkin, P. (2006). *Strategic Giving: The Art and Science of Philanthropy.* Chicago: University of Chicago Press.

Frumkin, P. (2002). *On Being Nonprofit: A Conceptual and Policy Primer.* Cambridge, MA: Harvard University Press.

Frumkin, P., and L. Treschan. (2005). Building Volunteer Capacity: The Drivers of Successful Corporate and Service Partnerships at City Year. In *Gifts of Time and Money,* edited by A. C. Brooks, pp. 33–58. Oxford: Rowman & Littlefield.

Fukuyama, F. (1995). *Trust: The Social Virtues and the Creation of Prosperity.* New York: Free Press.

Furco, A., P. Muller, and M. S. Ammon. (1998). *Civic Responsibility Survey.* Berkeley, CA: Service-Learning Research and Development Center, Graduate School of Education, University of California at Berkeley.

Galston, W. A. (2005). The Case for Universal Service. In *The AmeriCorps Experiment and the Future of National Service,* edited by W. Marshall and M. P. Magee, pp. 99–109. Washington, DC: Progressive Policy Institute.

Galston, W. A. (2001). Political Knowledge, Political Engagement, and Civic Education. *Annual Review of Political Science* 4: 217–234.

Garr, R. (1995). *Reinvesting in America: The Grassroots Movements That Are Feeding the Hungry, Housing the Homeless, and Putting Americans Back to Work.* Reading, MA: Addison-Wesley.

Gerstein, D. R. (1987). To Unpack Micro and Macro: Link Small with Large and Part with Whole. In *The Micro-Macro Link,* edited by J. C. Alexander, B. Giesen, R. Munch, and N. J. Smelser, pp. 86–111. Berkeley and Los Angeles: University of California Press.

Gerstein, L. H., D. A. Wilkeson, et al. (2004). Differences in Motivations of Paid versus Nonpaid Volunteers. *Psychological Reports* 94(1): 163–175.

Gibson, C. (2001). *From Inspiration to Participation: A Review of Perspectives in Youth Civic Engagement.* New York: Grantmaker Forum on Community and National Service and Carnegie Corporation.

Giordono, L., J. Jastrzab, et al. (2003). *Post-Program Analysis Design: Serving Country and Community: A Study of Service in AmeriCorps,* revised draft. Cambridge, MA: Abt Associates.

Glass, G. V., B. McGaw, et al. (1981). *Meta-analysis in Social Research.* Beverly Hills, CA: Sage Publications.

Goldsmith, S. (2005). National Service on a Community Scale. In *The Ameri-Corps Experiment and the Future of National Service,* edited by W. Marshall and M. P. Magee, pp. 87–96. Washington, DC: Progressive Policy Institute.

Goldsmith, S. (1993). *A City Year.* New York: W. W. Norton.

Gorham, E. B. (1992). *National Service, Citizenship, and Political Education.* Albany: State University of New York Press.

Granovetter, M. S. (1973). The Strength of Weak Ties. *American Journal of Sociology* 78(6): 1360–1380.

Grossman, J. B., and K. Furano. (2002). *Making the Most of Volunteers.* Philadelphia, PA: Public/Private Ventures.

Guterbock, T. M., and J. C. Fries. (1997). *America's Social Fabric: A Status Report.* Washington, DC: American Association of Retired Persons.

Hager, M. A., and J. L. Brudney. (2004). *Volunteer Management Practices and Retention of Volunteers.* Washington, DC: Urban Institute.

Hall, P. D. (2005). Historical Perspectives on Nonprofit Organizations in the United States. In *Handbook to Nonprofit Leadership and Management,* edited by R. D. Herman and Associates, pp. 3–39. San Francisco: Jossey-Bass.

Handy, F., and N. Srinivasan. (2004). Valuing Volunteers: An Economic Evaluation of the Net Benefits of Hospital Volunteers. *Nonprofit and Voluntary Sector Quarterly* 33(1): 28–54.

Hart, D., T. M. Donnelly, et al. (2007). High School Community Service as a Predictor of Adult Voting and Volunteering. *American Educational Research Journal* 44(1): 197–219.

Healey, J. F. (2002). *Statistics: A Tool for Social Research*. Belmont, CA: Wadsworth Group.

Hellenius, R., and S. Rudbeck. (2003). In-Kind Donations for Nonprofits. *McKinsey Quarterly* 4. Retrieved 11/28/2009 from http://www.mckinseyquarterly.com/In-kind_donations_for_nonprofits_1345.

Hennessy, J., and M. A. West. (1999). Intergroup Behavior in Organizations: A Field Test of Social Identity Theory. *Small Group Research* 30(3): 361–382.

Henton, D., J. Melville, and K. Walesh. (1997). *Grassroots Leaders for a New Economy: How Civic Entrepreneurs Are Building Prosperous Communities*. San Francisco: Jossey-Bass.

Hillygus, D. S. (2005). The Missing Link: Exploring the Relationship between Higher Education and Political Engagement. *Political Behavior* 27(1): 25–47.

Hirst, P. (1994). *Associative Democracy: New Forms of Economic and Social Governance*. Amherst: University of Massachusetts Press.

Hoad, P. (2002). Drawing the Line: The Boundaries of Volunteering in the Community Care of Older People. *Health and Social Care in the Community* 10(4): 239–246.

Hoegl, M., and H. G. Gemuenden. (2001). Teamwork Quality and the Success of Innovative Projects: A Theoretical Concept and Empirical Evidence. *Organization Science* 12(4): 435–449.

Hoffman, E. C. (1998). *All You Need Is Love: The Peace Corps and the Spirit of the 1960s*. Cambridge, MA: Harvard University Press.

Hoge, R., C. Zech, et al. (1998). The Value of Volunteers as Resources for Congregations. *Journal for the Scientific Study of Religion* 37(3): 470–480.

Hogg, M. A., and D. Abrams. (1988). *Social Identifications: A Social Psychology of Intergroup Relations and Group Processes*. New York: Routledge.

Hogg, M. A., and D. J. Terry. (2000). Social Identity and Self-Categorization Processes in Organizational Contexts. *Academy of Management Review* 25(1): 121–140.

Hunt, L. L., and M. O. Hunt. (2001). Race, Region, and Religious Involvement: A Comparative Study of Whites and African Americans. *Social Forces* 80(2): 605–631.

Husock, H. (2004a). *The AmeriCorps Budget Crisis of 2003(A): Why the National Service Movement Faced Cutbacks and How It Responded*. Cambridge, MA: Harvard University, Kennedy School of Government Case Program.

Husock, H. (2004b). *The AmeriCorps Budget Crisis of 2003(B): Why the National Service Movement Faced Cutbacks and How It Responded*. Cambridge, MA: Harvard University, Kennedy School of Government Case Program.

Husock, H. (2004c). *The AmeriCorps Budget Crisis of 2003 (Sequel): Why the National Service Movement Faced Cutbacks and How It Responded*. Cambridge, MA: Harvard University, Kennedy School of Government Case Program.

Ilchman, W. F., S. N. Katz, et al., eds. (1998). *Philanthropy in the World's Traditions.* Bloomington: Indiana University Press.

Independent Sector. (2001). *Giving and Volunteering in the United States: Findings from a National Survey 1992.* Washington, DC: Independent Sector.

Independent Sector. (1996). *Giving and Volunteering in the United States: Findings from a National Survey.* Washington, DC: Independent Sector.

Jackson, E. F., M. D. Bachmeier, et al. (1995). Volunteering and Charitable Giving—Do Religious and Associational Ties Promote Helping Behavior? *Nonprofit and Voluntary Sector Quarterly* 24(1): 59–78.

Jacobson, A. L., and S. Ramisetty-Mikler. (1999). *The HIPPYCORPS Initiative: Getting Things Done.* Dallas: University of North Texas, Center for Parent Education.

James, R. N., III, and D. L. Sharpe. (2007). The Nature and Causes of the U-Shaped Charitable Giving Profile. *Nonprofit and Voluntary Sector Quarterly* 36: 218–239.

James, W. (1962). The Moral Equivalent of War. In *Essays on Faith and Morals.* Cleveland, OH: World Publishing.

Janoski, T., M. A. Musick, et al. (1998). Being Volunteered? The Impact of Social Participation and Pro-Social Attitudes on Volunteering. *Sociological Forum* 13(3): 495–519.

Janoski, T., and J. Wilson. (1995). The Contribution of Religion to Volunteer Work. *Sociology of Religion* 56(2): 137–153.

Janowitz, M. (1983). *The Reconstruction of Patriotism: Education for Civic Consciousness.* Chicago: University of Chicago Press.

Jastrzab, J. (2000). *Evaluation of the Washington Service Corps: Final Report Executive Summary.* Cambridge, MA: Abt Associates.

Jastrzab, J., L. Bernstein, et al. (2001). A *Profile of AmeriCorps Members at Baseline.* Cambridge, MA: Abt Associates.

Jastrzab, J., J. Blomquist, et al. (1997). *Youth Corps: Promising Strategies for Young People and Their Communities.* Cambridge, MA: Abt Associates, 31.

Jastrzab, J., L. Giordono, et al. (2004a). *Serving Country and Community: A Longitudinal Study of Service in AmeriCorps, Appendices.* Cambridge, MA: Abt Associates.

Jastrzab, J., L. Giordono, et al. (2004b). *Serving Country and Community: A Longitudinal Study of Service in AmeriCorps, Early Findings.* Cambridge, MA: Abt Associates.

Jastrzab, J., J. Masker, et al. (1996). *Impacts of Service: Final Report on the Evaluation of the American Conservation and Youth Service Corps.*

Washington, DC: Abt Associates and Brandeis University Center for Human Resources.

John, P. (2005). The Contribution of Volunteering, Trust, and Networks to Educational Performance. *Policy Studies Journal* 33(4): 635–656.

Jones, G. R., and J. M. George. (1998). The Experience and Evolution of Trust: Implications for Cooperation and Teamwork. *Academy of Management Review* 23(3): 531–546.

Jospin, D. R. (2003). National and Community Service: Service as a Strategy to Promote Rural Development. Washington, DC: ICP Report.

Julian, D. A., A. Jones, et al. (1995). Open Systems Evaluation and the Logic Model: Program Planning and Evaluation Tools. *Evaluation and Program Planning* 18(4): 333–341.

Kahne, J., and J. Westheimer. (2002). The Limits of Efficacy: Educating Citizens for a Democratic Society. Paper presented at the annual meeting of the American Political Science Association, Boston, Massachusetts, August 28.

Karafantis, D. M., and S. R. Levy. (2004). The Role of Children's Lay Theories about the Malleability of Human Attributes in Beliefs about and Volunteering for Disadvantaged Groups. *Child Development* 75(1): 236–250.

Kearns, K., C. Park, et al. (2005). Comparing Faith-Based and Secular Community Service Corporations in Pittsburgh and Allegheny County, Pennsylvania. *Nonprofit and Voluntary Sector Quarterly* 34(2): 206–231.

Kemmelmeier, M., E. E. Jambor, et al. (2006). Individualism and Good Works—Cultural Variation in Giving and Volunteering across the United States. *Journal of Cross-Cultural Psychology* 37(3): 327–344.

Kennedy, J. F. (1963). Letter to the President of the Senate and to the Speaker of the House Transmitting Bill to Strengthen the Peace Corps.

Kerry, J. (2003). Reviving the Ideal of Citizenship. *Responsive Community* 13(3): 42–49.

Kirlin, M. (2004). *Civic Skill Building: The Missing Component in Service Programs?* Washington, DC: American Political Science Association Online.

Kotter, J. P. (1990). *A Force for Change: How Leadership Differs from Management.* London: Collier Macmillan.

Lah, D. (1986). *Youth Corps Profiles: The Young Adult Conservation Corps, the Wisconsin Conservation Corps, the Michigan Civilian Conservation Corps, the Texas Conservation Corps.* Philadelphia, PA: Public/Private Ventures.

Lam, P. Y. (2002). As the Flocks Gather: How Religion Affects Voluntary Association Participation. *Journal for the Scientific Study of Religion* 41(3): 405–422.

Lenkowsky, L., and J. L. Perry. (2000). Reinventing Government: The Case of National Service. *Public Administration Review* 60(4): 298–307.

Letts, C. W., W. P. Ryan, et al. (1998). *High Performance Non-Profit Organizations: Managing Upstream for Greater Impact.* New York: John Wiley and Sons.

Light, P. C. (2002). The Volunteering Decision: What Prompts It? What Sustains It? *Brookings Review* 20(4): 45–47.

Light, P. C. (1998). *Sustaining Innovation: Creating Nonprofit and Government Organizations That Innovate Naturally.* San Francisco: Jossey-Bass.

Light, R. J., and D. B. Pillemer. (1984). *Summing Up: The Science of Reviewing Research.* Cambridge, MA: Harvard University Press.

Lind, M. (1989). Youth Service: Euphemism for Cheap Labor. *St. Louis Post-Dispatch,* p. 3B.

Little, H. (1999). *Volunteers: How to Get Them, How to Keep Them.* Naperville, IL: Panacea Press.

Lowell, S., L. Silverman, and L. Taliento. (2001, February). Not-for-Profit Management: The Gift That Keeps on Giving. *McKinsey Quarterly,* no. 1: 147–155.

Magee, M. (2003, February 25). A U-Turn on National Service? *Progressive Policy Institute Backgrounder.*

Magee, M. (2002a). *Congress and National Service.* Washington, DC: Progressive Policy Institute.

Magee, M. (2002b, March 11). Scaling Up National Service. *Progressive Policy Institute Backgrounder.*

Magee, M., and W. Marshall. (2005). Has AmeriCorps Lived Up to Its Promise? In *The AmeriCorps Experiment and the Future of National Service,* edited by W. Marshall and M. P. Magee, pp. 1–50. Washington, DC: Progressive Policy Institute.

Magee, M., and W. Marshall. (2003). Thinking Bigger about Citizenship. In *United We Serve: National Service and the Future of Citizenship,* edited by E. Dionne, K. M. Drogosz, and R. E. Litan, pp. 73–83. Washington, DC: Brookings Institution Press.

Malekoff, A. (2002). The Power of Group Work with Kids: Lessons Learned. In *Stories Celebrating Group Work,* edited by R. Kurland and A. Malekoff. Binghamton, NY: Haworth Press.

Markovitz, C. E., G. Schneider, et al. (2007). *Study of 40 Years of VISTA's Impact on Volunteers: Final Report.* Cambridge, MA: Abt Associates.

Markus, G. B., J. P. F. Howard, and D. C. King. (1993). Integrating Community-Service and Classroom Instruction Enhances Learning—Results from an Experiment. *Educational Evaluation and Policy Analysis* 15(4): 410–419.

Marshall, W., and M. Magee. (2005). The Voluntary Path to Universal Service. In *The AmeriCorps Experiment and the Future of National Service,* edited by W. Marshall and M. P. Magee, pp. 111–119. Washington, DC: Progressive Policy Institute.

Marshall, W., and M. Magee. (2003, August 11). Break the Silence on Ameri-
    Corps Funding [Opinion]. *Christian Science Monitor.*

Mattis, J. S., R. J. Jagers, et al. (2000). Religiosity, Volunteerism, and Community
    Involvement among African American Men: An Exploratory Analysis.
    Journal of Community Psychology 28(4): 391–406.

McAdam, D. (1988). *Freedom Summer.* New York: Oxford University Press.

McBride, A. M., and M. Sherraden. (2004). Toward a Global Research Agenda on
    Civic Service: Editors' Introduction to This Special Issue. *Nonprofit and
    Voluntary Sector Quarterly* 33(4): 3S–7S.

McBride, A. M., M. Sherraden, et al. (2004). Civic Service Worldwide: Defining a
    Field, Building a Knowledge Base. *Nonprofit and Voluntary Sector Quarterly*
    33(4): 8S–21S.

McCain, J. (2001). Putting the National in National Service. *Washington Monthly*
    33(10): 14–17.

McCarthy, A. M., and M. L. Tucker. (1999). Student Attitudes toward Service
    Learning: Implications for Implementation. *Journal of Management Educa-
    tion* 23(5): 554–573.

McEntee, G. W. (2006). The New Crisis of Public Service Employment. *Public
    Personnel Management* 35(4): 343–346.

Meier, S. (2006). *The Economics of Non-selfish Behavior: Decisions to Contribute
    Money to Public Goods.* Northampton, MA: Edward Elgar.

Melchior, A. (1999). Summary Report: National Evaluation of Learn and Serve
    America. Waltham, MA: Center for Human Resources, Brandeis University.

Mesch, D. J., M. Tschirhart, et al. (1998). Altruists or Egoists? Retention in
    Stipended Service. *Nonprofit Management and Leadership* 9(1): 3–21.

Mettler, S. (2002). Bringing the State Back in to Civic Engagement: Policy
    Feedback Effects of the G.I. Bill for World War II Veterans. *American
    Political Science Review* 96(2): 351–365.

Metz, E., J. McLellan, and J. Youniss. (2003). Types of Voluntary Service and
    Adolescents' Civic Development. *Journal of Adolescent Research* 18(2):
    188–203.

Morgan, W., and M. Streb. (2001). Building Citizenship: How Student Voice in
    Service-Learning Develops Civic Values. *Social Science Quarterly* 82(1):
    154–169.

Moskos, C. C. (1988). *A Call to Civic Service: National Service for Country and
    Community.* New York: Free Press.

Moskos, C. C., and J. S. Butler. (1996). *All That We Can Be: Black Leadership and
    Racial Integration the Army Way.* New York: Basic Books.

Moskos, C. C., and P. Glastris. (2001, November). Now Do You Believe We Need
    a Draft? *Washington Monthly.*

Mummendey, A., and M. Wenzel. (1999). Social Discrimination and Tolerance in Intergroup Relations: Reactions to Intergroup Difference. *Personality and Social Psychology Review* 3(2): 158–174.

Musick, M. A., J. Wilson, et al. (2000). Race and Formal Volunteering: The Differential Effects of Class and Religion. *Social Forces* 78(4): 1539–1571.

Mutchler, J. E., J. A. Burr, et al. (2003). From Paid Worker to Volunteer: Leaving the Paid Workforce and Volunteering in Later Life. *Social Forces* 81(4): 1267–1293.

National and Community Service Act of 1990 (as amended through Public Law 106-170, approved 17 December 1999). U.S. Code 42, § 12501. (1999).

Neumann, G. (1995). *The Benefits and Costs of National Service: Methods for Benefit Assessment with Application to Three AmeriCorps Programs.* San Francisco: James Irvine Foundation.

Obama, B., and J. Biden. (2009). Helping All Americans Serve Their Country. Retrieved 1/5/2009 from http://www.barackobama.com/pdf/NationalServicePlanFactSheet.pdf.

O'Connell, B. (1983). *America's Voluntary Spirit: A Book of Readings.* New York: Foundation Center.

Oesterle, S., M. K. Johnson, and J. T. Mortimer. (2004). Volunteerism during the Transition to Adulthood: A Life Course Perspective. *Social Forces* 82(3): 1123–1149.

O'Flanagan, M., and L. Taliento. (2004). Nonprofits: Ensuring That Bigger Is Better. *McKinsey Quarterly*, no. 22: 113–122.

Oi, W. (1990). National Service: Who Bears the Costs and Who Reaps the Gains. In *National Service Pro and Con,* edited by W. M. Evers, pp. 81–103. Stanford, CA: Hoover Institution Press.

O'Neill, M. (2001). Research on Giving and Volunteering: Methodological Considerations. *Nonprofit and Voluntary Sector Quarterly* 30(3): 505–514.

Osborne, D., and T. Gaebler. (1993). *Reinventing Government.* New York: Plume.

Ostrander, S. A. (1995). *Money for Change: Social Movement Philanthropy at Haymarket People's Fund.* Philadelphia, PA: Temple University Press.

Ozorak, E. W. (2003). Love of God and Neighbor: Religion and Volunteer Service among College Students. *Review of Religious Research* 44(3): 285–299.

Pass, D. J. (1976). *The Politics of VISTA in the War on Poverty: A Study of Ideological Conflict.* Doctoral dissertation, Columbia University, New York.

Paxton, P. (1999). Is Social Capital Declining in the United States? A Multiple Indicator Assessment. *American Journal of Sociology* 105(1): 88–127.

Pearson, S. S., and H. M. Voke. (2003). *Building an Effective Citizenry: Lessons Learned from Initiatives in Youth Engagement.* Washington, DC: American Youth Policy Forum.

Perry, J. L., and M. T. Imperial. (2001). A Decade of Service-Related Research: A Map of the Field. *Nonprofit and Voluntary Sector Quarterly* 30(3): 462–479.

Perry, J. L., and M. C. Katula. (2001). Does Service Affect Citizenship? *Administration and Society* 33(3): 330–365.

Perry, J. L., A. Thompson, et al. (1999). Inside a Swiss Army Knife: An Assessment of AmeriCorps. *Journal of Public Administration Review and Theory* 9(2): 225–250.

Perry, J. L., and M. Thomson. (2004). *Civic Service: What Difference Does It Make?* Armonk, NY: M. E. Sharpe.

Proudford, K. L., and K. K. Smith. (2003). Group Membership Salience and the Movement of Conflict—Reconceptualizing the Interaction among Race, Gender, and Hierarchy. *Group and Organization Management* 28(1): 18–44.

Putnam, R. D. (2000). *Bowling Alone: The Collapse and Revival of American Community.* New York: Simon and Schuster.

Putnam, R. D. (1995). Bowling Alone: America's Declining Social Capital. *Journal of Democracy* 6(1): 65–78.

Putnam, R. D. (1993). *Making Democracy Work: Civic Traditions in Modern Italy.* Princeton, NJ: Princeton University Press.

Putnam, R. D., and L. M. Feldstein. (2003). *Better Together: Restoring the American Community.* New York: Simon and Schuster.

Racine, D. P. (1998). *Replicating Programs in Social Markets.* Philadelphia, PA: Replication & Program Strategies.

Rehnborg, S. J. (2005). Government Volunteerism in the New Millennium. In *Emerging Areas of Volunteering,* edited by J. L. Brudney, ARNOVA Occasional Papers Series, vols. 1 and 2, pp. 93–112. Indianapolis, IN: Association for Research on Nonprofit Organizations and Voluntary Action.

Rhoads, R. A. (1997). *Community Service and Higher Learning: Explorations of the Caring Self.* New York: State University of New York Press.

Rompf, E. L., and D. Royse. (1994). Choice of Social Work as a Career: Possible Influences. *Journal of Social Work Education* 30(2): 163–171.

Roosevelt, F. D. (1933). Three Essentials for Unemployment Relief. In *The Public Papers and Addresses of Franklin D. Roosevelt.* New York: Random House.

Roosevelt, F. D. (1932). Nomination Address. Democratic National Convention of 1932, Chicago, Illinois.

Rosenbaum, P. R., and D. B. Rubin. (1984). Reducing Bias in Observational Studies Using Subclassification on the Propensity Score. *Journal of the American Statistical Association* 79(387): 516–524.

Rosenbaum, P. R., and D. B. Rubin. (1983). The Central Role of the Propensity Score in Observational Studies for Causal Effects. *Biometrika* 70(1): 41–55.

Rosenblum, N. L. (1998). *Membership and Morals: The Personal Uses of Pluralism in America.* Princeton, NJ: Princeton University Press.

Rosenblum, S., and S. Leiderman. (1986). *Youth Corps Case Studies: The San Francisco Conservation Corps, Interim Report.* Philadelphia, PA: Public/ Private Ventures.

Rossi, P. H., and H. E. Freeman. (1993). *Evaluation: A Systematic Approach.* Newbury Park, CA: Sage Publications.

Sagawa, S. (1998). Ten Years of Youth in Service to America. In *The Forgotten Half Revisited: American Youth and Young Families, 1998–2008.* Washington, DC: American Youth Policy Forum.

Schambra, W. A. (1994, Summer). By the People: The Old Values of the New Citizenship. *Policy Review,* 32–38.

Schudson, M. (1998). *The Good Citizen: A History of American Civic Life.* New York: Free Press.

Schwartz, M. (1988). *In Service to America: A History of VISTA in Arkansas, 1965–1985.* Fayetteville: University of Arkansas Press.

Seligman, A. B. (1997). *The Problem of Trust.* Princeton, NJ: Princeton University Press.

Selingo, J. (1998). AmeriCorps at Five Years: A Success but Not in the Way Clinton Hoped. *Chronicle of Higher Education* 45(5): 38.

Shapiro, P. (1994). *A History of National Service in America.* Monograph No. M0078. College Park, MD: Center for Political Leadership and Participation.

Sherraden, M. W., and D. J. Eberly, eds. (1981). *National Service: Social, Economic and Military Impacts.* Elmsford, NY: Pergamon Press.

Shields, M. (1989, May 20). Volunteer Service Is a Fair Idea. *Washington Post,* A25.

Simon, C. A. (2002). Testing for Bias in the Impact of AmeriCorps Service on Volunteer Participants: Evidence of Success in Achieving a Neutrality Program Objective. *Public Administration Review* 62(6): 670–678.

Simon, C. A., and C. H. Wang. (2002). The Impact of AmeriCorps Service on Volunteer Participants: Results from a Two-Year Study in Four Western States. *Administration and Society* 34(5): 522–540.

Simon, C. A., and C. H. Wang. (1999a). *Impact of AmeriCorps on Members' Political and Social Efficacy, Social Trust, Institutional Confidence, and Values in Idaho, Montana, Oregon, and Washington.* Portland, OR: Northwest Regional Educational Laboratory.

Simon, C. A., and C. H. Wang. (1999b). *The Impact of AmeriCorps Service on Volunteer Participants: Building the Social Capital and Levels of Confidence in Public Institutions.* Reno, NV: American Political Science Association.

Skelton, N., H. C. Boyte, and L. S. Leonard. (2002). *Youth Civic Engagement: Reflections on an Emerging Public Idea.* Minneapolis, MN: Center for Democracy and Citizenship.

Skocpol, T. (2003). *Diminished Democracy: From Membership to Management in American Civic Life.* Norman: University of Oklahoma Press.

Skocpol, T. (1997). The Tocqueville Problem. *Social Science History* 21(4): 455–479.

Smith, D. H. (2000). *Grassroots Associations.* Thousand Oaks, CA: Sage Publications.

Smith, D. H. (1994). Determinants of Volunteering Association Participation and Volunteering—A Literature Review. *Nonprofit and Voluntary Sector Quarterly* 23(3): 243–263.

Spalding, M. (2003). Principles and Reforms for Citizen Service. *Heritage Foundation Backgrounder,* 1 April.

Stets, J. E., and P. J. Burke. (2000). Identity Theory and Social Identity Theory. *Social Psychology Quarterly* 63(3): 224–237.

Stukas, A. A., M. Snyder, and E. G. Clary. (1999). The Effects of "Mandatory Volunteerism" on Intentions to Volunteer. *Psychological Science* 10(1): 59–64.

Supphellen, M., and M. R. Nelson. (2001). Developing, Exploring, and Validating a Typology of Private Philanthropic Decision Making. *Journal of Economic Psychology* 22(5): 573–603.

Tajfel, H., and J. C. Turner. (1985). The Social Identity Theory of Intergroup Behavior. In *Psychology of Intergroup Relations,* 2d ed., edited by S. Worchel and W. G. Austin, pp. 7–24. Chicago: Nelson-Hall.

Thomson, A. M., and J. L. Perry. (1998). Can AmeriCorps Build Communities? *Nonprofit and Voluntary Sector Quarterly* 27(4): 399–420.

Tierney, J., and J. B. Grossman. (2000). *Making a Difference: An Impact Study of Big Brothers Big Sisters.* Philadelphia, PA: Public/Private Ventures.

Tocqueville, A. de. (2002). *Democracy in America.* Chicago: University of Chicago Press.

Tocqueville, A. de. (1983). Of the Use Which the Americans Make of Public Associations in Civil Life. In *America's Voluntary Spirit: A Book of Readings,* edited by B. O'Connell, pp. 53–58. New York: The Foundation Center.

Tschirhart, M. (2002). Diversity and Service-Learning: A Call for More Research. *Journal of Nonprofit and Public Sector Marketing* 10(2): 139–150.

Tschirhart, M. (1998). Understanding the Older Stipended Volunteer: Age-Related Differences among AmeriCorps Members. *Public Productivity and Management Review* 22(1): 35–48.

Tschirhart, M., D. J. Mesch, et al. (2001). Stipended Volunteers: Their Goals, Experiences, Satisfaction, and Likelihood of Future Service. *Nonprofit and Voluntary Sector Quarterly* 30(3): 422–443.

Turner, D. (2004, May 3). DeLay Quietly Trying to Kill AmeriCorps. *Buffalo News.*

Turner, J. C., M. Hogg, et al. (1987). *Rediscovering the Social Group.* Oxford: Blackwell.

Van Til, J., and G. H. Gallup Jr. (1997). AmeriCorps: Twenty Questions and Their Answers from a National Study. *Cantigny Conference Series.* Wheaton, IL: Rutgers University and George H. Gallup International Institute.

Van Willigen, M. (2000). Differential Benefits of Volunteering across the Life Course. *Journal of Gerontology: Social Sciences* 55(5): 308–318.

Verba, S., K. L. Schlozman, et al. (1993). Race, Ethnicity and Political Resources. *British Journal of Political Science* 23: 453–497.

Verba, S., K. L. Schlozman, et al. (1995). *Voice and Equality: Civic Voluntarism in American Politics.* Cambridge, MA: Harvard University Press.

Vogt, W. P. (1997). *Tolerance and Education: Learning to Live with Diversity and Difference.* Thousand Oaks, CA: Sage Publications.

Waldman, S. (2005). Putting Faith in Service. In *The AmeriCorps Experiment and the Future of National Service,* edited by W. Marshall and M. P. Magee. Washington, DC: Progressive Policy Institute.

Waldman, S. (1995). *The Bill: How the Adventures of Clinton's National Service Bill Reveal What Is Corrupt, Comic, Cynical—and Noble—about Washington.* New York: Viking.

Waldzus, S., A. Mummendey, et al. (2002). Towards Tolerance: Representations of Superordinate Categories and Perceived Ingroup Prototypicality. *Journal of Experimental Social Psychology* 39(1): 31–47.

Walters, J. (1996). Clinton's AmeriCorps Values. *Policy Review* 75: 42–47.

Warren, M. E. (2001). *Democracy and Association.* Princeton, NJ: Princeton University Press.

Weichselbaum, S. (2003, September 11). Cutbacks Come Due for AmeriCorps Volunteers. *Washington Post,* DZ03.

Weinstein, J. L. (2003, August 26). AmeriCorps Cuts to Be Deep, but Not Disastrous. *Press Herald.*

Weir, M., and M. Ganz. (1999). Reconnecting People and Politics. In *The New Majority: Toward a Progressive Politics,* edited by S. B. Greenberg and T. Skocpol, pp. 149–171). New Haven, CT: Yale University Press.

Weisbrod, B. A. (2001). An Agenda for Quantitative Evaluation of the Nonprofit Sector: Need, Obstacles, and Approaches. In *Measuring the Impact of the Nonprofit Sector,* edited by P. Flynn and V. A. Hodgkinson, pp. 273–290. New York: Kluwer Academic / Plenum Publishers.

Westat Inc. (1999). Evaluation of the First Year of the AmeriCorps Education Awards Program. Rockville, MD: Westat.

Wilson, J. (2000). Volunteering. *Annual Review of Sociology* 26: 215–240.

Wilson, J., and M. A. Musick. (2003). Doing Well by Doing Good: Volunteering and Occupational Achievement among American Women. *Sociological Quarterly* 44(3): 433–450.

Wilson, J., and M. A. Musick. (1999). Attachment to Volunteering. *Sociological Forum* 14(2): 243–272.

Wilson, J., and M. A. Musick. (1997). Who Cares? Toward an Integrated Theory of Volunteer Work. *American Sociological Review* 62(5): 694–713.

Wofford, H. (2002, September 22). The Politics of Service: How a Nation Got Behind AmeriCorps. *Brookings Review.*

Wofford, H., and S. Waldman. (1996). AmeriCorps the Beautiful? *Policy Review* 79: 28–36.

Wolf, J. F. (1983). Career Plateauing in the Public Service: Baby Boom and Employment Bust. *Public Administration Review* 43(2): 160–165.

Wuthnow, R. (1991). *Acts of Compassion: Caring for Others and Helping Ourselves.* Princeton, NJ: Princeton University Press.

Youniss, J., J. McLellan, and M. Yates. (1997). What We Know about Engendering Civic Identity. *American Behavioral Scientist* 40(5): 620–631.

Youniss, J., and M. Yates. (1997). *Community Service and Social Responsibility in Youth.* Chicago: University of Chicago Press.

Zaff, J. F., and E. Michelsen. (2002, October). Encouraging Civic Engagement: How Teens Are (or Are Not) Becoming Responsible Citizens. *Child Trends Research Briefs.*

Zaff, J. F., K. A. Moore, et al. (2003). Implications of Extracurricular Activity Participation during Adolescence on Positive Outcomes. *Journal of Adolescent Research* 18(6): 599–630.

Index

DATE DUE

OCT 2 5 2011	

DEMCO, INC. 38-2931